THE DEEPEST SENSE

DATE DUE

THE DEEPEST SENSE

A Cultural History of Touch

Constance Classen

UNIVERSITY OF ILLINOIS PRESS
Urbana, Chicago, and Springfield

LIBRARY OF CONGRESS CATALOGING-IN-PUBLICATION DATA
Classen, Constance
The deepest sense : a cultural history of touch / Constance Classen.
p. cm. — (Studies in sensory history)
Includes bibliographical references and index.
ISBN 978-0-252-03493-0 (hardcover : alk. paper) —
ISBN 978-0-252-07859-0 (pbk : alk. paper) —
ISBN 978-0-252-09440-8 (e-book)
1. Touch—History.
2. Senses and sensation—History.
3. Social history. I. Title.
GN279.T68C56   2012
612.8'8—dc23   2011034118

FOR EMMA VICTORIA

CONTENTS

Acknowledgments ix

The Inside Story xi

1 . A PLACE BY THE FIRE 1

The Common Touch 1

A Place by the Fire 7

The Walled City 12

Hard at Work........................ 16

The Rites of Pleasure 20

2 . A TOUCHABLE GOD 27

A Tactile Cosmology 27

Mystical Touch 29

Gestures of Piety 31

The Cult of Relics.................. 35

Corpus Christi 41

Ordeals by Fire 43

3 . PAINFUL TIMES 47

Suffering Bodies and
    Healing Hands.................... 47

Blind Touch 51

Leprosy, the Black Death,
    and Dancing Mania 56

The Uses of Pain.................... 60

The Torments of Hell 64

Sorrow and Compassion 68

4. A WOMAN'S TOUCH 71
   Male and Female Bodies........... 71
   A Woman's Touch................... 75
   Women's Work..................... 77
   Texts and Textiles.................. 81
   Mystical Raptures
     and Pain Craft 85
   The Witch's Touch................. 90

5. ANIMAL SKINS 93
   Animal Bodies...................... 93
   Animal Companions 98
   Beasts, Wild Men, and Slaves 103
   Animal Souls 109
   Experimentation and the
     Campaign Against Cruelty 117

6. TACTILE ARTS...................... 123
   The Aesthetics of Touch 123
   The Feel of Art.................... 126
   Crafty Ladies 133
   Touch in the Museum............. 136

7. THE MODERN TOUCH.......... 147
   Petrarch's Vision 147
   The Decline of Sacred Touch 148
   New Sensory Worlds.............. 153
   The Persistence of Touch......... 158
   The Finishing Touch 165

8. SENSATIONS OF A NEW AGE .. 167
   The Drill........................... 167
   The School, the Prison,
     and the Museum 171
   The Feel of the City.............. 178
   The Electric Creed............... 183
   Touch at Home 186
   The Stuff of Dreams.............. 191

   Bibliography 199
   Index 221

Illustrations follow page 122

ACKNOWLEDGMENTS

I am very grateful to everyone who assisted me during the years of preparation for this book. Among my colleagues in the field of the history of the senses I owe thanks to Mark Smith, who proposed I embark on the present study and Richard Newhauser, who responded with such enthusiasm to it. David Howes offered invaluable guidance and encouragement during the writing process and George Classen served as an insightful reviewer. Jonathan and Emma were always supportive of my work and the two of them, along with Mishi, provided wonderful company during the long months of writing. *Gracias también a mi querida mamá por todo su apoyo.*

I wish to thank everyone who read the manuscript before publication for their positive responses and helpful suggestions. I appreciate, as well, the support and interest of my editors at the University of Illinois Press, Kendra Boileau and Willis Regier. The technical assistance given by Pierre-Louis Houle is much appreciated. I would like to take this opportunity to thank the many individuals from institutions around the world who have invited me to speak on the subject of the cultural life of the senses. I am grateful to the Canadian Centre for Architecture, and to Phyllis Lambert and Mirko Zardini in particular, for inviting me to be a visiting scholar at the Centre and thereby enabling me to deepen my knowledge of the histories of art and architecture.

Part of the research for this book was funded by grants from the Social Sciences and Humanities Research Council of Canada. While most of the book is based on new research, chapter 4 makes use of some material from chapters 3 and 4 in my book *The Color of Angels: Cosmology, Gender and the Aesthetic Imagination* (Routledge, 1998) and the sections on craftwork and museums in chapter 6 build on my essays "Feminine Tactics" and "Touch in the Museum" in my edited anthology *The Book of Touch* (Berg, 2005).

THE INSIDE STORY

Among men it is in virtue of fineness of touch, and
not of any other sense, that we discriminate the
mentally gifted from the rest.

—THOMAS AQUINAS
Commentary on Aristotle's De Anima

Until the eighteenth century at least, touch remained
one of the master senses . . . It verified perception,
giving solidity to the impressions provided by the
other senses, which were not as reliable.

—ROBERT MANDROU
Introduction to Modern France

If a history could be written of touch, what would it embrace? Hot fire and cold
wind, smooth silk and rough wool, spinning wheels and threshing flails, relics
and frolics and the healing touch of a king? A world of meaning can lie within the
simplest gesture, a kiss, or the touch of a hand. If such a history could be written, why hasn't it? Touch lies at the heart of our experience of ourselves and the
world yet it often remains unspoken and, even more so, unhistoricized. Indeed,
in many historical accounts the past is so disembodied that it appears little more
than a shadow play, a procession of ghosts who surely never felt the pinch of a
shoe nor the cut of a sword. This omission of tactile experience is noticeable not
only in the field of history, but across the humanities and social sciences. It seems
that we have so often been warned not to touch that we are reluctant to probe
the tactile world even with our minds.

Touch—and sensory experience in general—is often downplayed or disregarded even within such fields as the history of the body or the history of medicine.
(Compare, for example, the centrality of touch in Daniel Defoe's 1722 literary
rendering of the Great Plague to its marginalization in recent historical accounts.)

The decision to omit tactile data is probably not a choice contemporary historians have made as individuals. The decision would seem to have already been made for them by a general, unspoken consensus among academics.

We can find this attitude already in the historical writing of the nineteenth century when the notion that "high" culture requires the suppression of the "lower" senses was formalized. Touch was typed by the scholars of the day as a crude and uncivilized mode of perception. In the sensory scale of "races" created by the natural historian Lorenz Oken, the "civilized" European "eye-man," who focused on the visual world, was positioned at the top and the African "skin-man," who used touch as his primary sensory modality, at the bottom. Societies that touched much, it was said, did not think much and did not bear thinking much about— except perhaps by anthropologists. To achieve respectability, societies needed to be seen to have risen above the "animal" life of the body. To achieve respectability, historians had to show that in their work they had done the same.

The potential benefits of reversing this tendency are considerable. Exploring the history of touch makes the past come alive. It clothes the dry bones of historical fact with the flesh of physical sensation. Sensuous history is more interesting and more memorable. An embodied approach saves historical figures from being perceived as lifeless puppets who move across the stage of the past without any real feelings. When we allow historical figures to be of flesh and blood we make it possible to relate to them as fellow beings and, therefore, to make meaningful comparisons between their lives and situations and our own (see Hoffer 2005: Introduction).

The ways in which sensuous description can make history—and indeed any cultural account—come alive might in itself be enough to justify the historical study of touch. Yet, however valuable this descriptive dimension may be, it cannot in itself reveal the significance of touch in other times and places. To understand the sensory life of a society one must look at the cultural values that inform its ways of sensing the world. The history of the touch involves not just a search for experience, but for meaning.

In this book the quest for tactile meaning begins in the Middle Ages. The reason for this is that the early Middle Ages was often included among the "uncivilized" hands-on societies that did not bear much thinking about. This was a time when, it was said, "Europe lay sunk in a night of barbarism which grew darker and darker . . . a barbarism more awful and horrible than that of the primitive savage, for it was the decomposing body of what had been a great civilization" (Briffault 1919: 164). The very use of the term "Dark Ages" to refer both to the centuries im- mediately following the fall of Rome and to the entire medieval period conveyed the notion of an age when people groped about blindly, feeling their way through life. Indeed, according to this sensory classification of historical periods, it was only in the Enlightenment, the eighteenth-century age of reason, that the light of learning finally dispelled the shadows of past ignorance and enabled people to think clearly about the world.

The term Dark Ages, with its pejorative connotations, is no longer generally used by historians, who now concede that, though most of the medieval population may have been unlettered, they were not intellectually benighted. In the words of the eminent historian Keith Thomas, "It would be utterly wrong to think that [premodern] illiterates lived in some sort of mental darkness" (1986: 105). Early admissions that the darkness of the Middle Ages was pierced by a few rays of light have led to assertions that the Middle Ages had its own "enlightenment(s)," prefiguring that of the eighteenth century. In recent decades so much work has been done on the cultural achievements of the Middle Ages that the period might now be said to be positively basking in the sun.

Despite all of the recent scholarship on the Middle Ages, there nevertheless remains much to be learned about the tactile values that shaped the sensibility and sociality of the period, the embodied life that so repelled earlier historians that it seemed akin to savagery. By exploring the corporeal sensations and symbols of the Middle Ages, *The Deepest Sense* attempts to both give readers a feel for medieval life and to demonstrate the social and religious centrality of touch during this formative period of Western civilization.

The emphasis in much of the present book is on the persistence of collective practices and beliefs involving touch over the *longue durée*. At points throughout the book and specifically in the last chapters, however, the reader's attention is directed to the interplay of tactile practices and cultural change as the West undergoes its long transition from the structures of medieval life to those of modernity (here used in the sociological sense to refer to the period beginning with the eighteenth century). Among the subjects considered are the decline of the medieval "tactile" cosmology, the development of a culture of comfort, the "discovery" of the nervous system, and the industrialization of touch. As the reader moves through the book from topic to topic and from period to period the plot thickens and broader issues of social control and representation come to the fore.

The eight chapters of the book explore different tactile realms, from the feel of the world to the (dis)comforts of home, from the rites of pleasure to the disciplinary uses of pain, and from the gestures of faith to the postures of the drill. Each chapter provides a general overview of its subject matter together with intimate accounts of tactile experiences. Where citations are made from medieval texts, translations or modernizations have been selected that give a good "feel" for the original. Reading through poignant descriptions of the devastation occasioned by the Black Death in the fourteenth century or the harsh conditions of nineteenth-century prison life, we find that history, far from being a dry and lifeless subject, touches us to the quick.

To some, exploring the history of touch may seem like an attempt to reassert old stereotypes of earlier periods as crude and unenlightened—as dark ages. However, it is precisely this engrained association of touch with irrationality and primitivism that must be overcome before one can appreciate the tactile values of any particular period. As regards the Middle Ages, it bears noting that many people of the time were proud of the accomplishments of their age and quite ready to use tactile metaphors to express it. The eleventh-century Abbot Guibert of Nogent, paraphrasing a biblical text, declared that "our little fingers are thicker than the backs of our fathers," to signal the superiority of his own period (Guibert of Nogent 1984: 10). A medieval critic of the later gloomy assessment of the age might well have responded like one of the characters in a seventeenth-century play by Shadwell : "I am not so dark either, I am sharp, sharp as a needle!" (1927: 263).

If the aim of the history of touch is not to denigrate premodernity as a primitive world of mindless sensations, neither is it to romanticize it as a purveyor of warm tactile experiences in contrast to the cold visual values of modernity. The intention is rather to explore how the corporeal practices of any particular period relate to the cultural context of the time, and how this relationship changes under the influence of new factors. As the following chapters show, touch does not simply recede from cultural life in modernity, it is reeducated, and while it retreats from some domains, it expands into others.

The topic of touch is, of course, capacious, and the first question to ask before undertaking its study is what one means by touch. While the sense of touch may be most closely associated with physical contact, it can also include sensations of heat, pain, pleasure, and movement, among others. To the extent possible, I have tried to consider a range of tactile sensations in this work, while at the same time taking into account those aspects of touch that were of particular relevance in the periods under study.

Touch is not only highly complex in itself, it is also closely related to the other senses (as well as to the emotions). Indeed, all of the senses can be, and have been, thought of as having tactile dimensions—even sight involves eye movement. It is not my aim here to try to disentangle tactile experience from its multisensorial context, but rather to foreground sensations that have customarily been understood to be so basic to bodily existence that they have been taken for granted.

The Deepest Sense does not intend to offer a comprehensive history of the culture of touch. There are, inevitably, gaps in the material covered—tactile, cultural, and temporal. The historical investigation I have initiated here might be taken backward to antiquity or forward to the present day, or across to other cultures. It might be fleshed out—reshaped—in numerous ways by further research. While I have done my best to produce an informed and thought-provoking guide to the tactile past, the exploration of past worlds of touch provides more than a handful for any historian.

I have generally given less attention to topics that have already been the subject of extensive research, such as the history of sexuality. On the other hand, I have developed areas that thus far have received little consideration within the history of the body and the senses, such as the relationship between humans and animals. While I refer to scientific theories of perception within their cultural context, I do not try to employ modern data about the physiology of touch to explain the practices of the past. Sander Gilman has noted that works on touch tend "to return over and over again to the physiological 'realities' for their understanding of the history or culture of touch" (1993: 198). This remains the case today when concepts and conclusions drawn from neuroscience tend to creep into, if not dominate, cultural investigations of the senses across the humanities and social sciences. Yet to rely on science for a true understanding of perception is both to disregard the ways in which science is itself a social construct and to detract from the significance of culturally specific models of sensation.

The history of touch presented here is grounded in the work of the Annales School, which aimed to broaden our understanding of the past by investigating collective beliefs and practices within their social, physical, and economic environments. One of the founders of that school, Marc Bloch, explored medieval structures of corporeal behavior and social organization in works such as *The Royal Touch* (1973) and *Feudal Society* (1989). Another of its founders, Lucien Febrve, provocatively suggested in 1947 that "a series of fascinating studies could be done on the sensory underpinnings of thought in different periods" (1982: 436). Other Annales historians—such as Philippe Ariès, Robert Mandrou, Jacques Le Goff and Emmanuel Le Roy Ladurie—would take up the challenge, at least in part, and bring perception into the historical domain. The first full-length history of the senses, *The Foul and the Fragrant: Odor and the French Social Imagination*, was written by Alain Corbin (1986). This seminal work was later followed by an influential exploration of the significance of sound in nineteenth-century rural France titled *Village Bells* (1998; see also Corbin 1995 and 2005).

Some sixty years after Febvre first called for a historical investigation of perception, work on the history of the senses is flourishing. The most recent books on the subject include Robert Jütte's *A History of the Senses* (2005) and Mark Smith's *Sensing the Past* (2007), along with a number of specialized studies (e.g., Woolgar 2006; Cowan and Steward, 2007; Nichols, Kablitz, and Calhoun 2008; Schleif and Newhauser 2010). When it comes to works on individual senses, however, there is a marked disparity in the amount of scholarly attention each has received. While the cultures of sight and hearing have been the subject of numerous important studies, much less has been said about the senses of smell, taste, and touch. Yet the so-called lower senses have not been left completely unhistoricized. As regards the history of touch, works dealing with issues in the field include Marjorie O'Rourke Boyle's (1998) examination of the significance of hands and posture in the sixteenth century, Laura Gowing's (2003) study of women's corporeal experience in the seventeenth century, Elizabeth Harvey's (2002) anthology of essays on touch during the same period, and my own edited collection of writings on touch in history and across cultures, *The Book of Touch* (Classen 2005a). Mark Paterson (2007) has recently explored the history of philosophical treatments of touch and its relevance to the haptic technology and digital culture of the present day. While not explicitly on touch, Stephen Connor's *Book of Skin* (2004) reminds us that the cultural meanings and sensory qualities of the human skin are multifold.

Along with the work of the Annales historians, another formative influence on this book has been the methodological approach known as the anthropology of the senses. In the 1990s Canadian anthropologist David Howes, along with others, advocated that attention be paid to how sensory experience is collectively patterned to shape people's understanding of and interaction with the world (see Howes 1991; 2003; 2005). A knowledge of the groundbreaking work of the anthropology of the senses is now essential for any one wishing to explore the life of the senses in cultural context.

A distinguishing feature of an anthropological approach to the senses is that it makes it possible to transcend the bounds of language. The historian of the senses undertakes what could be called deep anthropology, seeking the unspoken messages of our bodies and exploring our most intimate relationships. Often people, particularly in societies that feel no compulsion to "put it all into words," don't talk about their experiences. A lack of words, however, does not mean a lack of feelings or of social significance. Many feelings are difficult to put into language, they are too subtle or too powerful or too complex. The anthropology of the senses sensitizes us to the multiple ways in which humans communicate and express themselves through nonlinguistic modalities.

Historians, unlike anthropologists, must rely a great deal on texts for their material, though an exploration of the visual images and material artifacts of the period under study can contribute enormously. Even when dealing with texts, however, those who seek sensory references will find plenty to occupy them. Take for example, the following passage concerning the life of the castle and the countryside written in 1518:

> Whether perched on a peak or situated in a plain, the castle was built not
> for pleasure but for defense, surrounded by moats and trenches, cramped

within, burdened with stables for animals large and small, dark buildings for bombards and stores of pitch and sulfur, swollen with stores of armaments and machines of war. Everywhere the disagreeable odor of powder dominates. And the dogs with their filth—what a fine smell that is! And the comings and goings of the knights, among them bandits, brigands and thieves. Usually the house is wide open, because we do not know who is who and do not take much trouble to find out. We hear the bleating of the sheep, the mooing of the cows, the barking of the dogs, the shouts of men working in the fields, the grinding and clatter of carts and wagons. And near the house, which is close by the woods, we even have the cry of the wolf. (Ulrich von Hutten, cited by Braunstein 1988: 540).

In this passage, castle life is presented as a conglomeration of (rather disagreeable) sensations. The reader goes from feeling cramped—closed in by encircling trenches and swollen rooms—to being exposed—open to all and sundry. The ambience is pervaded by odors and sounds—of war, of work, of animals. All of these sensations (few of which, notably, are visual) are set on edge by the fearsome howl of the wolf just outside the bounds of human settlement. Such passages set to rest the notion that the sensory life of the past is unavailable to the historian, and also dispel any romantic ideas of premodern sensuality.

Despite the sensory richness of many period accounts, it is still often the case that people leave no record of their feelings. The corporeal practices and sensory values that define life may be so pervasive they are taken for granted and left unmentioned. The history of touch is, consequently, often an inferred history. It must move sideways from a suggestive phrase to a characteristic practice to an informative artifact or site, and even inward to one's own distinctive yet shared corporeal experience, rather than in a linear fashion from narrative to narrative, event to event. It is not just a history from below. It is a history from inside and a history from in between—the kind of history one needs to explore the cultural dimensions of our deepest sense.

THE DEEPEST SENSE

CHAPTER ONE

A Place by the Fire

THE COMMON TOUCH

Much of medieval life was lived in common with others. This was particularly the case when large groups of people lived under one roof, as in a castle or a monastery, but also held true of people living within villages or settlements. Keeping close to others allowed individuals to reap the benefits of common labor and also provided much needed security. During a time when food shortages, banditry, feuds, and warfare were commonplace, strong social ties meant a stronger chance of survival. Marc Bloch wrote of feudal society: "The best-served hero was he whose warriors were all joined to him either by the new feudal relationship of vassalage; or by the ancient tie of kinship" (1961: 124). The worst-served person, by contrast, was one with no such social ties: "The unattached person during the Middle Ages was one either condemned to exile or doomed to death" (Mumford, 1938: 29). It was a time when it was dangerous to stand alone as an individual and dangerous to venture outside the pale—the enclosing boundaries of one's community.

The identification of the individual with the group was so strong during the Middle Ages that a whole kin group or village might be held responsible for the acts of one of its members. In one case of 1260, a French knight named Louis Defeux took a man who assaulted him to court. The assailant explained that the assault was in retaliation for an attack he had suffered from Defeux's nephew. The judge, seeing the justice of this defense, ruled in favor of the assailant (126–27). The social body to which Louis Defeux belonged was responsible for the original crime and therefore any adult male member (i.e., person of authority) belonging to the social body was liable to receive retribution for it. Even when the importance of feudal and kin relationships declined in the later Middle Ages with the rise in importance of cities—which had their own complex networks of interdependence—the ideal of corporate unity remained a powerful social and symbolic force.

The unity of the social body, which ideally enabled it to stand together in good times and bad, was promoted through a number of communal practices. One of these was eating together. Eating as a group not only made the most efficient use of food and fuel resources, it also strengthened social bonds. Feasting in the great hall of a manor house or castle, the lord and his men reinforced their sense of corporate identity. The customary sharing of bowls and cups during meals further fostered a feeling of unity. As all were members of one social body there was no reason why plates should not be common.

This common feasting was, furthermore, a hands-on experience. In the Middle Ages all food, aside from soups and stews that required spoons, was finger food (Flandrin 1989: 266–67). Tactile table manners centered on ensuring that the hands of diners were reasonably clean before being dipped in a common bowl (and that fingers were not licked between dippings). As Norbert Elias pointed out in *The Civilizing Process,* rather than thinking of such practices as indicative of a barbaric social formation, we need to investigate how they responded to the needs and values of the time (1994: 55). Picking up food directly with one's hands out of a common bowl indicated that no artificial barriers or niggling suspicions separated oneself from one's food and one's fellows. In an age when survival depended on an intimate knowledge of the land and when the strength of the individual lay in the strength of the group, cultivating this sense of integration with the social and physical environment was all important.

When the use of forks began to spread among the nobility in the seventeenth century, the users were considered by many to be as ridiculous and offensive as someone would be in our own day who insisted on shaking hands using a stick. One French satire of 1605 described the use of forks as follows: "They never touch the meat with their hands but with forks which they raise to the mouth as they reach forward with their necks. . . . They take the salad with forks . . ., however difficult it may be to pick up, and they would rather touch their mouths with this little forked instrument than with their hands" (cited by Flandrin 1989: 269).

It was said of a Byzantine princess who introduced the use of forks to Italy that her early death was a direct result of her "excessive delicacy" in refusing to pick up her food with her hands. Not only was the use of forks seen as affected, it was also condemned as impious. The stern comment of one Italian priest was that "God in his wisdom has provided man with natural forks—his fingers" (Giblin 1987: 46).

Along with eating, another practice that was frequently communal in the Middle Ages was bathing. Soaking together in a common tub was a pleasant way to foster intimacy among family members and neighbors. At times the conviviality of eating was added to that of bathing and food and drink would be served to the bathers seated around the tub. In this case the practice of eating out of a common bowl was supplemented by that of *being* in a common bowl.

Church officials expressed concern about shared baths leading to lewd behavior—and, indeed, many medieval bath houses were sites of prostitution. Supporters of the practice, however, upheld the fundamental innocence of the institution, in which whole families participated. One seventeenth-century account of public bathing in Basel records: "The members of the lower classes [and] the polite citizens undressed in the house and walked naked across the public road to the Bath house. . . . Yes, how often the father runs naked from the house with a single shirt together with his equally naked wife and naked children to the bath" (V. Smith 2007: 172). The communal nakedness of the tub was supplemented by communal touching. Such touch, however, was not necessarily considered to be detrimental to good morals. In the sixteenth century the Protestant reformer Ulrich von Hutten said of the practice of public bathing in Germany, "Yes, they touch one another in a friendly fashion [but] . . . nowhere is honour stronger than here. . . . They trust one another and live in good faith free and humbly without deception" (169). It was worthwhile then to risk the possibly harmful consequences of an overly free use of touch to create a environment of openness and trust.

Not even at night did individuals necessarily retreat into their own private space. Medieval beds were often not just matrimonial, but familial, with as many family members as possible crowding into one large bed (Barthélemy and Contamine 1988: 497). Servants, furthermore, would often sleep in or beside their master's or mistress's bedroom. At night the great hall of the manor house might be turned into one vast dormitory for knights and servants, who would sleep on the table boards and floors. Apprentices, students, and soldiers would customarily sleep together and travelers might well be expected to share a bed at an inn. One charming twelfth-century carving from the cathedral of Autun in France shows the three Magi, exhausted from their long journey, cuddled together in one bed. One of the kings, whose hand is being touched by an angel, has a look of startled wakefulness, while his companions slumber peacefully beside him. (Similar images can be found in other medieval churches, such as the Cathedral of Amiens.)

Sleeping together not only economized on furniture and floor space, it also provided warmth and security—two values that were highly prized in the Middle

Ages. Moreover, sharing a bed was a way to forge alliances and cement friendships. It was recorded of Richard the Lionhearted that he and his ally King Phillip II of France ate out of the same plate and slept in the same bed. Whatever personal satisfaction these practices might have given Richard, they doubtless also had a strategic significance.

Just as eating together required good manners, so did sleeping together. Erasmus advised, "If you share a bed with a comrade, lie quietly; do not toss with your body, for this can lay yourself bare or inconvenience your companion by pulling away the blankets" (cited in Elias 1994: 64). The emphasis on not laying oneself bare came from the fact that most people slept naked, a situation that would have increased the intimacy of any contact that took place.

Common forms of social touching in the Middle Ages included embracing, kissing, and holding hands. These acts were not limited to male-female or parent-child interaction: men might kiss men and women hold hands with women. While such tactile tokens of goodwill were in general use throughout Europe, certain regions were particularly effusive. Describing a trip he made to England in the late fifteenth century, Erasmus wrote, "When a visit is paid, the first act of hospitality is a kiss, and when guests depart, the same entertainment is repeated; whenever a meeting takes place there is kissing in abundance; in fact whatever way you turn, you are never without it. Oh Faustus, if you had once tasted how sweet and fragrant those kisses are, you would indeed wish to be a traveller . . . for your whole life, in England" (Erasmus 1962: 203). Evidently modern representations of England as a physically uneffusive society did not have their roots in the Middle Ages.

A few contemporary scholars have seen in the medieval practice of men kissing men signs of a homosexual orientation. One historian, for example, has said of the practice that "two men who . . . kiss each other are surely more likely to be having sex than two men who do not" (Guy-Bray 2002: 11). Following this logic, however, one might as well say of present-day society that two men who shake hands with each other are more likely to be having sex than two men who do not. When assessing the significance of tactile practices of any kind it is essential to situate them within their particular cultural context.

In the Middle Ages both handholding and kissing could be employed as ritual and legal signs of contractual obligations. When a man formally placed his hands inside the hands of another man, it meant that he was offering him his services as his vassal in exchange for certain material and social benefits. This *immixtio manuum* or insertion of hands physically enacted the tradition that placed everyone in a household "in the hand" of its lord. Gloves were not permitted during the ceremony because a true union could only be accomplished through skin-to-skin contact (Duby 1988: 13; Burrow 2002).

An exchanged kiss on the mouth, the "kiss of peace," often followed hand-holding as a way of sealing a contract. As the spirit was closely associated with the breath in premodernity, a kiss was thought to unite both body and spirit. For this reason kissing was regarded by some, especially within the Church, as a more binding act than holding hands. One account from twelfth-century France records how, when a nobleman offered his hand to seal a transaction with a group of monks, the monks insisted instead on a kiss, which they held to be both more "Christian" and a better guarantee of good faith (Petkov 2003: 48–49).

A good illustration of the moral and legal weight given to this kiss of peace can be seen in the attempts to effect a formal reconciliation between the exiled Archbishop Thomas Becket and King Henry II in 1169. The king agreed to accept Becket back in his "love and grace" but refused to kiss him. Henry argued that in a fit of anger he had sworn never to kiss Becket again. Becket, following Pope Alexander's advice, insisted on having the security of a kiss. Henry offered to have his young son kiss the archbishop instead. This offer was rejected on the grounds that the kiss had to be proffered personally by the king to serve as a valid warranty. In the end Becket returned to England without the kiss only to be murdered by Henry's knights a few days later. No kiss of peace evidently meant no guarantee of safety (63–65).

Such corporeal rites of commitment as the kiss and the hand clasp would have been more meaningful and more binding to many than a mere signed document. Written documents, in any case, would have been unintelligible to the majority of the population who were illiterate. In the Middle Ages information was generally communicated through the medium of the human body, either through speech or through other sensory signs (such as kisses) and not through the impersonal and disembodied medium of a written text. Learning, likewise, customarily took place through doing and not through reading. One did not learn how to cook by reading a cookbook or how to farm by reading a manual on agriculture. Hands-on training was required. The scanty use of writing during this time helped to shape the interpersonal dynamics of the period and increase social interdependency.

The worst crime in this era of social interdependence was betrayal. The most severe punishments—being flayed, hanged and quartered, or burnt alive—accordingly were meted to those who were deemed traitors, either to their earthly or heavenly lord (Bellamy 1970: 13). In Dante's *Inferno,* traitors are consigned to the innermost circle of Hell as the worst of sinners. In the very center of Dante's Hell a three-headed Satan gnaws on three of history's most notorious traitors: Brutus and Cassius, who conspired to assassinate Julius Caesar, and Judas, who betrayed his Lord with the very sign of fealty: a kiss.

Throughout the Middle Ages were challenges to the idealized model of a hierarchized social body with all members from the head down working together for the common good. Discordances might arise over something as seemingly minor as seating rights in church pews. It was in the later medieval period, however, that serious social rifts became particularly notable and widespread. This is the period of the peasants' rebellions. Among the various reasons for the breakdown in social order at this time was the growing divisiveness of society. The more the nobles distinguished themselves from the peasantry, the less contact they wanted with them and the more marginalized the peasants felt. When in the fourteenth century lords and ladies began to abandon the great hall to dine privately in their rooms, it was taken as one more sign of social disintegration. William Langland wrote about this in *The Vision of Piers Plowman:*

> Woe is in the hall in all times and seasons
> Where neither lord nor lady likes to linger
> Now each rich man has a rule to eat in secret
> In a private parlour . . . (1935: 115)

The growing literacy of the educated classes strengthened class divisions as written texts, rather than personal relations, were increasingly used to order society (Chartier 1989: 159). Keith Thomas has written that the effect of the spread of literacy during this period "was to consolidate the authority of the educated classes over their inferiors and to impoverish and disparage other forms of expression" (1986: 121).

Nowhere is this point brought out more clearly than in Shakespeare's historical play *Henry VI, Part 2* (see Sousa 1996). In this play the nobility are accused of employing the power of writing to oppress the poor: "Thou has put [poor men] in prison, and because they could not read thou hast hanged them, when, indeed, only for that cause they been most worthy to live" (IV.vii.43–48). According to this perspective, it is not the poor who should be punished for being illiterate but the literate nobility. The schoolteachers are also declared to be at fault, for it is they who "corrupted the youth of the realm" (IV.vii.34–39) by teaching them how to write in the first place. The solution to this unjust state of affairs is said to be to replace impersonal written directives with direct, embodied government: "Away, burn all the records of the realm," the leader of the rebellion proclaims, "my mouth shall be the parliament of England" (IV.vii.41).

Shakespeare based his play on two late medieval revolts—the Peasants' Revolt of 1381 and Jack Cade's Rebellion of 1450. In the Peasants' Revolt, legal records were burnt and the traditional acts of vassalage mocked. When the leader of the Revolt, Wat Tyler, met with the king, "he half bent his knee" and "shook [the king's] hand roughly and forcefully" (Galbraith 1927: 147). During Jack Cade's Rebellion the traditional kiss of peace was parodied when the severed heads of noblemen were put on pikes and made to kiss each other. Such rough handling indicated that the old bonds of alliance were being broken and that the common touch could destroy—as well as uphold—the social order.

A PLACE BY THE FIRE

In the Middle Ages home was where the hearth was. The fireplace provided families with life-sustaining heat and enabled them to have hot, cooked meals. As we know from *Piers Plowman* people of the time liked their food "hot or hotter, against a cold stomach" (Langland 1935: 87). The hearth not only kept people physically warm, it also drew the household together and was the center for social interaction in the home. The warmth of the fire became human warmth as those gathered around it talked and ate and worked together.

The conservation of heat within a house was a major concern in the colder regions of Europe. For the sake of warmth, as well as for reasons of economy, most houses were small, with few internal divisions. Windows were also kept small to reduce draughts within the house (glass windows did not become affordable for ordinary homes until the seventeenth century). Covering walls with animal skins or hangings and floors with straw or rushes—which had the added benefit of soaking up spills—helped to insulate the house. Yet, away from its warm, cheerful hearth the medieval home in winter was notoriously cold.

On winter days people would spend as much time as they could near the hearth, which was usually located in the center of the room. One domestic scene from the early sixteenth-century Grimani Breviary depicts a family warming itself round a fire inside a snow-covered hut. The woman is spinning wool and the boy has gone only a few paces away from the fire to urinate through the open doorway. Outside a woman draped in a shawl and blowing on her cold hands is returning to the gratifying blaze indoors. In the distance a farmer drives a donkey, lost in a wilderness of snow (see Orme 2001: 2).

The association of the hearth with physical and social comfort can be seen in the frequent request of the elderly that their children provide them with "a place by the fire." Moralists warned parents, however, not to place overmuch trust in filial promises of a home in their old age. One medieval story told of an old man who was denied not only a place by the fire by his son but even a blanket. When the grandson is given a sack to place over the chilled body of his grandfather the boy tears it in two, declaring that he will keep half for his own father when he grows old (Gies and Gies 1990: 121–22). The moral of the story: keep your parents warm and comfortable in their old age and your children will keep you warm and comfortable in yours.

To be left out in the cold was the worst of fates for it combined a potentially deadly physical hardship with a psychologically devastating social exclusion. Beggars and misfits were left out in the cold, heretics were driven out into it. This last was the fate of the members of an unorthodox sect who were driven out of Oxford in 1166: "Then with their clothes cut off to the waist they were publicly flogged and with resounding blows driven forth from the city into the intolerable cold, for it was wintertime. None shewed the slightest pity on them and they perished miserably" (cited in Hassall 1957: 82).

For all the social and practical importance of the hearth, however, it had serious shortcomings. For one thing, it often filled the room with irritating smoke. An old adage declared a smoky fireplace, a leaky roof, and a scolding wife to be the three things that could drive a man from home. (A woman, presumably, had no choice but to remain within.) The medieval fireplace, furthermore, was notably inefficient at heating a room. People who sat facing a fire would have hot fronts but their backs were quite likely to be cold.

As late as the sixteenth century homes were still so chilly that on a trip to Switzerland Montaigne was surprised to find how pleasantly warm the stove-heated houses were—despite a certain malodor: "Once you have swallowed a certain smell in the air that strikes you as you come in, all that remains is a gentle and even warmth." (2003: 1078). Indeed, so frigid were most house interiors that people might wear more clothing indoors than out, where activity and sunshine would help keep them warm. Montaigne noted that with their pleasantly warm rooms the Swiss could reverse this pattern: "Whereas we put on our warm furred dressing gowns when we enter the house, they on the contrary stay in their doublets and go bareheaded in the heated room, and get dressed warmly to go back into the open air" (ibid.).

The enduring penchant for "long, full gowns with many folds" had much to do with the protection such clothing offered from the cold (Mandrou 1976: 27). This style of clothing, in turn, helped to shape characteristic ways of walking and holding one's body: "The way a man walked to avoid tripping over the many folds, the way he held his arms well away from his body to be able to extricate his hands more easily and hold up the drooping folds was determined by it. Inevitably he moved slowly and took long strides" (27–28). Such dignified bearing was by no means universal. The author of the fourteenth-century *Cloud of Unknowing*, for example, noted a range of idiosyncratic corporeal practices among his contemporaries: "For some people are so burdened with quaint and unseemly posturing in their behaviour, that when they have to listen to anything, they waggle their heads from side to side and up and down most oddly. . . . Others, when they have to speak, use their fingers, either poking on their own fingers or their chest, or the chests of those to whom they are speaking. Others yet can neither sit, stand, nor lie still, they have to be tapping with their feet, or doing something with their hands" (*Cloud of Unknowing* 1981: 223). Such accounts of extravagant bodily practices indicate that an emphasis on group solidarity did not necessarily translate into corporeal uniformity; there was plenty of room for individual variation in postures and gestures (see further Bremmer and Roodenburg 1991).

Clothing was a key indicator of social status. While the aristocracy might favor "long, full gowns with many folds," peasants usually wore shorter clothes that were more suited to physical activity and less wasteful of cloth. The coarse, scratchy wool of a peasant's tunic was a tactile sign of the hardships peasants could expect to encounter in life as well as of their low social status and supposedly coarse natures. The smooth silk that caressed the bodies of the rich and noble, by contrast, signaled the life of ease to which they were entitled, as well as their supposedly more refined and delicate natures. Class distinctions were impressed on the skin through the use of symbolically potent textiles.

In some countries sumptuary laws were enacted in the late Middle Ages that specifically limited certain materials to the social elite. In England, for example, silk was technically restricted to the nobility above the rank of viscount while the wearers of velvet had to be at least members of the court. In actual practice the cast-off finery of the wealthy did sometimes make its way onto the backs of the lower classes through gifts to servants or through the thriving market in second-hand clothes. Even a beggar might enjoy a touch of luxury as the medieval rhyme tells us:

> Hark, hark, the dogs do bark,
> The beggars are coming to town.
> Some in rags and some in jags [fashionably slashed garments],
> And one in a velvet gown.

Generally, however, the softer the cloth, the higher the social rank.

Greater wealth, however, did not always mean greater bodily comfort. Fashion and social ostentation often required a sacrifice of comfort. One example of this is the weighty cloth of gold (made by using silk threads wound with gold wire) that was favored by medieval royalty on ceremonial occasions. Another is the long, pointed shoes that came into fashion in the fourteenth century. To hold their shape, the toes of these shoes were stuffed with hair or moss. Aside from the minor inconveniences they caused, which no doubt included a good deal of tripping, the shoes permanently deformed the feet of many medieval men and women (Mays 2005). Finally, it should be kept in mind that many wealthy and powerful individuals wore hair shirts or other devices for bodily mortification under their fine vestments as part of their devotional practice.

As regards furniture, the bed was the most important item in the sparsely furnished medieval home. The best beds consisted of a frame, which lifted the sleepers off the cold, hard ground, a soft feather mattress, fine linen sheets, a downy quilt, and a bedspread lined with fur. Bed curtains and a canopy added the final touch, sheltering sleepers from cold draughts and bothersome insects and creating a sense of intimacy. The poor made do with a sack of straw, perhaps placed directly on a dirt floor, and coarse wool blankets. A French miniature from the fifteenth century shows a beggar lying on a straw mattress, covered with a ragged blanket through which his legs (one of which is bandaged) protrude. Holes in the walls and roof, letting in the cold and the rain, complete this picture of painful poverty (Barthélemy and Contamine 1988: 490–94).

To a certain extent the poor would have grown accustomed to cold and rough sensations through habitual exposure to them. Montaigne (1943: 202) writes, "Someone or other was asking one of our beggars whom he saw in the depth of winter as cheery in his shirt as someone muffled to the ears in sables, how he could endure it. 'And you, sir,' he answered, 'you have your face uncovered; now I am all face.'" The frigid air that the rich man can only bear on his face the beggar claims to be able to bear all over his body. While not groundless, however, the notion of the hardiness of the poor would have been socially convenient for the better-off classes, as it implied there was no need to lessen hardships that were not really felt.

Aside from beds, other furniture within the home might consist of a chest for storage, stools or benches, and a trestle table. The table board would be set on its trestles when it was time for a meal and later dismantled and put to the side of the room. (An Anglo-Saxon riddle described the table as a richly dressed quadruped at dinner and a despoiled cripple afterwards.) Chairs were few, as they were symbolic artifacts of authority and not simply places to sit. Lords and bishops sat in chairs. The king, of course, had the most symbolically potent chair of all—the throne. The chair set the sitter off from his fellows; ordinary people crowded companionably together on benches.

The outdoor complement to the medieval home of higher rank was the walled garden. In the garden one could warm oneself in the sun and enjoy the scents and sounds of nature, sheltered by its walls from the wind and from outsiders. A splashing fountain provided a cool contrast to the warmth of the sun, while a turf bench offered a soft and fragrant place to sit. It was a good place, medieval pictures tell us, for ladies to sit with their babies or their needlework—in contact with nature and yet still within the protective boundaries of the home.

One great advantage to the world outdoors in the Middle Ages was its good visibility, for their small windows kept house interiors dim even at midday. Indoors or outdoors, however, when night fell the whole world grew dark. Medieval fireplaces, lamps, and candles were but poor sources of illumination and indeed, the resources they consumed were generally considered too valuable to be squandered for the sake of mere brightness. Hence, "from curfew to the opening of the gates, the town, with all its lights and fires extinguished, shrank fearfully into darkness" (Mandrou 1976: 55). Nighttime was the realm of the unknown and the dangerous, of thieves, predatory animals, demons and ghosts. Nighttime was also the realm of touch, when sight failed and the tactile senses attained their full potential.

In the Middle Ages a great deal of time was spent in the dark, particularly in winter. It was essential to be able to feel one's way around: to make one's way home, to dress oneself, nurse one's children, make a fire, prepare food, in the dark. Placing furniture against the walls, as was the custom in medieval homes, helped to avoid accidents when moving about dark rooms. "At nighttime," A. Roger Ekirch writes in his history of the night, "persons embraced a way of doing things distinct from the rhythms and rituals of the visible world." (2005: 119). In the darkness, the members of a household communicated with each other by touch as well as by voice, patting and prodding and pinching. In this one sense, at least, the Middle Ages were indeed dark ages.

For those outside at night a stick or staff extended the tactile reach of the hand. Descartes would write of this, "No doubt you have had the experience of walking at night over rough ground without a light, and finding it necessary to use a stick in order to guide yourself. . . . You may have been able to notice that by means of this stick you could feel the various objects situated around you, and that you could even tell whether they were trees or stones or sand or water or grass or mud" (55).

As time passed, affordable plate-glass windows and better means of illumination brought more light into the home, reducing the practical importance of touch and opening up new possibilities for the eyes. Even so, being able to find one's way by touch in the dark remained a useful skill well into the modern era (122).

As time passed houses also grew warmer. In the late Middle Ages the construction of chimneys led to an increase in the amount of heat and a reduction in the amount of smoke in homes. In *Piers Plowman* Langland mentions a "chamber with a chimney" as being a room preferred by the lord and his family over the great hall, which was rather draughty (1935: 115). The increased domestic comfort produced by the introduction of chimneys accompanied a general improvement in living conditions. In 1557 William Harrison remarked that the old men in his English village "noted three things to be marvellously altered in England within their sound remembrance." The first was "the multitude of chimneys lately erected." The second was the "amendment of lodging" or improvement in home comforts. Regarding this, the men recalled that in their youth they had "lien full oft upon straw pallets . . . and a good round log under their heads":

> If it were so that our fathers or the goodman of the house had within seven years after his marriage purchased a mattress or flock-bed, and thereto a sack of chaff to rest his head upon, he thought himself to be as well lodged as the lord of the town, that peradventure lay seldom in a bed of down or whole feathers, so well were they contented with such base kind of furniture. . . . Pillows . . . were thought meet only for women in childbed. As for servants, if they had any sheet above them it was well, for seldom had they any under their bodies to keep them from the pricking straws that ran oft through their hardened hides (1994: 200–201).

The third great change, according to the village elders, concerned another domestic refinement: the use of pewter dishes and silver or tin spoons instead of the old wooden platters and spoons.

Harrison himself saw the recent improvements as contributing to a decrease in general hardiness: "Now we have many chimneys, and yet our tenderlings complain of rheums, catarrahs, and [colds]. Then we had none but [open hearths] and our heads did never ache" (276). In contrast to the "hardened hides" of old, sixteenth-century bodies seemed tender and vulnerable, softened by an array of new domestic comforts.

THE WALLED CITY

The typical medieval city was a walled city. The walls were tangible markers of corporate strength and at the same time enclosing arms that protected and contained the city's inhabitants. In the morning people would stream through the city's gates to work in the fields outside. At dusk they came streaming back in, gathering together like sheep in a corral. To be without the walls was to be vulnerable, exposed to the danger and disorder of the outside world.

As medievalists have noted, "building walls was a reflex of the medieval mind" (Barthélemy and Contamine 1988: 438). In a tradition that dated back to antiquity, even the human body might be conceptualized as a miniature walled city or castle, inhabited by the soul. An illustration of this idea occurs in a fifteenth-century architectural treatise by Francisco di Giorgio Martini, which shows a walled city in the shape of a human body with a fortress crowning the head and towers around the feet and elbows (Pepper 2002: 115).

Religion presented the walled city of the soul as a city besieged by vices that were always ready to rush in through the gateways of the senses and take control. Peter Damian expounded on this theme in one of his letters in which he advised Christians to "close then . . . these gates of the senses of the body, and block up the phalanxes of the onrushing vices, and open them up for the troops of the spiritual virtues" (cited in Vinge 1975: 65). The metaphor worked because people at the time could well imagine, if they had not personally experienced, the state of being besieged by hostile forces within a walled city.

An important sensory effect of city walls was that, from ground level, they blocked vision by limiting external views. Even within the city, while a cathedral or a castle might stand out as a landmark, views were limited. "Cities were mazes of twisting, tiny streets, impasses, and courts; squares were small, and there were few broad vistas . . ." (Barthélemy and Contamine 1988: 439). When the second stories of houses extended over a narrow corridor a street might become almost a tunnel. A surviving example of such a street is the seven-foot-wide Ruelle des Chats in the French city of Troyes. In this "Cat's Alley" the housetops lean toward each other until they almost touch, blocking the entry of sunlight. Walking through a neighborhood of such twisting streets and dark lanes one might well find the senses of touch and smell to be as informative as the sense of sight.

The textures of the medieval city were of natural materials, stone, wood, clay, and straw. The difficulty of transporting materials over long distances meant that cities were built by local craftsmen out of the particular materials at hand. This gave cities their own local look and feel. Buildings were rarely set back from streets, and many a medieval house wall must have received the touch of a passing hand. When a horse and cart came trundling along a narrow street, pedestrians might well find themselves obliged to press their whole bodies against those walls to make room.

The central streets in the city were paved with stones, the rest were dirt. On a dry day medieval feet—perhaps bare—would kick through dust and pebbles, while on a wet day, they would slog through mud or slip on the rounded tops of cobblestones. Streets also provided a ready supply of stones to throw at foreigners, beggars, or dogs. Describing a chain of tactile incidents, one medieval account tells of a man who, bitten by a dog, picked up a stone to throw at him, slipped, hit his head on a wall and died (Gies and Gies 1990: 103).

Walking along medieval streets meant coming into contact with a certain amount of waste, from household rubbish to workshop waste. Some of the refuse would be retrieved by scavengers, some would be eaten by animals, and some would be washed away by rain. The rest would be ground into the street to become part of the texture of city life.

The feel of the medieval city, however, depended not only on its physical makeup, but also on the activity that occurred within its walls. At busy times of day streets would be jammed with pedestrians and the occasional rider. Some people might travel in horse-drawn carts but this was an uncomfortable way to journey over unpaved roads, and was furthermore regarded as only suitable for the old and infirm. Moving through the city one would have contrasting sensations of being squeezed by a narrow street and then liberated as one exited into an open square. Perhaps one would be humbled or awed by the sudden appearance of a towering church around a street corner (Mumford 1938: 62).

Carpenters, cobblers, potters, and other tradespeople would often invade the street with their activities and wares. In larger cities whole streets might be dedicated to certain trades. Thus in the medieval city of Coventry there were streets named Ironmongers Row, Potter Row, Great Butchery, and Spicer Stoke (meaning "the place of the grocers"). Each of these different streets (though not entirely restricted to the practice of the trade that gave it its name) would have had a different look, smell, and sound along with a different feel. Streets that ran with the blood of slaughtered animals and echoed with their cries would have made a quite different impact on pedestrians than streets strewn with the sawdust of carpenters' workshops and ringing with hammer blows (see B. Smith 1999: ch. 3).

Special events, such as fairs, brought an added bustle to city life, as well as providing a much appreciated break from everyday chores. Fairs gave the inhabitants of relatively isolated medieval communities the opportunity to buy luxurious or exotic goods, such as silverware, spices, and silks. Along with the fairs came performers—and pickpockets. The fair was a time for new corporeal experiences, whether pleasant or unpleasant, a time to wonder at a juggler's dexterity or to realize with horror that one's purse had been stolen while one was fingering a fine woolen cloth from Flanders.

Much of the success of fairs depended on the weather, for these were basically open-air events. A thirteenth-century account of St. Edward's fair in London describes the hardships faced by merchants during rainy weather: "All those who exhibited their goods for sale there suffered great inconvenience because of the lack of roofs apart from canvas awnings; for the variable gusts of wind, usual at that time of year, battered the merchants so that they were cold, wet, hungry and thirsty. Their feet were dirtied by the mud and their merchandise spoiled by the rain" (cited in Herrin 1999: 41). Perhaps the most famous of these medieval trading fairs were held outside Troyes in the summer and fall. The fair held in the summer was known as the "Hot Fair" and the one in the fall as the "Cold Fair." These names suggest the extent to which climate and weather influenced people's perceptions in an age of outdoor life.

Religious festivals produced their own transformations of urban life. On saints' days tapestries might be hung from windows and herbs strewn in the streets to exhale pungent aromas when trodden underfoot. There was likely to be the excitement of participating in a procession, and perhaps the satisfaction of beating a drum or of helping to carry a revered image of a saint (Mumford 1938: 63–84). In medieval England Good Friday entailed "creeping to the cross" barefoot or on one's hands and knees, while May Day, marking the end of the cold, dark days of winter, was celebrated with dancing and bonfires. During Carnival the city entered a topsy-turvy world of make-believe social disorder, in which the sense of touch was temporarily permitted unaccustomed liberties: masked revelers could play pranks on strangers, mock kings could be beaten and overthrown, men could dress as women or parade their masculinity. A verse sung by keymakers during Carnival in Florence suggestively boasted:

> Our tools are fine, new and useful;
> We always carry them with us;
> They are good for anything,
> If you want to touch them, you can. (Burke 2009: 265)

Carnivalesque celebrations of disorder provided communities with an accepted and contained way to release pent-up emotions and experiment with other identities (Humphrey 2001). There was always a risk, however, that the mock disorder of carnival might spill over its prescribed boundaries and provoke real social disorder. A carnival game of hand-to-hand combat in fourteenth-century Siena, for example, led to a citywide riot, a burnt church, and four deaths (Cohn 2004: 62–63).

It was not only fairs and festivals that might transform the medieval city. City life was also frequently affected by wars and epidemics, fire, floods and famines. During the Black Death (probably bubonic plague) in the fourteenth century, cities blazed with bonfires to clear the air of infection, while their fearful inhabitants holed up in their houses with stockpiles of food or else defied death with boisterous parties. Giovanni Boccaccio wrote that in Florence the plague spread like wildfire, filling the city with corpses: "So many corpses would arrive in front of a church every day and at every hour that the amount of holy ground for burials was certainly insufficient . . ., [so that] huge trenches were dug in all of the cemeteries of the churches and into them the new arrivals were dumped by the hundreds; and they were packed in there with dirt, one on top of another, like a ship's cargo, until the trench was filled" (1977: 8). City walls offered no protection against this evil visitation. Indeed, it was particularly those who lived within the city walls who were the hardest hit, so that "men and women in great numbers abandoned their city . . . as if the wrath of God could not pursue them with this pestilence wherever they went but would only strike those it found within the walls of the city!" (6).

As a result of the high death rate many cities that had been straining at their bonds found themselves, at least for a while, with room to spare within their encircling walls.

HARD AT WORK

Dawn. Cocks crow, birds sing, and bells ring. Time to stretch stiff limbs, scratch at insect bites, awaken drowsy bedfellows, and leave the warmth of the bed for the cool morning air. On with the coarse, woolen clothing. A hunk of bread washed down by beer makes a peasant's breakfast. Outside the ground is wet with dew. Time to fetch water from the well, time to sweep out the dust, time to take the sheep to pasture, time to get to work.

The rhythms of work in premodernity were primarily set by the rhythms of nature and agriculture. The seasonal cycle dictated what was done when for the vast majority of people. In the winter when the sun rose late and nature slowed down, laborers had more hours for rest and leisure (though there were still winter crops and farm animals to care for and firewood to cut and gather). In the summer and early autumn, days were long and long hours of work were needed to help bring in the harvest. Only when the sun hung hot and heavy in the midday sky would harvest workers seek a cool refuge to rest and eat.

Whatever the season, Sundays were days of enforced rest. Legends told of people who had transgressed this divine law and found their hands permanently fastened to whatever tool they had been using on the Lord's Day. In many churches images showed a doleful Christ surrounded and attacked by pitchforks, axes, and hammers, graphically instructing churchgoers that to work on Sundays was to hurt Christ himself (Rigaux 2005).

Farm work was acknowledged to be very hard work, for both humans and beasts. It took strong arms to guide the plow as it cut through stony ground, and the oxen who did the heavy pulling would be pricked with the sharp point of a goad to drive them ever onwards. A furlong, about two hundred meters, was the length of a field that oxen could plow before needing a rest. Even after a field was plowed, clumps of earth might still need to be broken up by hand (Gies and Gies 1990: 137).

The material world was recalcitrant. It resisted the touch of the human hand; it could not simply be stroked or cajoled into productivity. In the medieval fantasy land of Cockaigne tame deer and rabbits allowed themselves to be caught by hand and ripe fruit dropped into people's mouths. In the real world, attaining food involved force: digging and cutting and killing. While knights fought with enemies and priests fought with Satan, laborers were understood to "fight" with the land. The earth had to be broken with a plow, root vegetables had to be torn from the ground, grain had to be cut down with scythes and flogged with flails.

The tenth-century *Colloquy* by Aelfric described the harshness of agricultural labor from the plowman's point of view: "I work so very hard. At daybreak I drive the oxen to the field and yoke them to the plough; even in the bitter winter I dare not stay at home for fear of my lord. . . . I must plough a whole field or more every day. . . . The boy who drives the oxen with a goad for me is hoarse from the cold and from shouting" (Aelfric 1961: 20). Recently unearthed bodies of medieval laborers show the permanent physical effects of "the excruciating labors of plowing, lugging forty-pound seed bags, and harvesting with the scythe" in their skeletal deformations (W. Jordan 1996: 14).

In the metaphor of society as a body, peasants were the lowly feet, carrying the rest of the body by their efforts. The hard and rough work of the peasantry was understood by the higher orders of society—the nobility and the clerics—to be in keeping with the supposedly hard and rough nature of the laborer, a notion expressed in the stereotype of the "coarse peasant." The laborer's physical intimacy with the land identified him with it: like the land he was said to be difficult to cultivate and always ready to lapse into his former uncouth ways (Freedman 1999: 15, 60, 218–19).

Yet farm work was, at least verbally, honored as honest and productive toil, worthy of heavenly, if not earthly, reward. Manual labor could be traced back to the prototypical labors of Adam and Eve—a lineage that could not be claimed for the "finer" accomplishments of the higher orders. As the famous phrase from the Peasants' Revolt of 1381 asserted: "When Adam delved and Eve span, who then was the gentleman?" (Hassal 1957: 166). The implied answer was that the soft-living "gentleman" was a superfluous invention of a corrupt posterity.

However, while farming was understood to be particularly hard on the body, it was by no means the only hard work in the Middle Ages. The labors of the knight might result in worldly glory and posthumous fame, but they were undeniably physically demanding. The knight started his career with a symbolic beating when he was "dubbed"—struck—by his sponsor. This was often no mere tap but a heavy clout (Bloch 1989: 312). All the blows and falls suffered by the knight-in-training were considered necessary not only to hone his skills but to prepare him for the even harder knocks of real warfare. As the chronicler Roger of Hoveden wrote: "A youth must have seen his blood flow and felt his teeth crack under the blow of his adversary and have been thrown on the ground twenty times—thus will he be able to face real war with the hope of victory" (cited by Norman 1971: 151–52). Besides withstanding battle blows, the body of the knight had to bear the considerable weight of medieval armor and weaponry and cope with all the hardships—including cold, rain, thirst, and hunger—of life on the march. The medieval romance *Sir Gawain and the Green Knight* describes some of these knightly tribulations in harsh detail:

> For fighting troubled him less than the rigorous winter,
> When cold clear water fell from the clouds

And froze before it could reach the faded earth.
Half dead with the cold Gawain slept in his armour
More nights than enough among the bare rocks,
Where splashing from the hilltops the freezing stream runs,
And hung over his head in hard icicles. (*Sir Gawain* 1992: 43)

In between the labors of farming and knighthood were the myriad labors of craftwork (not to mention the work of the merchant). Virtually every element of material culture in the preindustrial era was the result of bodily toil—toil that might be scarcely less arduous than the work of the plowman. It was said of the work of weaving, for example, "there is no sense that is not consumed in weaving. It tires [weavers'] feet, hurts their hands, deafens their ears, destroys their eyes and torments their intellect" (Mocarelli 2009: 108).

Before the job of weaving could commence, a series of labors had to take place. The sheep who produced the wool had to be reared, the wool had to be sheared off the sheeps' backs, then it had to be cleaned and carded with spiked teasel flowers. After weaving the wool was cleaned again and softened by trampling. The woven cloth was then stretched on a tenter frame and left to dry. Only now could it be made into clothing. As William Langland wrote:

Cloth that comes from the weaver is not good for wearing
Until it is trod under foot or taken in the stretcher,
Washed well with water, wiped with teasels,
Tucked, and given to the tenter hooks, and to the tailor's finishing.
(1935: 208)

Every stage in the production process depended on manual labor, for labor-saving mechanical devices were still in an early stage of development: "In the countryside or in the workshops . . . human manual work remained the principal source of energy" (Le Goff 1988: 214). What one ate, what one wore, what one lived in or sat on was the result of a series of tactile contacts reshaping the world into new forms. It was a handmade life.

The hard nature of work was understood to be ordained by God, who had decreed that men should suffer to earn their bread (Gen. 3: 17–19). All true labor was thought to involve toil and tedium, whether "dyking or delving or travailing at prayers" (Langland 1935: 85). Not even such supposedly light labors as reading and writing were exempt from this rule. Medieval authors likened writing to agriculture, the writer plowed through difficult material to bring forth the fruits of knowledge (Kimmelman 1999: 127). Like plowing, writing could be physically demanding. One medieval scribe wrote of the toil writing took on his body: "A man who knows not how to write may think this is no great feat. But only try to do it yourself and you will learn how arduous is the writer's task. It dims your eyes, makes your back ache, and knits your chest and belly together—it is a terrible ordeal for the whole body" (Drogin 1989: 50).

Reading, while perhaps not such an ordeal as writing, was no mere matter of gliding one's eyes over a page. Medieval readers had to deal with poor illumination, cramped script, uncomfortable seating, and temperature extremes. Readers, furthermore, did not simply look at their books, but customarily read them aloud, metaphorically chewing over the words and digesting their meaning (see Carruthers 2008: 205). Evidence suggests that reading, even to oneself, involved both a performance of and a corporeal response to the text. Indeed, one should not underestimate the strength of the impressions made on readers by the texts they mulled over. On reading Saint Augustine's *Confessions* Petrarch "cried, struck his forehead, and wrung his hands" (Braunstein 1988: 616). Reading and writing were in this way experienced as bodily processes and not simply acts of the intellect.

The whole process of learning how to read and write was in itself a physical trial. The badge of the schoolmaster was his birch or rod. One indication that this was not just a symbolic staff of office is that "when the degree of 'master of grammar' was conferred in sixteenth-century Cambridge, the new graduate demonstrated his prowess by ceremonially flogging a 'shrewd' (i.e. naughty) boy" (Orme 2006: 146). In "The Schoolboy's Lament" we hear a medieval scholar complaining of the beatings he receives: "the byrchyn twgges be so sharpe" ("Schoolboy's Lament," 1999: 398). It was asserted time and again that learning required the assistance of beatings, not only to ensure that scholars attended to their work, but to make what they learnt memorable. Beatings and whippings were thought to almost literally drive knowledge into the body. Wisdom that was mere external show was no wisdom at all but rather, as Aelfric put it "just like a sepulchre, which looks good from the outside but is full of stench inside" (Aelfric 1961: 43).

In the semi-oral society of the Middle Ages, embodied memory might well be thought superior to, or at least an important adjunct to, written records. One legal custom involved beating a boy when a transaction was made so that even in his old age he would be able to recall the details of the agreement if necessary (Drogin 1989: 15–17). Similarly the philosopher Ramon Llull asserted that the reason new knights were ceremonially struck was so that their knightly vows would have a lasting impression on them (Llull 1926). The pain that accompanied learning made what one learnt part of one's innermost bodily experience. In this way the sharpness of birch twigs supposedly made for a sharp mind.

In the ordinary course of events hard work was expected to bring rewards, if only the minimal reward of continued existence. There were times, however, when this did not prove true. Such was the case in the fourteenth century when Europe moved from its long and fruitful "medieval warm period" into its "little ice age."Temperatures dropped, harvests failed, and hunger took hold of the poor man "and so wrung him by the ribs that his eyes watered" (the fate of slackers according to Langland [1935: 82]). Populations weakened by hunger were easy prey for the diseases that swept across Europe during this age of pain. There seemed no point in plowing and sowing and harvesting when death might come at any moment. The calamity might have been brought on by sin, as the preachers claimed, but as the godly and the ungodly suffered alike increased devotions often seemed of little earthly use. In times such as these neither hard work nor hard praying appeared to avail against hard fortune.

THE RITES OF PLEASURE

After a hard day's work the fortunate laborer would enjoy the soft pleasures of bodily comforts. The hardness of the work, indeed, made the softness of the comforts all the more pleasurable. Huizinga noted that, due to the greater ease of modern life, "we . . . can hardly understand the keenness with which a fur coat, a good fire on the hearth, a soft bed, [and] a glass of wine" were enjoyed in the Middle Ages (1948: 1).The fifteenth-century housekeeping manual *The Goodman of Paris* describes the loving care a man, who has traveled "in rain and wind, in snow and hail, now drenched, now dry, now sweating, now shivering, ill-fed, ill-lodged, ill-warmed, and ill-bedded," might expect from his wife on his return home:

> He is upheld by the hope that he hath of the care which his wife will take of him on his return, and of the ease, the joys, and the pleasures which she will do him, or cause to be done to him in her presence; to be unshod before a good fire, to have his feet washed and fresh shoes and hose, to be given good food and drink, to be well served and well looked after, well bedded in white sheets and nightcaps, well covered with good furs, and assuaged with other joys and desports, privities, loves, and secrets whereof I am silent. And the next day fresh shirts and garments. (*Goodman* 2006: 171–72)

For every hardship the husband suffers during the course of his labors a corresponding comfort awaits him at home. Now he is cold, but then he will be warm; now he is dirty, then he will be clean; now he is hungry, then he will be fed; now he has but a poor bed, then he will be well bedded. The final touch to this list of pleasures is provided by the "joys and desports" the husband will enjoy with his wife when covered with soft furs in his comfortable bed.

If a man had no such comforts awaiting him at home, or perhaps even if he had, another place where he might counter the hardships of life with soft delights was the public brothel or bathhouse. A thirteenth-century account of the baths at the German town of Erfurt gives a glowing description of the pleasures to be had there: "A pretty young girl will massage you absolutely in all good faith with her soft hands. An expert barber will shave you, without letting the smallest drop of sweat fall on your face. When you are tired from the bath you will find a bed to rest on. Then a pretty woman . . . will tidy your hair skilfully with a comb. Who would not kiss her, if he wishes to and she puts up no resistance?" (cited in Le Goff 1988: 356).

Such accounts of soft delights were customarily related from the man's point of view. The woman was presented as the provider of pleasures, not the receiver, though she might also partake of them. *The Goodman of Paris* (1928, 171) suggests that this is an equitable arrangement as women did not suffer the hardships encountered by men in their work.

The sensuous pleasures described above were not without their corresponding social controls. There was a widespread attitude that all physical pleasures, and especially sexual ones, were sinful, the sign of a soul pursuing worldly rather than heavenly benefits. Thus the Church promoted sexual restraint even within marriage. Moreover, any sexual activity that could not result in conception was considered unnatural and condemned. Such activity included masturbation and what are now thought of as homosexual acts, but which in the Middle Ages and Renaissance were generally included among a range of "abuses" of sexuality rather than considered signs of a particular sexual "orientation" (Bray 1995: 16–17).

Nonetheless, as many tales and records indicate, people throughout the Middle Ages often engaged in unauthorized sexual activity in spite of Church teachings. Many communities, in fact, were tolerant of at least certain forms of such activity, including prostitution and premarital petting. These might be allowed as customary practices or as necessary "safety vents" for hot-blooded youths. In the late Middle Ages, however, changes in social attitudes along with concerns over the spread of sexually transmitted diseases led to a greater restriction of unsanctioned sexual behavior (Rossiaud 1995; Karras 2005).

It was in the late Middle Ages, as well, that the simple pleasures of pastoral life came to be extolled as superior to the artificial luxuries of city and court life. A trendsetter in this regard was Philippe de Vitry's fourteenth-century ballad "Le dit de Franc Gontier" in which Franc Gontier and his wife enjoy a simple al fresco meal of fruit, cheese, and bread, exchange loving kisses, then return to their happy labors of woodcutting and clothes-washing. Not everyone bought into this myth of bucolic bliss, however. In the fifteenth century, François Villon composed a "Contrediz de Franc Gontier" in which a plump priest reclines on an eiderdown:

> Near a good fire, the room well-strewn with mats,
> With Dame Sidonie lying at his side,

All white and tender, smooth and nicely groomed,
Drinking spiced wine by day as well as night,
Laughing, sporting, caressing, giving kisses. . . .
No treasure matches living at one's ease. (1994: 155).

In fact, while frugal pastoral pleasures might appeal on paper, Villon's ideal of "living at one's ease" more nearly matched the popular concept of the good life.

Judging by the dominant role of food in medieval fantasies such as the tales of Cockaigne, the most basic pleasure of the period was that of feasting. In the hungry Middle Ages, the pleasure of the feast lay not only, or even primarily, in the enjoyment of rare and sumptuous dishes, but in filling one's stomach to satiety. "When the belly is full, the head is happy," declared a proverb of the time (Pleij 2001: 128). Collective feasting was especially pleasurable, for it combined the excitement of a party with a reassuring sense of social solidarity and communal abundance. Alongside the feasting itself came other pleasures—roaring with laughter at a foolish joke, exuberantly flaunting the codes of polite behavior, singing and dancing and making love, and perhaps simply drifting off into a contented, full-bellied stupor—as depicted in the painting by Bruegel the Elder titled "The Land of Cockaigne."

Any important event, from a wedding to a saint's day, might provide an occasion for a feast, if sufficient food were available. The customary season for feasting, however, was the start of winter, when the harvest was in and the animals that could not be fed through the cold months were slaughtered. That was the time for real stuffing, for countering the cold, dark emptiness of winter with the warm glow of corporeal fullness.

Feasts and festivals were also enjoyed as a respite from everyday toil. On holidays—and, indeed, during any period of leisure—the tedium of work might be replaced by fun and games. The colder climate of Europe's "Little Ice Age" enabled more people to enjoy the kinesthetic thrills of skating and sledding. Other medieval sports and games included running and catching games such as prisoner's base; hopscotch (sometimes played with a friend on one's back); circle games in which the players held hands; wrestling matches; "mob football," in which large groups would struggle over an inflated pig's bladder; and various forms of hand-to-hand combat. It was always possible for combat games to get out of hand and turn into real fights and even riots, but this by no means diminished their popularity (though it might lead to legal restrictions).

Certain games, such as "Hoodman Blind" and "Hot Cockles" ("hautes-coquilles") required that one player be blinded and obliged to rely on his or her sense of touch alone. In Hoodman Blind a player whose face was covered by a hood ("hoodwinked") tried to catch and identify by touch one of the other players, who would be hitting him or her with their hoods. In Hot Cockles players knelt and hid their faces in the laps of other players and then tried to guess who was striking them (Wilkins 2002). Temporarily blinding the central player in these two popular games both gave a greater license to touch and allowed people to demonstrate their tactile acuity. That such games were enjoyed by many adults as well as by children indicates the pleasure people took in the corporeal sensations of rough-housing. Such happy grabbing of other bodies also suggests the extent to which bodies might be seen as public, rather than private, property in the Middle Ages.

Physical prowess was highly admired, as one learns from the number of medieval stories depicting a hero performing prodigious feats of strength. The Icelandic "Grettir's Saga" provides some fine accounts of medieval wrestling matches engaged in by the hero Grettir. In one, Grettir wrestles with a local strongman, Thord: "[Thord] ran at Grettir at his briskest; but Grettir moved no whit from his place: then Grettir stretched out his hand down Thord's back, over the head of him, and caught hold of him by the breeches, and tripped up his feet, and cast him backward over his head in such wise that he fell on his shoulder, and a mighty fall was that." After this easy victory Grettir takes on Thord and his brother at once, grappling with them until "they were all blue and bruised." The enthusiastic spectators "thought this the best of sport" and concurred in declaring Grettir the strongest of men (*Story of Grettir* 1869: 216–17).

For those who were not village strongmen but still wanted to experience the pleasures of physical power there was always someone weaker and more vulnerable to dominate. Indeed, for many in the Middle Ages, having a good time meant giving others a hard time. This was especially true of festive occasions when blind men might be made to fight each other, Jews forced to run races naked, and dogs tossed in blankets (see Burke 2009: 266–67). The absurd nature of such events and the discomfiture of their participants made for the diversion of the instigators and spectators, who would also have relished the sense of superiority provided by their dominant position.

Such "diversions," whether engaged in by individuals or whole communities, made strong statements about who was powerful and who was powerless within society. They also exemplified the premodern love of practical jokes. The best expression of this kind of "fun" (in the word's original meaning of "hoax") could be found in the castle at Hesdin in Artois. In the fifteenth century Hesdin was filled by Phillip "the Good," duke of Burgundy, with mechanical contrivances designed to fool and assault visitors. These included "three figures which can be made to squirt water at people . . . a device over the entrance of the gallery which, when a ring is pulled, showers soot or flour in the face of anyone below . . . and another contrivance, at the exit from the gallery, which buffets anyone who passes through well and truly on the head and shoulders." The castle further offered a room "where water can be made to spray down just like rain." When visitors moved to a dry part of the room to escape the rain they found themselves "precipitated into a sack of feathers below" (Vaughan, 2002: 138). Presumably visitors enjoyed experiencing, or at least marveling at, the sudden soakings and buffetings they received or, having heard what lay in store for them, they would not have come. In any case, as one English visitor remarked, it all made for the "singuler pleasir" of the duke himself (Williams 2004: 98).

The most prestigious amusement to be had in the Middle Ages was the tournament, which centered on arranged battles between groups of knights. In tournaments and jousts (combats between two knights) it was no longer just a matter of proving one's superior strength and skills, but of displaying and accumulating wealth and social status. This was especially the case in the later Middle Ages when tournaments became public spectacles and troops of colorfully dressed knights and ladies would parade through city streets before a tournament. It was also the last great celebration of hand-to-hand combat before the triumph of gunpowder on the battlefield would rob warfare of its intimacy.

Many footloose young noblemen spent their youth on the tournament circuit, traveling from one event to another, winning renown and prize money or incurring humiliations and debts. One tournament celebrity in the twelfth century was Henry, the charismatic young king of England, who earned the reputation of being "the bravest and most daring of tourneyers" (Crouch 2005: 25). Bravery was a necessary attribute for tournament players, for though tournaments were considered a form of "recreation," real weapons were used and participants not infrequently paid for their fun with their lives.

By now it is obvious that pleasure in the Middle Ages did not just consist of "soft" bodily comforts, such as warm fires and full stomachs. Many of the rites of pleasure, including wrestling and jousting, demanded just as much hard physical effort as work itself. The great difference was that it was hard work with a thrill. This was particularly the case with one of the favorite amusements of the Middle Ages, hunting. Along with the tangible reward of a slain animal, hunting offered the excitement of chasing, cornering, and killing. These actions might be experienced either personally or vicariously through hunting dogs and hawks. Yet, whether undertaken on horseback or on foot, with weapons or with hounds and hawks (a privilege of the elite), hunting might entail considerable labor. In the sixteenth-century "The Noble Art of Venerie," the author says of hunting with dogs: "Although the pastime be great, yet many times the toyle and paine is also exceeding great: and then it may be called eyther a painful pastime, or a pleasant payne" (cited by Strutt 1801: 18). The toil was not so burdensome, however, to prevent hunting from being a medieval passion. And, in fact, the nobility could leave a good deal of the hard work to servants or even do as Queen Elizabeth I did in her later years—shoot at animals enclosed in a paddock (Bergman 2007).

Another common activity involving violence and death often described as highly pleasurable was warfare. "War is a delightful thing for a young man of courage," wrote Jean de Bueil (1887: 118) in the fifteenth century. A twelfth-century poem attributed to Bertran de Born openly celebrates the gratifications of the battlefield:

> I tell you: no pleasure's so large
> (Not eating or drinking or sleep)
> As when I hear the cry: "Charge!"
> Or out of the darkened deep
> A horse's whinnying refrain
> Or the cry: "Help! Bring aid!"
> As big and little in turn cascade
> Into ditches across the plain,
> And I see, by the corpses whose sides
> Are splintered, flags unfurling wide. (Born 1990: 91–92)

It may be that bravado played a role in the "happy and joyful" response medieval knights reputedly gave to news of war (Kaeuper 1999: 162–63), yet texts such as Born's do seem to express real joy, and even aesthetic delight, in the battle experience.

For some, the feeling of solidarity that united comrades-in-arms constituted one of the great pleasures of war. Jean de Bueil wrote in 1465:

> War is a joyous thing. We love each other so much in war. If we see that our cause is just and our kinsmen fight boldly, tears come to our eyes. A sweet joy rises in our hearts, in the feeling of our honest loyalty to each other, and seeing our friend so bravely exposing his body to danger . . . we resolve to go forward and die or live with him and never leave him on account of love. This brings such delight that anyone who has not felt it cannot say how wonderful it is. (Cited in Elias 1994: 160. For a modern counterpart see Das 2005).

The pleasure that Born and like-minded men took in warfare, however, was not primarily of this nature. No particular bonds of allegiance seemed to be involved in the matter. There was no righteous rejoicing at the defeat of the wicked. Rather we see expressed the heady joy, unadulterated by any feeling of pity, of allowing one's aggressive and destructive tendencies free play, that is, the pleasure of "slicing and smashing" and "hack[ing] at arms and heads" as Born puts it (1990: 91).

Though the clerics might complain, no social penalties were imposed for engaging in such enthusiastic violence within the context of warfare. "The pleasure in killing and torturing others was great, and it was a socially permitted pleasure" (Elias 1994: 163). It could even be deemed a useful pleasure as it served to disable and cow one's opponents. Warriors apparently had little reason, therefore, to restrain their violent impulses, though in the later Middle Ages codes of chivalry would provide some curbs to the excesses of war. No doubt the knowledge that at any moment he himself might be at the receiving end of a slicing sword or a smashing mace quickened the warrior's pleasure at his moment of godlike power.

Pleasure, moreover, need not be thought to end with death. For the righteous, among whom warriors might well trust to be included, there was the hope of a joyful afterlife in Heaven. The sense of touch seems to have played a minor role in conceptualizations of this afterlife, however. Heaven is frequently described as a place of dazzling light, of divine fragrance, and of glorious music, but rarely as a place of wondrous touch. Perhaps touch was too earthy a sense for the "airy" spiritual life of Heaven. Perhaps the chroniclers of Heaven preferred to err on the side of caution for, if the blessed in Heaven made use of their sense of touch, might not that lead them to pluck forbidden fruits? It was much safer to depict Heaven as regaling saints with golden visions and angelic music.

Hence, among the jeweled walls and golden streets of the heavenly city there were no cozy fireplaces and no comfortable beds—no need for any comforts, it would seem, in a place with no discomforts. Certainly there was no joyful battling such as cheered the afterlives of slain warriors in Norse mythology. Yet tactile pleasures were not entirely abandoned in the medieval vision of Heaven, even if they must be understood as partaking of a different nature from those experienced on earth. Now and then in mystical treatises we hear of divine embraces or of heavenly flames. God's love warms souls with a "lovely and most merry burning fire" declared the medieval English mystic Richard Rolle (2000: 184). Perhaps, then, in Heaven, too, one could hope for a good place by the fire.

CHAPTER TWO

A Touchable God

A TACTILE COSMOLOGY

At its heart, the cosmology of the Middle Ages was tactile. Heaven may have seemed to be all light and music and fragrance but the primordial qualities of the universe were held to be the contrasting forces of hot, cold, moist, and dry. All of these qualities could only be experienced through touch, making touch the only sense open to the fundamental nature of reality.

In the created world these four primary qualities were understood to combine to form the four elements: the union of hot and dry created fire; that of hot and moist made air; cold and moist combined to form water; and together cold and dry produced earth. As the heaviest of these elements, earth lay at the ponderous center of the cosmos, forming the basis of our world. Water lay on top of earth; above water was the lighter air; and fire, the lightest of all, was understood to form a flaming region above the air. This cosmic model explained why earthly flames leapt into the sky: they sought their natural sphere above the air. Similarly, a handful of earth, if thrown up in the air would fall down again to its natural home, the Earth. Like was seen to be drawn to like (see Lewis 1964).

Above the cosmic realm of fire lay the rotating spheres of the planets and the stars, one encompassing the other, all free from the mutability that characterizes the Earth and its atmosphere (collectively known as the "sublunar" world). Encompassing all of the planetary spheres was the sphere known as the Prime Mover that, by its own movement, set the other spheres in motion. Surrounding this was the Empyrean, the heavenly dwelling of God and all the saved souls. Hell, the dwelling-place of the Devil and the damned souls, was usually positioned inside the Earth. In contrast with Heaven, which offered only delight, Hell was conceptualized as a place of pure pain.

This notion of the cosmos consisting of sphere nesting within sphere was masterfully expressed in the early fourteenth century by Dante. Dante's literary cosmology includes not only the customary planetary spheres, but also nine concentric enclosures within the underworld of Hell, nine within the outerworld of Heaven, and seven rings or terraces around the "Mountain of Purgatory." In the central pit of Hell, Satan can be found encased up to his chest in cold, heavy ice. On top of the Mountain of Purgatory is the Garden of Eden, signifying an original state of innocence. In the center of Heaven God appears in a fiery, interactive trinity of rings. The contrast between the heavy, immobile ice at the core of Hell and the light, dynamic fire at the center of Heaven in Dante's vision emphasizes the opposing tactile values of the two extremes of the cosmos.

To the medieval mind the universe was immense, it was awe inspiring, but it was orderly: the careful craftwork of God. Like the cosmos itself, human beings were understood to be the handiwork of the deity, who, in Job's words, knits our bodies with bones and muscles and clothes them with flesh and skin (Job 10: 8–11). A number of medieval images, indeed, show God as a sculptor, fashioning Adam's body directly with his hands (Boyle 1998: 19–20).

Like the cosmos, the human body was grounded in the primary qualities of hot, dry, cold, and moist. Within the body these qualities combined to create four bodily humors: blood, yellow bile (choler), black bile (melancholy), and phlegm. The particular combination of humors within any individual was thought to shape that person's character and physical nature. This made it possible to tell at a touch the nature of anyone's character. A warm, hard body signified a hot and dry choleric individual who would be energetic and hot-tempered. A cool, soft body, by contrast, indicated a cold and moist phlegmatic individual who would be passive and mild-tempered.

Within the cosmic system, each person was understood to move in a web of astral influences—direct lines of power sent down to Earth by the planets. These influences (the word literally means astral powers) affected the health and fortune of human beings. The question of how the ancient theory of planetary influences could be reconciled with the Christian notion of free will occupied many a medieval theologian. Some argued that, whereas weak-willed individuals would be caught in the astral net, persons of strong will would be able to break the bonds and forge their own destinies. Whatever the opinions of the experts, however, it was generally understood that the space within which people acted was permeated by powerful forces, some of them emanating from the planets, others of magical, demonic, or divine origin. Medieval space was never empty. Humans were continuously in contact with both natural and supernatural forces.

Humans imitated the cosmic pattern of concentric enclosures on a worldly level with their walled cities, their walled homes, and walled gardens. Not until modernity would these cosmic and urban enclosures be opened up and the human mind exposed to the terror and wonder of infinite, uncontained space. Not until modernity would one lose the imaginative possibility of feeling one's way from boundary to boundary, cosmic level to cosmic level, until one finally came to rest inside the walls of the city of God.

MYSTICAL TOUCH

According to Christian belief, the God who crafted the cosmos and its inhabitants had himself entered the created world in the form of his son, Jesus. The physical nature of Jesus' body brought God firmly into the realm of human experience and tangibility. In an astounding juxtaposition of divine power and mortal frailty, the Christian God could be approached as a broken body on a cross, as a baby nursing at his mother's breast, or as a young man embracing a friend. This last is movingly depicted in the fourteenth-century German carving titled "St. John Resting on Jesus' Chest" in which Jesus holds one of John's hands and places a protective arm around his shoulders (Museum Mayer van den Bergh, Antwerp). The carving, in itself eminently tactile, presents the image of an intimately touchable God.

It was in the later Middle Ages that Jesus's corporeality became a particular focus of Christian devotion. This development was influenced by a growing cultural emphasis on individual experience, an interest in physiology, and a transition in popular theology from a more supernatural to a more naturalistic portrayal of Jesus. As part of this transition believers were encouraged to imaginatively experience Christ's sufferings in their own person. A number of wrenching accounts of the Passion provided a stimulus for such meditation. The Swedish mystic Birgitta wrote of (and to) the crucified Christ: "The bones of your hands, of your feet, and of all your precious body were dislocated from their sockets to your great and intense grief; the veins and nerves of all your blessed body were cruelly broken; you were so monstrously scourged and so injured with painful wounds that your most innocent flesh and skin were all intolerably lacerated" (Birgitta of Sweden 1990:228).

One story related that Birgitta had prayed that she might learn the exact number of wounds Jesus had received. The answer was 5,475—an accumulation of pain scarcely imaginable. For devotional purposes, however, it conveniently translated into the recitation of fifteen prayers a day for a year (Krug 1999: 110).

Tactile language was employed in medieval religious texts not only to evoke sensations of pain, but also to convey the immediacy of God's love. Using touch as a metaphor for faith, Bernard of Clairvaux suggested that touch can grasp spiritual truths that are inaccessible to the more superficial sense of sight. While God cannot be perceived by sight, "faith . . . grasps what cannot be measured, takes hold of the uttermost, and in a way encompasses even eternity itself in its broad breast." "Christ urges us: 'touch me with the hand of faith, the finger of desire, the embrace of love'" (cited in Rudy 2002: 57). John of the Cross, who similarly made rich use of tactile symbolism, composed a paean to God's hand: "O gentle hand! laid so gently upon me, and yet, if Thou wert to press at all, the whole world must perish" (John of the Cross 2007: 40–41). Hadewijch of Brabant, in her discussion of the tactile qualities of divine love asserted simply that "[Love's] most secret name is Touch" (cited in Rudy 2002: 81).

Not everyone, however, was equally captivated by the mystical potential of the sense of touch. Some mystics warned against trying to approach God through concrete symbols, asserting, rather, that one should strive to free one's mind of outward forms and sense objects. In this regard the author of *The Cloud of Unknowing* wrote: "So leave your outward senses and do not work with them, neither exteriorly nor interiorly. For all those who set themselves to be spiritual workers inwardly, and yet think that they ought either to hear, smell, see, taste or touch spiritual things, either within or outside themselves, surely they are deceived" (*Cloud of Unknowing* 1981: 255). Nonetheless, even the high-minded author of *The Cloud of Unknowing* could not resist employing tactile metaphors to describe how the soul "wrestled" with the Unknowable—"which can be better felt than seen" (252).

Biblical narrative, and in particular the Gospels, provided much of the basis for medieval speculations about the religious significance of touch. Jesus healing with a touch, having his feet anointed, washing his disciples' feet, kissed by Judas, scourged by Roman soldiers—all of these biblical scenes were the subject of extensive commentary and meditation. Two passages from the Gospel of John dealing with touch in relationship to the risen Christ particularly exercised the medieval mind. In the first (John 20: 17) Jesus tells Mary Magdalene not to touch him (or more accurately, not to cling to him). In the second, Thomas refuses to believe in Christ's resurrection until he has touched his wounds (John 20: 24–29). When Jesus later appears to the disciples he invites Thomas to do so: "Reach out your hand and put it in my side." A now fully convinced Thomas calls out in response: "My Lord and my God!" Theologians puzzled over what these passages revealed about faith and about the nature of Christ's resurrected body, and why Mary was forbidden to touch while Thomas was invited to do so. Mary's touch, it was generally decided, was too familiar and too worldly—she wished to embrace Jesus as though he were still a mortal man. Thomas, on the other hand, perhaps due to his "high-minded" masculine nature, was better able to manifest a proper attitude of reverence toward the risen Christ (Boyle 1998: 120–21).

Significantly, while John never states that "doubting" Thomas did actually touch Jesus he was almost invariably understood to have done so, and thus he was depicted in works of art (Most 2005). Mary Magdalene, by contrast, was customarily portrayed as having her desiring touch warded off by Jesus. However, the medieval imagination was not content to leave Mary Magdalene untouched. Legend asserted that Jesus had gone on to touch her forehead with his hand, so powerfully, indeed, that he left his prints on her skull. The author of the fifteenth-century Digby Play of the Mary Magdalene further mused: "Although it seemed at first that the Lord held back from her . . . I can hardly believe that she did not touch him familiarly before He departed, kissing His feet and His hands" (cited in Boyle 1998: 121). The Middle Ages wanted to touch.

GESTURES OF PIETY

For most people the role of touch in religion did not primarily concern mystical experience or theological commentaries but embodied practice. It was through the practice known as the laying on of hands that believers were admitted to full communion, priesthood was conferred, and rites of healing performed. Everyday religious practice involved a number of essential ritual gestures: crossing oneself, bowing, kneeling, placing one's hands together in prayer, and giving the kiss of peace. While the particulars of such practices underwent modifications over the centuries (and were sometimes the subject of fierce debates), in general their basic forms remained the same.

Premodern practices of witchcraft, whether real or imaginary, inverted traditional corporeal practices of piety. Among satanic sects celibacy was reputedly replaced with fornication, fasting with feasting, kisses on the mouth with kisses on the buttocks, and swallowing the host with spitting it into a latrine. Certain "satanic" practices, however, were simply copied wholesale from Christian devotional techniques. One medieval Devil-worshipper asserted that he had worn a hair shirt for five years in "the obedience of Lucifer" (Hergemöller 2004: 178–79. Standard Christian piety, it would seem, provided an array of ritual gestures that could be rejected, accepted, or inverted by opposing sects.

At times the pious might take the performance of ritual gestures to extremes, as in the case of the twelfth-century Mary of Oignies: "First of all without pause . . . she bent the knee 600 times; secondly reading the entire psalter upright, she offered to the Blessed Virgin the angelic salutation, kneeling, at the conclusion of each psalm; thirdly, when the spirit of devotion moved her yet more strongly, striking herself 300 times with the rod of discipline, she made a genuflexion at each blow . . . and with the three last blows, she drew blood freely. Finally she consummated the sacrifice with 50 more simple genuflexions" (J. D. Miller 2002:

45–46). Likewise it was said of the twelfth-century Aybert of Crespin that he bent his knees a hundred times a day, and prostrated himself fifty times "raising his body by his fingers and toes," while repeating each time the Hail Mary (89). Such accounts not only indicate the considerable athletic abilities of many medieval ascetics, they also show the religious importance attached to the repetition of ritual gestures.

In some cases a symbolic significance and even practical benefits were associated with the completion of a specific number of gestures and prayers. In return for saying 5,475 prayers in accordance with the supposed 5,475 wounds of Christ, for example, one could hope to be blessed with good health on Earth, and a reduced period in purgatory. The important thing in this case was apparently to use matching numbers to establish a firm numerical link between oneself and God. Serial prayers were also said to produce spiritual wreaths of roses, crowns, garments, and many other items for the adornment of Jesus and the saints. The thought that with one's prayers one was creating tangible goods added power and meaning to the familiar recitations—even if such goods were only tangible in a mystical sense (see Krug 1999: 110; Lentes 2002).

To keep track of repetitions of prayers, pebbles, knotted strings, and prayer beads (which would come to be called rosaries) were used. In the eleventh century we hear of Lady Godiva (of folkloric fame) bequeathing a string of gems that she had fingered while counting her prayers to a local statue of the Virgin (J. D. Miller 2002: 95). Such mnemonic devices added a visual and tactile dimension to the vocal repetitions of prayers, allowing supplicants to see and feel the accumulation of their spiritual efforts.

Ritual gestures might also be employed as a way of disciplining the body, as was clearly the case with the exercises practiced by Mary of Oignies. Other means of disciplining the body included fasting, sexual abstinence, sleep deprivation, and the self-infliction of pain. The influential monastic Benedict of Aniane (750–821) provided a model of such behavior. His biographer related that Benedict ate only enough food to avert death, spent nights in prayer standing barefoot on the cold ground, slept as infrequently as possible, and "never indulged his body in baths" (Ardo 1979: 52). Many ascetics would go even further in their disciplinary practices and torment their body with hair shirts and whippings.

Such extreme asceticism was customarily taken to indicate exceptional piety and an almost superhuman disregard for the body. The seeming ability to withstand pain and do without sleep and food was, indeed, closely associated with the exhibition of such miraculous signs of bodily transcendence as levitation and walking on water. The saintly body, the hagiographies plainly indicate, is not bound by the natural laws that regulate the lives of ordinary mortals.

Church officials, particularly in the later Middle Ages, often tried to discourage practices of extreme asceticism, fearing that they led to spiritual pride and physical infirmity. Thus the thirteenth-century guide for female recluses *Ancrene Wisse* states: "Let no one . . . wear any iron or hair, or hedgehog-skins; let her not beat herself with them, nor with a leaded scourge, with holly or briars, nor draw blood from herself without her confessor's leave; let her not sting herself with nettles anywhere, nor beat herself in front, nor cut herself, nor impose on herself too many severe disciplines to quench temptations at one time" (Savage and Watson 1991: 202). Some even questioned the value of lengthy prayer sessions on the basis that their prolixity fostered spiritual aridity rather than zeal. Peter the Venerable, who was in the forefront of the movement to reduce "hateful multiplicity" in religious practice, wrote that he himself had been obliged to compose a shorter hymn to Saint Benedict "owing to the boredom of the singers" (Constable 1996: 203, n.178). Of course, the tedium of repeating the same words and gestures many times over gave the practice an extra value as a technique of self-discipline.

While Church authorities generally prescribed moderation with regard to penitential practices, there is no doubt that the disciplinary heroics of medieval ascetics were widely admired. When Thomas Becket, after being murdered by Henry II's knights, was discovered to be wearing a vermin-infested hair shirt under his ecclesiastical vestments, his reputation for sanctity was assured. On discovering the murdered archbishop's rough inner garments "the monks gazed at one another, astounded at this proof of a hidden piety" (Hassall 1957: 86).

After Becket's murder, it was the turn of Henry II (who was at least indirectly responsible for the crime) to undertake an exemplary act of penitence. Barefoot, and wearing nothing but a hair shirt and a cloak, Henry walked through the streets of Canterbury to Becket's shrine to be ritually beaten by the bishops, abbots, and monks assembled there. After this dramatic public act of humiliation Henry was pardoned by the Church.

An important precedent for Henry II's act had taken place in 1070 in Canossa when excommunicated Holy Roman Emperor Henry IV had desired a papal pardon. On that occasion Henry IV had waited at the pope's gates standing barefoot in the snow, fasting, and wearing a penitential hair shirt. These physical acts belonged to a corporeal language of contrition that was well understood by everyone and that spoke louder than words. Far from necessarily being seen as demeaning, the hair shirts and bare feet of the two Henrys could rather be admired as constituting the kind of grand gestures that one might expect of a king.

Experiencing pain, nonetheless, was understood to be more than just a means of subduing the body and expressing penitence. It was also a way of approaching

God. Not content with merely meditating on Christ's Passion, many mystics in the later Middle Ages wanted to feel it for themselves. Thus we find numerous accounts of stigmata, marks resembling the wounds of Christ, appearing on the bodies of the holy from the thirteenth century on. At times these marks were self-inflicted, but at other times they appeared to arise spontaneously after profound meditation on the Passion. The first stigmatic, Francis of Assisi, for example, received wounds on his hands, feet, and side after having a vision of the crucified Christ.

The Augustinian nun Clare Montefalco manifested particularly striking physical signs of her mystical identification with the crucified Christ. An autopsy performed by her sister nuns after her death in 1308 found within her heart a minute image of the crucifixion formed out of cardiac nerves and muscles, along with other miniature symbols of the Passion. The nuns were not unduly surprised at their discovery for Clare had often told them that she carried Christ's cross within her heart. Indeed, it was with the purpose of discovering some such tangible wonder that they had undertaken their operation. The dissection of Saint Clare's corpse clearly indicates the extent to which the symbolic and the concrete were entwined in the Middle Ages and the cultural importance given to perceptible evidence of interior dispositions.

Significantly, the close physical identification with Christ manifested by many mystics provided a way of bypassing priestly authority and gaining direct access to Christ's holy body. It further allowed the mystically minded to feel they were contributing to the expiation of sin by sharing in Christ's redemptive pain. This particular belief lay at the heart of the flagellant movement, which reached its height in the fourteenth century. The spread of the Black Death at this time was widely interpreted as a manifestation of divine wrath that required in response an extraordinary communal manifestation of penitence. By whipping themselves in large numbers in the streets the flagellants aimed to fulfill this requirement. So certain were they of the salvational power of their actions that they claimed that, but for their suffering, "all Christendom would meet perdition" (Tuchman 1978: 114).

While their center of activity was Germany and the Low Countries, the flagellants enacted their exciting displays of self-mortification throughout Europe. The following account describes a group of Dutch flagellants who visited London in 1349: "Each had in his right hand a scourge with three tails. Each tail had a knot and through the middle of it there were sometimes sharp nails fixed. They marched naked [from the waist up] in a file one behind the other and whipped themselves with these scourges on their naked and bleeding bodies. Four of them would chant in their native tongue and another four would chant in response like a litany" (cited in Hassall 1957: 156).

To many the flagellants provided something more concrete, more vital, and more ostentatiously holy than the traditional rituals of the Church. In some cases groups of flagellants actually denounced traditional Christian rites, took possession of churches, and encouraged the populace to stone priests. The flagellants' bodies alone were now the route to salvation.

When sinfulness did not convince as the cause of the plague, and penance and attacks on the Church did not seem to suffice as its cure, another cause and treatment readily suggested itself to the flagellants and their followers. The plague was said to have been started by Jews poisoning wells, and so in many towns the flagellants attacked and in some cases annihilated the Jewish community there (Tuchman 1978: 114–16).

By the latter fourteenth century Church and State had had enough of these turbulent acts of piety. Public flagellation was outlawed and its leaders executed. Nonetheless, throughout the premodern period the flagellant movement would experience revivals whenever times seemed troubled. In situations where the ordinary gestures of life might well appear useless, flagellation offered its devotees a heady sense of taking matters into their own hands.

THE CULT OF RELICS

The most highly valued form of religious touch was that which brought one in direct physical contact with holiness. Hence, anyone reputed to be saintly, from Bernard of Clairvaux to a zealous flagellant, was likely to be an object of devotional touch. The desiring touch of the masses, in fact, might be directed not only at reputed saints, but at any striking public figure, especially one who met with a dramatic death. This occurred in the twelfth century with the English revolutionary William Longbeard. After Longbeard was hung as a traitor, pieces of his body, his clothing, and even dirt from the foot of the gallows were collected as relics by enthusiastic Londoners (Mackay 1980: 724). It is evident from such occurrences that what led one to be considered a source of supernatural power was not necessarily an exemplary religiosity, but the impact one's reputation, acts, and death made on the popular imagination. The Church, however, only enshrined and fostered devotion to the relics of the officially holy.

From the medieval point of view, a dead saint was in some ways even better than a living saint. Death was believed to intensify, as well as put the final dramatic seal on, a person's sanctity. Furthermore, a dead body could be a material artifact in a way a living body could not. Living saints often tired of being touched and sometimes tried to avoid contact with the public. The bodily remains of a saint, by contrast, could be counted on to always be on hand. As material artifacts, saintly relics could furthermore be bought and sold, making them highly valuable possessions.

The cult of saintly relics was enormously popular in the Middle Ages. Cathedrals and monasteries vied with each other over the size and importance of their relic collections—and occasionally even stole relics from each other (Geary 1990). In some cases several churches claimed to possess the relics of the same saint. Mistaken documentation or outright counterfeiting was responsible for some of this duplication. Otherwise, it might be due to the practice of dividing the bodies of important saints into numerous pieces for greater spiritual and monetary gain. Hence, a number of skull-shaped reliquaries could each contain a piece of the same saintly skull with the result that several churches could claim to possess that saint's head (Finucane 1995: 29).

The enormous attention paid to relics makes it clear that they were the most potent objects possessed by the medieval Church. In an age in which tangible signs meant more to most people than written texts, relics provided an essential material link to the power of the Divine. An oath sworn on relics, in fact, was often seen as more binding than one sworn on the Bible or a missal (book of service), for breaking such an oath meant incurring the wrath of the saint whose bones had thus been offended (25–26). When William the Conqueror wanted to ensure the allegiance of Harold, earl of Wessex, he had him swear with his hand on a missal open at a passage from one of the Evangelists. After the oath had been sworn, William removed the missal and the cloth on which it lay to reveal a chest full of holy relics. The revelation that Harold had (albeit unwittingly) sworn not just on a biblical text but on holy relics was intended to impress on him and everyone else that his oath was of the utmost sacrality.

Virtually every notable medieval saint had an important material afterlife as a notable relic. This afterlife as a relic might begin even before sainthood had been officially conferred; hence the bodies of potential saints were often closely guarded by their devotees. In the case of the dying Francis of Assisi, armed guards were posted around the building where he lay to ensure that his body would not be stolen after death. Two centuries earlier, when Saint Romuald left his monastery in Catalonia to go to Italy, certain impetuous Catalan peasants were said to have attempted to kill him to retain possession of his holy body for their community (Le Goff 2004: 46). An important relic was believed to be a blessing for a whole region, making the resting place of a saintly corpse a matter of considerable public concern.

Dying candidates for sainthood must have known very well that their followers were eagerly awaiting their last breath to take possession of their bodies. On his deathbed, Thomas Aquinas "can hardly have been unaware of eyes contemplating his body, minds thinking what a splendid relic he was about to become" (Brentano 1968: 229). Indeed, shortly after death, Thomas's body performed its first miracle. A monk was healed of an eye affliction by lying down on the body and pressing his eyes to those of the corpse (Torrell 2005: 297). Like that of many another saint, Thomas's body would be partitioned into a number of precious relics by his devout disciples.

While the bodies of saints were generally considered the best relics, objects that had been worn or touched by a saint made for good "second-class" relics. An early example of a second-class relic in action is described in the New Testament where it is said that "when handkerchiefs or cloths which had touched [Paul's] skin were applied to the sick, their diseases were cured and evil spirits departed from them" (Acts 19: 11–12). Third-class relics were objects that had been touched by first- or second-class relics. Generally, the further away the relic was from the original power source, the less powerful it was considered to be and therefore the less valuable.

Objects that had reputedly touched Jesus's body were accorded a very high value as relics. One such was the Holy Nail (purportedly one of the nails used in the crucifixion) that was kept in the church of Saint-Denis in Paris. When in 1232 the nail fell out of its reliquary while some pilgrims were kissing it, "the anguish and sadness" caused by its loss was said to be "so great that it can hardly be told." On hearing of the loss of the Holy Nail, King Louis IX was so distraught that "he began to scream aloud that he would have rather had the best city of his kingdom ruined and destroyed" (Le Goff 2009: 80–81). This outpouring of grief was due not only to the loss of a precious relic but also to the fear that it signaled a loss of divine protection, perhaps even the downfall of the whole kingdom.

As records of practices indicate, the way in which the power of relics was accessed was above all through touch. If the relic could not be touched directly, then its container, whether a tomb or a reliquary, was touched. (The higher one's social status, the greater tactile access to a prized relic one was likely to have.) Pilgrimages were thus made to shrines for the express purpose of touching, or coming in as close contact as possible to, the saintly bones contained therein. (One surviving memorial of this practice is the tomb of Saint Osmond at Salisbury that had holes through which pilgrims could insert their hands [Tatton-Brown 2002: 94]). Visitors to Mary Magdalene's shrine in France, for example, eagerly handled the fingers that were said to have once embraced Jesus's feet and stroked the locks of the hair that had wiped them dry. The shrine even claimed to possess the saint's skull, still showing a piece of skin miraculously marked with Jesus's fingerprints (Boyle 1998: 122).

The particular ways in which a relic might be touched varied considerably. One twelfth-century example shows a whole sequence of ritual touches taking place on the occasion of the exhumation of the body of Saint Edmund. "[The abbot] proceeded to touch the eyes and the nose . . . and afterwards he touched the breast and arms and, raising the left hand, he touched the fingers and placed his fingers between the fingers of the saint; and going further . . . touched the toes of the feet and counted them as he touched them" (Binski 1996: 15). What was the abbot doing here? Ritually awakening the "sleeping" saint? Checking the integrity of the long-dead corpse? Manifesting the completeness of his devotion? Gathering sanctity from as many points as possible? Or taking an inventory of the number of pieces in this valuable relic? (This would have been necessary if any of the abbey's members were like the monk who stole teeth belonging to the body of William of Norwich when it was moved in the twelfth century [Finucane 1995: 25].)

Whatever the reasons for the abbot's meticulous touching of Saint Edmund's body, the extreme care he manifested was not necessarily the norm. In the same century, in fact, the Bishop of Lincoln went so far as to bite off a piece of the supposed arm of Mary Magdalene, which constituted one of the treasures of the monastery of Fécamp in France. When the monks complained, the bishop replied that if he could touch the body of Christ during Mass, surely he should be allowed to use his teeth on the bones of a saint. (28). (No doubt it would have given such a dedicated relic hunter as the Bishop of Lincoln satisfaction to know that one day his own body would become a valuable relic.) In general, however, kissing was considered the most respectful, as well as the most efficacious, way of touching a sacred object.

What benefits did medieval Christians hope to receive by touching relics? The primary spiritual benefits would have been a strengthening of faith and an increase of personal holiness through a direct infusion of saintly virtue. More important in many cases, however, were the physical benefits touching a relic was believed to confer. As we shall see in the following chapter, relics were deemed to have powerful curative properties. Many visitors to shrines therefore touched relics in the hope that the holiness of the saint's body would effect a "wholeness" in their own bodies, and they would be miraculously healed of their afflictions.

It was also a common belief that holding a relic, particularly of a female saint, during childbirth ensured a safe delivery. Thus in medieval England, "the abbey in Bruton, Somerset was fortunate to possess both the girdle of the Virgin Mary, in red silk, and that of Mary Magdalene, in white silk, used by labouring women. Women in Burton-on-Trent leaned upon the staff of St Moodwyn while in labour. In Norwich women borrowed St Ethelrede's ring to help them in childbirth" (Fissell 2004: 15–16).

Relics were, in fact, believed able to generally protect from harm those who were in contact with them. The contact, however, needed to last out the period of potential harm. In the case of childbirth this was usually a matter of hours. In the case of a journey it could be a matter of months. Medieval travelers, hence, often carried some small relic on their persons, often in a bag strung around the neck. A knight, similarly, might seek protection against the adversities of war, as well as superior prowess on the battlefield, by enclosing a relic in the pommel of his sword. In this way it would be not only the knight who grasped the sword, but also the saint whose relic lay inside. When William the Conqueror fought and defeated Harold of Wessex (who had broken his oath of allegiance) in 1066, he was wearing a bag of relics around his neck.

Neither their holiness nor their reputed supernatural powers, however, could always protect relics themselves from ill treatment. Such ill treatment took an official form when relics were ritually humiliated by being placed on a rough penitential cloth on the floor in front of the altar. On the surface this ritual was intended to express that an injustice had been done to the Church and to petition retribution from God and from the wrongdoers. The underlying idea, however, was that the punitive nature of the rite would stir the slumbering bones into fulfilling their protective role toward their sanctuary and their community. In the eleventh century the monks of Saint-Médard of Soissons placed their relics on the church floor for a whole year because a local nobleman had appropriated a village claimed by the monastery. Only when the nobleman returned the village (after receiving a hearty beating from the saints in a vision) were the holy bones relocated in their place of honor (Geary 1983: 136).

Though only ecclesiastics could properly perform rites of humiliation, lay persons might unofficially undertake this bone badgering themselves. One medieval account told of a group of peasants who struck the altar containing the relics of Saint Calais because the saint had not protected them from being abused by a local nobleman. "'Why don't you defend us, most holy lord?' they cried as they beat the altar, 'Why do you ignore us, sleeping so?'" (Geary 1983: 135; Snoek 1995: 366). Such acts were not only a way of petitioning—and coercing—particular saints to act in one's favor, they also made a compelling public statement that could result in community support for the aggrieved and in the shaming of the aggressor. Relics were potent political tools.

Occasionally, however, the bones of the saints were said to punish those who handled them irreverently. While a "submissive" female saint, such as Mary Magdalene, might put up with rough handling, this was not the case with stronger-minded saints. As one monk put it, "The more mighty and worshipful [saints] are, the more caution is needed lest they be offended" (cited in Finucane 1995: 35). When, in the twelfth century, the abbot of Bury St. Edmunds picked up the skull of Saint Edmund, he prayed that the saint would not damn him because "I, a miserable sinner, now touch thee" (27). The abbot's anxiety was likely increased by the knowledge of the fate of one of his predecessors who "wasted away with a permanent palsy of both hands" after handling Edmund's corpse too roughly (28).

The belief that relics could express their disapproval if they wished led to the related belief that if they did not protest being disturbed it was because they recognized the justice of the action. This provided a convenient means of justifying the theft of relics—by not resisting their removal the saintly bones were supposedly consenting to their abduction.

The foregoing examples demonstrate that the relics of saints were not simply thought of as vessels for a greater or lesser amount of sacrality. Rather they were understood to retain part of the saint's personality, and to be able to feel and respond to the treatment they received. The saint whose relics a community possessed was, in fact, expected to act like the head of a household, protecting his people in exchange for their service and offerings.

Another striking feature of the cult of relics was the apparent lack of any sense of disgust or feeling of reticence in the people who touched, wore on their persons, and at times even put into their mouths, parts of corpses. Granted that high mortality rates made people very familiar with death in the Middle Ages, one still wonders at this willingness to have such intimate and prolonged contact with human remains. After all, the Romans (who were no strangers to death), had been so wary of their dead that they buried them outside the city walls.

Religious factors would seem to have played a large part in shaping this acceptance of dead bodies. Death had a central role to play in Christianity, with its story of the man-god who dies and returns to life. Surely no Christian could think of Jesus's corpse as contaminating or disgusting. Saint's bodies, full as they were thought to be with spiritual purity, could likewise hardly be treated as polluting or revolting. Ordinary corpses might decompose and stink, but saintly bodies were imagined to be incorruptible and fragrant (see Classen 1998: ch. 2). Handling the relic of a saint, hence, was understood to be quite a different thing from handling ordinary human remains. Once the bodies of saints were allowed into churches and churchyards, ordinary corpses, so to speak, followed, for Christians wanted to be buried near these sources of holy power. This brought the dead into the city and into close and familiar contact with the living (Ariès 1974: 15–16).

The physical integrity of the saint's body after death was taken to be the logical outcome of their spiritual integrity during life. A saint whose body showed obvious signs of decomposition after death was quite likely to lose popular (though not necessarily official) support—a fact that sometimes deterred monastic communities from disinterring the bodies of their revered dead to better enshrine them. To understand the particular appeal the remains of saints had in the Middle Ages one has to think of the saint's body not as a lifeless corpse, but as a supernatural force (called *virtus*) manifested in a personalized material form—a supernatural force that had the power to grant one good health, good fortune, and a good end—all through the medium of a touch.

CORPUS CHRISTI

An eminently tangible source of supernatural power in the Middle Ages was the Eucharist, which was understood to be, in some mysterious way that theologians struggled to elucidate, the actual body of Christ. For those who doubted the real presence, accounts of eucharistic miracles told of hosts that bled or transformed into flesh or a living body. One tale told of a Jew who caused a consecrated host to bleed by stabbing it with a knife. When he threw it into a cauldron of boiling water it reportedly changed into a beautiful child. Another story told of a woman who laughed when Gregory the Great administered the host to her "because you called this bread, which I made with my own hands, the 'Body of the Lord'" (Lansing 1998: 103). After Gregory prostrated himself in prayer the bread changed into a (perhaps accusatory) finger-shaped piece of flesh. He prayed again, the flesh changed back into bread, and the scoffer devoutly swallowed the wafer and her words. These miracle stories warned Christians not to take the Eucharist lightly or be deceived by its mundane appearance.

While ordinary folk might bake the bread that became the body of Christ with their own hands, only priests were allowed to handle the consecrated host. This gave the clergy a tactile and spiritual advantage over the rest of humanity. A special healing power was sometimes attributed to priestly fingers, sanctified as they were by touching the consecrated host. "As true as I today have touched the body of Christ with these fingers, so say I to you, recover from this affliction," a medieval abbot is recorded saying as he touched the neck of a woman with a throat infection (Snoek 1995: 350). This touch of holiness was deemed to make the fingers of a saintly priest particularly potent relics.

If the nonordained could not handle the Eucharist, however, they could swallow it. Swallowing, indeed, was the most efficacious act one could perform with the Eucharist, as it was believed to only begin its work of grace when it reached the warm, welcoming cavity of the stomach and was digested. This most intimate of tactile acts gave great comfort and delight to many, who could thus feel that they were both physically and spiritually united to Christ. The mystic Angela of Foligno, for one, had a strong experience of this interior sensuous and spiritual delight, saying that swallowing the host gave her "an extremely pleasurable sensation" that caused her to "tremble violently" (Angela of Foligno 1999: 61).

However, consuming the Eucharist also caused many considerable anxiety. If the host was truly the body of Christ, was it not irreverent to be crushing it with one's teeth? What if a crumb of the host fell down and was lost? Was Christ's body to lie among the dust and be eaten by mice? These and related issues were given lengthy consideration by medieval theologians. A cloth could be held under the chins of communicants to prevent the loss of sacred fragments. The consumption of the holy blood of Christ might be limited to priests so as to minimize spillage. Communion could henceforth be denied to infants to avoid any spitting up of the sacrament. Even so, troubling questions remained concerning the fate of the Eucharist once inside the body. Jesus himself had stated that "everything that enters into the mouth goes into the belly and is passed out in stool" (Matt. 15:17). Did this occur as well with the Eucharist? To refute this impious line of thought medieval theologians worked hard to develop complex theories concerning the assimilation of food, and especially of the Eucharist, into the body (P. Reynolds 1999: 5). This process was part of the scholastic drive to apply reason and logic to symbols and mysteries.

From a modern (and perhaps classical) perspective the simplest solution to many of these trying difficulties would seem to be to interpret the Eucharist as representing, rather than containing, Christ's body. This did not suit the medieval mentality, however, which craved real contact, not encounters with "empty" symbols. Indeed, an oath was devised in the eleventh century for theologians who were inclined to be less than literal in their understanding of the nature of the Eucharist: "I believe that the bread and wine which are laid on the altar are after the consecration not only a sacrament but also the true body and blood of our Lord Jesus Christ, and they are physically taken up and broken in the hands of the priest and crushed by the teeth of the faithful, not only sacramentally, but in truth" (Rubin 1991: 19–20).

Also in the eleventh century Peter Damian emphasized the personal and historical character of the body consumed in the Eucharist by stating that it was "that same body which the blessed Virgin bore, which she cherished at her bosom, girded in swaddling clothes, nurtured with maternal care" (cited in Rubin 1991: 22). According to this perspective, the Eucharist created a bond not only between communicants and Jesus but also between communicants and the Virgin Mary. When taking communion believers touched the same flesh that Jesus's mother had touched. In fact, the flesh that she had brought forth from her body, they now took into their bodies, symbolically reversing the process of birth. Giving strength to the analogy, the consecrated host was sometimes kept in a pyx designed to represent the Virgin Mary (142–45).

As "the very body of Christ" the host was often given a role similar to that of a relic. Attempts by individuals to access the power of the Eucharist for private purposes included sewing the host into clothing to safeguard a traveler, applying it to the body for medicinal purposes, and using it for love magic (Snoek 1995: 377). One twelfth-century nun related how Christ had complained to her in a dream that the peasants had "concealed my body in a stall so their cattle will not succumb to the plague" (Kieckhefer 2000: 79).

Some of these practices had their roots in earlier centuries when consecrated hosts were often carried by travelers, used for healing, or buried with the dead. Saint Augustine, for example, relates the circumstance of a blind man being healed by having a poultice made of the Eucharist applied to his eyes. Another instance of such extra-official use of the elements of the Eucharist was the practice of signing solemn documents using pens dipped in "the blood of the Saviour"—consecrated wine. By the high Middle Ages, however, such usages had come to be regarded as inappropriate. The Eucharist was kept safeguarded under lock and key and grave sanctions imposed for any illicit handling.

The increased reverence paid to the Eucharist in the late Middle Ages led to the practice of the elevation of the host during Mass, at which point all worshippers were to fall on their knees in adoration. In the thirteenth century a feast especially dedicated to the Eucharist, Corpus Christi, was instituted that centered on the exposition and adoration of the consecrated host. This feast, with its associated processions, plays, and pageantry would become one of the most popular festivals of the fourteenth and fifteenth centuries. However, while Corpus Christi gave people plenty to see, it did nothing to increase tactile access to the Eucharist that it celebrated. Indeed, as will be discussed later, the institution of the feast of Corpus Christi can be seen as part of a cultural shift in emphasis from the tactile to the visual mediation of the divine.

ORDEALS BY FIRE

The importance of entering into physical contact with a sacred person or object in the Middle Ages, beyond the satisfaction of thereby acquiring firsthand knowledge of it, lay in the popular understanding of the nature of touch. Medieval philosophy confirmed what bodily experience made evident: the action of touch is reciprocal, one cannot touch without being touched in return. In the case of temperature, one cannot touch coldness without becoming colder or heat without becoming hotter. As Thomas Aquinas put it, "The hand touching something hot gets hot" (1970: 131). The power of the sacred was understood to function similarly to heat. By touching a source of spiritual "heat" one became, at least temporarily, spiritually "hot" oneself. No other form of sensory engagement could offer this transfer of power.

The sacred, indeed, was often conceptualized as fiery in the Middle Ages, and fire was accorded certain attributes of the sacred: it could transform, destroy, regenerate, and purify. In medieval cosmology fire was considered to be the purest and highest of the elements. This notion was inherited from antiquity when, as Augustine wrote, fire might be perceived not only as an element, but as "endowed with life and wisdom" and as "actually God" (cited by Le Goff 1984: 10). No doubt other pre-Christian traditions about the sacrality of fire also contributed to its potent symbolism in the Middle Ages.

As powerful as it was, however, worldly fire could not compare to the holy "fire" contained in sacred bodies, which had its source in Heaven. In story after story, when it came to a contest between saint, relic, or consecrated host and earthly fire, the former emerged victorious. Churches caught fire but the consecrated hosts within them remained unburnt. When heretics tried to throw hosts into the fire they met with the same result—or else with the transformation of the host into the Christ child. On one occasion Saint Dominic reputedly placed a host in a fire himself to prove its supernatural character to the incredulous. As regards saints, the Romans were said to have found Saint Agnes unburnable, whereupon they were obliged to dispatch her in an ordinary way with a sword. Saint Patrick escaped unscathed when his hut was set on fire while Catherine of Siena was not burnt though she fell on red-hot coals. The fact that there were notable exceptions to the supposed fireproof nature of saints—such as the burning at the stake of Joan of Arc—does not seem to have undermined popular belief in the notion. Relics were said to display similar fireproof qualities and might even be used to ward off fires. In the twelfth century, for instance, a man claimed he had driven fire away from a house with a relic of Becket tied to the end of a pole (Finucane 1995: 25).

When the question arose, as it did at times, of whether a relic was truly saintly, the best way of determining the issue was deemed to be to put it to the test of fire. A questionable relic would be placed in a brazier of burning coals. If it survived intact it was taken as proof that its purity was greater than that of fire and that it was hence the authentic relic of a saint. One suspects that a good number of relics must have been destroyed as a result of such fiery examinations, however the instances in which this happened apparently were not deemed worthy of recording. The extant accounts present the tested relic as emerging triumphantly intact from its ordeal. (It may be that the heat of the fire was occasionally adjusted in accordance with the officiants' desire to see the relic survive [Head 2000].) In 1031 Bishop Meinwerk of Paderborn lay the relic of Saint Felix on three separate fires to conclusively prove its holiness. The arm of the martyr Arnulf is said to have actually jumped unharmed out of the flames. Even a host might be put through this test to check whether it had been consecrated (Snoek 1995: 329–33).

The practice of testing relics by fire was similar to the ordeal by fire sometimes used to try people. In the latter practice the innocence of the accused was taken to be proven if he or she made a rapid recovery after grasping a red-hot iron or walking over heated ploughshares. The Old Testament provided an influential precedent for this in the story of the three devout boys who survived being cast into a fiery furnace by an irate King Nebuchadnezzar (Dan. 3: 8–30). Paul provided a Christian justification for the trial by fire when he wrote that "fire shall try every man's work of what sort it is" (1 Cor. 3: 13).

In at least one instance the practices of trying a relic and trying a person by fire were brought together. This occurred in the case of Peter Bartholomew, an eleventh-century pilgrim who took part in the First Crusade. Peter Bartholomew was guided by a vision to unearth what he said was part of the lance that had pierced Jesus's side in the cathedral at Antioch. To authenticate both the lance and his own visionary powers, Peter asked to undergo an ordeal by fire while holding the lance. Peter's ordeal was particularly difficult as he had to walk through blazing "olive branches stacked in two piles, four feet in height, about one foot apart and thirteen feet in length" (cited by Asbridge 2004: 291). The size of the conflagration was probably related to the fact that both a person and a relic were being tested, as well as to the controversial nature of both.

Peter Bartholomew died a few weeks after his ordeal by fire. His detractors thought his death due to his failing to pass the test, but his supporters argued that it was actually caused by the enthusiastic handling he received afterwards from onlookers: "As he emerged [from the fire] Peter waved to the crowd, raised the Lance, and screamed out, 'God help us.' Whereupon the crowd seized him, seized him I say, and pulled him along the ground. Almost everyone from the mob pushed and shoved, thinking Peter was nearby and hoping to touch him or snatch a piece of his clothing. The mob made three or four gashes on his legs in the tussle, and cracked his backbone" (291). It would seem that the ordeal of passing through a crowd that deems you a saint might be even worse than the ordeal by fire. The lance survived intact, but the death of its champion made its authenticity suspect. However, the Crusaders could always console themselves with pieces of the "True Cross" and other saintly souvenirs they picked up in considerable numbers in the Holy Land.

The counterpart of using fire to prove the sanctity of a relic or saint consisted of using fire to destroy works, people, and at times animals, deemed to be ungodly. The importance of using fire as the medium of destruction was not simply, as one might think, to punish heretics and witches with an intensely painful death or to produce a dramatic public spectacle of condemnation—a kind of preview of the fires of Hell. Fire was employed to purify the corruption that the condemned object or being was said to have brought into the world. Fire also had the advantage of totally destroying what it consumed so that no undesirable remains might be left, no proper burial be possible, and no possible relics be collected by the misguided. People condemned as heretics, such as Joan of Arc, were often burnt twice over, to ensure that nothing remained of them but ashes (Sells 1994: 140).

The purificatory power of fire also came into play in the medieval realm of purgatory in which those who died in a mildly sinful state were cleansed by fire.

(Grave sinners went straight to Hell where fire served only to punish, since purification, at that point, was of no avail.) The ultimate ordeal by fire was, according to apocalyptic literature, to occur on the Day of Judgment, when fire would consume the world. Those who had already been purified by the fires of purgatory, would, like the saintly relics that survived burning intact, be able to pass right through the devouring blaze and enter Heaven. In the early Middle Ages Saint Columban put the whole process of human existence with its final fiery test in a nutshell: "You have been created from the earth, you tread the earth, you will be laid to rest in the earth, you will rise in the earth, you will be tried in fire, you will await the judgement, and then either torture or the kingdom of heaven will be yours forever" (cited in Le Goff 1984: 100).

CHAPTER THREE

Painful Times

SUFFERING BODIES AND HEALING HANDS

Pain—caused by hunger and thirst, heat and cold, injuries, overwork, and ill-ness—was a commonplace of premodern life. In many cases there was not much people could do about it: work was hard, winter was cold, illness was often incurable. Worst of all, food, the heart-warming, belly-filling stuff of life, was all too commonly scarce. Described by Saint Basil as "the supreme human calam-ity" (Holman 2001: 77), hunger reached its agonizing peak in periods of famine. According to one source, every morning on the streets of Padua could be found the bodies of some thirty people who had died of starvation overnight during the famine of 1528 (Camporesi 1989: 26). Other, more impoverished regions would have fared much worse (Le Goff 1988: 239–44).

The severity of the suffering experienced by many is conveyed by the intensity of the language used to describe it: the sick man enveloped by an "atrocious storm of pain," the afflicted nun whose head "boiled like a pot on fire," the injured child who "hurt so acutely, that he suffered from bodily contortions, screaming and weeping as though insane" (Cohen 2003: 206, 207, 212). Even if one were spared intense experiences of pain, life was full of minor physical annoyances, such as itches, rashes, and insect bites. Among its advice for housewives, *The Goodman of Paris* gives six different methods for ridding a home of fleas. Indeed, "one of the [author's] infallible rules for keeping a husband happy was to give him a good fire in winter and keep his bed free from fleas in the summer" (Power 2006: 10). Away from home the situation might well be worse. When in the fifteenth century the middle-class Margery Kempe joined a company of poor pilgrims, she was shocked to see that "when they were outside the towns, her companions took off their clothes, and, sitting about naked, picked themselves for vermin." This was no doubt an important social activity for the group, as well as a health measure, but the more modest Margery would have none of it, with the result that she was "dreadfully bitten and stung both day and night" (Kempe 1936: 281).

While poverty was almost synonymous with suffering, even the wealthy were susceptible to common ailments, from flea bites to smallpox. Young King Henry, the dashing twelfth-century tournament player, died not of wounds incurred on the playing field but of the very commonplace illness of dysentery. In fact, even the plenteous diet of the wealthy might have dire consequences: Henry's great-grandfather, Henry I, reportedly died from eating a "surfeit of lampreys" (a favorite dish of the nobility), while the young king's brother John was said to have brought about his own demise by overindulging in peaches and cider (M. Evans 2007: 65–66). Such accounts of the sad fate of gluttonous royals, while not necessarily accurate, drove home the point that pampering afforded no security against a painful end.

There was a reason for this unhappy state of affairs according to the contemporary understanding of the world, and that reason was that pain was the result of human sinfulness. There had been no hunger, no illness, no cold in the Garden of Eden. By rebelling against God's will, humans had exchanged a perfect world for a fallen one and doomed themselves to a painful existence from which not even the rich and powerful could ultimately escape.

The notion of earthly suffering being ordained by God put something of a damper on attempts to alleviate pain. In the twelfth century Bernard of Clairvaux stated flatly that "to consult physicians and take medicines befits not religion" (R. Porter 1999: 110). Nonetheless, while physicians were sometimes caricaturized as atheists, caring for the sick was included within the exercise of Christian charity and so not utterly divorced from godliness. Indeed medieval monasteries were often important medical centers as monks honed their healing skills on each other and founded hospitals for the public. However, not all forms of suffering held an equal claim to alleviation. The pains of childbirth, though acknowledged to be intense, had been instituted by God (Gen. 3: 16) and thus, theologians decreed, should not be lessened (though medieval medicine did, in fact, offer some suggestions for relief). Injuries and illness held stronger claims to treatment, as the suffering they caused was not so evidently part of the ordinary God-given course of human life.

Physicians made use of the sense of touch both in the diagnosis and treatment of disease. Along with astrology and uroscopy (the scrutiny of a patient's urine), pulse-reading was an essential diagnostic tool. Physicians placed four fingers on a patient's wrist when pulse-reading, carefully noting the precise qualities of the pulse. Following the early medical writings of Galen, many different pulse types were distinguished, including the *pulsus serratus* (one that is tense and rapid like a saw) and the *pulsus myurus* (one that tapers off at the end like a rat's tail) (Naqvi and Blaufox 1998: 16). Touch could also be put to use in assessing a patient's temperature and palpating the body for abnormalities. (To make a good impression on patients during such handling physicians were advised to have "clean hands and well-shapen nails" [Rowling 1973: 180].)

The roles of touch in treatment, in turn, were myriad. Surgeons, the "manual laborers" of medicine as they were deemed, had the hands-on job of opening up the patient's body to drain fluids, perform operations, and cauterize wounds. (Surgeons were advised to have "light hands, expeditious in operating, lest you cause the patient pain [194].) Physicians, the "medical masters," might prescribe tactile treatments ranging from cupping to massages to hot baths. Included among the popular treatments of the time were many that would later be deemed mere charms, such as wearing a ring made of mistletoe or writing the names of the three Magi in one's own blood to cure "the falling sickness," epilepsy. However, the distinction between a sound and a superstitious medieval medical practice from a modern perspective is not necessarily straightforward. When a medieval physician decreed that a wound should be kept clean, for example, it might be more out of concern that the "evil" qualities of dirt might hinder the healing process than from the recognition of any modern notion of the danger of infection (Woolgar 2006: 58).

Using the medical texts of antiquity as a guide, medieval physicians emphasized the importance of maintaining a bodily equilibrium through such means as diet, exercise, and the proper evacuation of bodily fluids. When something went wrong within the body, therefore, the prescribed treatment was often aimed at restoring this corporeal balance. For example, plants and foods classified as hot by nature would be used to counteract diseases characterized as cold, while blood would be let to relieve a body considered to be overloaded with harmful fluids.

Many people, however, did not have the opportunity or means to consult a trained physician. Such people went for their cures to a knowledgeable housewife or to a local folk healer. A good number of the treatments they received would, nonetheless, have been substantially the same as those employed by physicians, for the knowledge of basic medical procedures was widely disseminated in premodernity. Indeed, while folk healers might not have known how to characterize and interpret as many different kinds of pulse beats as a physician, they might well have had a superior knowledge of herbal remedies.

For an alleviation of their woes, whether caused by illness, injury, or misfortune, many people put their faith not so much in the power of medicine as in the power of saints. Jesus provided a biblical model of miraculous healing in the cures he reputedly effected with a word or touch. The saintly were believed to carry on this tradition and to similarly be able to heal with a touch. In this case the customary practice was for the holy healer to say "I touch you, God heals you" while laying hands on the patient. This phrase absolved the healer of any heretical pretensions to personal healing power.

In England and France sovereigns—who were held to have a touch of the saintly due to their supposedly divine ordination—were widely believed to be endowed with the ability to heal scrofula. In a typical healing ceremony, a monarch would touch scrofulous patients while a priest read a suitable biblical text. Afterwards each patient would receive a gold coin. (This coin itself might be attributed healing powers, having been ritually touched by a king.) The seeming ability to cure scrofula grew to be so closely associated with kingship in England and France that it served as a sign of a divine right to reign. Thus when Elizabeth I appeared able to heal scrofula with a touch it was taken as proof of the legitimacy of her rule in spite of the Papal Bull excommunicating the upstart Protestant sovereign (Thomas 1997: 195; Bloch 1973).

Louis IX of France—the future Saint Louis—was especially assiduous in offering the benefits of his touch to the ailing: "He would more eagerly and more attentively visit those who were the sickest, and he would even touch their hands and the places where they were ailing, and the more the disease was serious—whether an abscess or something else like that—the happier the king would be to touch the sick person" (cited in Le Goff 2009: 719).

In comparison to the numbers of people wishing to be cured of one affliction or another, however, saints and monarchs with healing hands were few and often inaccessible. Most people, therefore, turned to saintly relics for their miraculous cures. A good number of the multitudes of medieval pilgrims who traveled to the shrines of saints went in hope of being healed. If the anticipated cure did not materialize at one shrine, another shrine might be tried. For example, one ailing Englishman from Attenborough went to Compostella early in 1201 hoping to be cured at the shrine of Saint James. While there he felt better but grew worse again after returning home in the spring. He spent the next months trying out different shrines until in September he was finally cured after a visit to Saint Gilbert's shrine at Sempringham (Finucane 1995: 85).

While such "shrine-hopping" suggests an easy mobility, travel in the Middle Ages was often arduous and must have significantly increased the suffering of many ailing pilgrims. Traveling to shrines was particularly difficult for disabled pilgrims who might have to make their way on crutches, be carried on litters or in wheelbarrows, or push themselves along on wheeled platforms down dusty, rutted roads (86).

While some saints were seen as good all-purpose healers, others were linked to specific ailments. Saint Sebastian, for example, was invoked to cure pestilence, while Saint Apollonia was appealed to for dental problems. Often the connection between saint and ailment was based on the particular torture the saint had suffered during his or her martyrdom. Saint Sebastian was shot with arrows, an experience thought to be similar to the sufferings of the plague, and Saint Apollonia was tortured by having her teeth broken, which allied her with sufferers from toothache. The notion may have been that, having personally experienced a particular bodily torment, a saint would be sympathetic to others suffering from a similar ailment. More simply a connection could have been based on the common principle that like is drawn to like.

Occasionally a visit to a saint's shrine would be accompanied by a vision in which the saint directly acted to heal the patient. In the case of Saint Martin, one story told of a woman who dreamt of the saint after visiting his shrine hoping for a cure for a paralyzed hand. In her dream she felt the saint moving his fingers among hers and she awoke to find her condition improved. In another story a nun with paralysis in one hand and both feet dreamt of an old man gently stroking her. In the morning her feet were cured. Now mobile, she was able to follow the inspiration of another dream and visit Saint Martin's church, whereupon her hand was healed as well (Moreira 2000: 133–34). In England a paralyzed monk who fell asleep after praying to be healed at the tomb of Saint Cuthbert "seemed to feel a great, broad hand rest on the seat of the pain in his head. At this touch, the entire area of his body affected by the disease was gradually eased of its pain, and health was restored right down to his feet" (Bede 1990: 264). Such stories depict how the sacred power flowing from a saint's body was believed to revitalize a disabled body through the medium of touch, even a visionary touch.

While exceptional curative powers were attributed to saintly bodies, corpses in general were believed to have certain healing abilities. Many an ailment in the Middle Ages (and long afterwards) was treated with a touch from a dead man's hand. It would seem that in this case it was the power of death itself—the power to undo—that was being invoked and applied to a particular bodily disorder. When it came to vanquishing disease, a touch of death, it seemed, could be a good thing.

BLIND TOUCH

Blindness was a not uncommon condition in the Middle Ages, when malnutrition, disease, and injury resulted in the loss or severe impairment of sight for many. Interestingly, blinding seems to have been one of the preferred punishments for overthrown monarchs. Where the outright execution of a king might be seen as too offensive to God and man, blinding served to both physically and symbolically disempower a monarch. This happened, for example, to the eleventh-century

Byzantine emperor Romanus IV who was blinded after being deposed. The same fate befell Magnus IV of Norway in the twelfth century—he, however, was more thoroughly disempowered by also having a foot cut off and being castrated. There was a biblical precedent for the blinding of defeated monarchs: King Zedekiah of Judah had his eyes put out after opposing Nebuchadnezzar II of Babylon (2 Kings 25: 1–7). In Greek mythology the ill-fated King Oedipus dethroned and blinded himself after discovering that he had killed his father and married his mother.

While a serious social handicap, blindness did not necessarily lead to social exclusion or to complete dependency. Many common chores and handicrafts, reliant as they were on manual skills for their execution, could be undertaken by the blind as well as the sighted. A few blind individuals would become renowned for their exceptional abilities at craftwork. One such was the carpenter Martin Castelein, who in the mid-fifteenth century was famed in Belgium for his woodworking skills, which included making an organ with wooden pipes. Other blind men, such as Francisco Salinus in Spain and Ludovico Scapinelli in Italy, made a name for themselves as musicians or writers (Levy 1872). The age-old tradition of the blind seer was sometimes invoked to explain how such apparently disadvantaged individuals could manifest such extraordinary abilities.

However, a number of negative stereotypes hampered the attempts of blind individuals to earn the respect of their peers. The reliance of the blind on touch led to blindness being linked with sensuality. The blind were often depicted as being enclosed in their bodies, unable to raise their thoughts above base desires and therefore concerned only with physical gratification. Furthermore, premodern medical lore held that blindness itself could result from an overindulgence in sexual activity, which would drain vital fluid away from the eyes (see Classen 1998: 71–72). Sight and touch were often placed in symbolic opposition to each other, and the blind, it seemed, having no sight, must be all desiring touch.

Along with their supposed sensuality, the mishaps that might occur due to their inability to see gave the blind a reputation for being buffoons: they stumbled, they groped, and they were readily deceived by the guileful. A number of premodern comic stories and plays, such as the French *Three Blind Men of Compiègne* centered on the misadventures of blind beggars. Occasionally people wished to see real-life enactments of the farcical situations they heard about in stories and saw performed on the stage. This occurred, for example, in 1425 in Paris, when a variation of the ever-popular party game of Hoodman's Blind was acted out with people who were really blind: "The last Sunday of August, there was an entertainment at the Hotel d'Armagnac on the rue Saint-Honoré for which four armored blind men were placed in a lists, each one a baton in hand, and in the lists there was a piglet they could have if they were able to kill it. And so it was, and this made for a battle so strange, because they administered so many great blows to each other, that they were the worse for it, because however much they thought to strike the piglet, they struck each other" (cited by Weygand 2009: 17). A brutal engagement, for both people and piglet, but one that evidently afforded much amusement to the spectators. Perhaps, indeed, the blind men, like the clowns who enacted similar diversions at fairground entertainments, had been encouraged by the organizers of the event to whack at each other to this very end.

An elaborate development of the motif of the blind buffoon occurs in the sixteenth-century Spanish novel *The Life of Lazarillo de Tormes* (1971). This story recounts how in his boyhood, Lazarillo Tormes goes to work as the guide of a blind beggar. He is quickly engaged in a battle for dominance with the beggar, a battle that is played out on the body and through the senses. The beggar (who is never named) begins the battle by asking Lazarillo to listen to the sounds supposedly issuing from a stone bull and then knocking the boy's head against the statue (thereby literally knocking "sense" into him). Lazarillo learns to profit from the alms given the beggar by placing the more valuable coins in his mouth and passing on only coins of lesser value. The beggar, however, can tell by touch that he is being defrauded and blames his assistant.

On one occasion Lazarillo steals and eats a sausage meant for the beggar, substituting an old turnip in its place. The beggar pokes his nose into the boy's mouth to smell out the truth of the matter whereupon Lazarillo throws up the stolen sausage. A thorough beating is the result. Lazarillo finally resolves to leave his blind master and to pay him one last trick at the same time. He tells the beggar to leap over a ditch that blocks their path but neglects to mention that on the other side stands the stone pillar of a house. The beggar knocks his head with such force against the pillar that he falls down half dead (now becoming the one to have sense "knocked into him"). Lazarillo's parting words to him are "What! You smelled the sausage and you couldn't smell the post?" (37). Lazarillo's keen wit has triumphed over the beggar's keen senses of touch, hearing, and smell, and the duped blind man is left in the customary role of the hapless buffoon.

The sightlessness that made the blind stand out as objects of derision in premodern culture also made them notable objects of pity and of charity. Such charity at times extended beyond a gift of food or money to include personal care. Louis IX was said to have personally tended to blind beggars, washing their feet and helping them eat: "He guided the hands of the poor man to the platter and taught him how to hold it. And when there was a blind or paralyzed person and there was fish before him, the blessed king took the piece of fish and diligently removed the bones with his own hands, dipped it in sauce, and then put it in the mouth of the sick person" (cited in Weygand 2009: 18). Certainly, for the most part the blind could have washed their own feet and helped themselves to food, but what we see played out here is a ritual enactment of Christian charity. King

Louis plays the role of Christ and the blind are cast in the role of the benighted sinners he succors with a loving touch.

The association of blindness with sin was strong in Western tradition. It was based on biblical references, a common perception of disabilities as divine punishments, and the symbolic association of sin with darkness. The passage in the Gospel of John in which Jesus cures a blind man was readily understood to symbolize the spiritual illumination of a sinful unbeliever (see Farmer 1997: 132–47). This was even more the case with the biblical passages concerning the blindness of Saint Paul, whose cure at the hands of a Christian coincided with his conversion to the new religion (Acts 9: 1–17). Unbelievers, most notably Jews, were characteristically described as "blind," unwilling or unable to see the light of redemption as revealed by Christianity (Barasch 2001: 83).

In the seventeenth century the blind poet John Milton would challenge the customary association of blindness and sin by declaring that "I am conscious of nothing, or of no deed, either recent or remote, whose wickedness could justly occasion or invite upon me this supreme misfortune" (Lewalski 2003: 313). A popular story about the poet stated that the future James II once asked Milton if he did not think his blindness to be a punishment for the sin of polemicizing against Charles I, beheaded by the Cromwellians. The annoyed poet reportedly replied that if worldly calamities signify heavenly displeasure, then the late king must have been an even greater recipient of divine wrath "for I have lost only my eyes, but he lost his head!" (Bedford 2002: 69).

Challenging the related association of blindness with ignorance, Milton asserted that though he was blind (and perhaps because he was blind), he had a better grasp of the truth than many of the sighted. To an anonymous author who used Milton's blindness to criticize his politics he wrote: "As far as blindness is concerned, . . . I would prefer, if necessary, my blindness to . . . yours. For yours, drowning the deepest senses, blinds your mind to what is sound and solid; mine, with which you reproach me, takes away only the colour and surface of things" (cited by Parker 1996: 595).

Milton here suggests that the knowledge of what is "sound and solid," a knowledge associated with the sense of touch, is deeper and hence superior to the superficial information, the "colours and surfaces" provided by the sense of vision. This was a theme developed by Shakespeare in *King Lear* in which the Earl of Gloucester realizes his errors of judgment only after being blinded. "I stumbled when I saw," Gloucester declares remorsefully (IV. I), implying that the intellectual missteps of the sighted might be far worse than any physical missteps of the blind.

While Milton thought that the anonymous writer who criticized him was Alexander More, the actual author of the text was Pierre Du Moulin. Writing afterwards of his secret amusement at Milton's misattribution, Du Moulin caricaturized Milton as a classic blind buffoon. "I looked on in silence, and not without a soft chuckle, at seeing . . . the blind and furious Milton fighting and slashing the air, like the hoodwinked horse-combatants in the old circus, not knowing by whom he was struck and whom he struck in return" (cited in Masson 1877: 220). Even the literary endeavors of the blind, one sees, could be recast as physical comedy unintentionally performed by those who, because sightless, know not what they do.

Nonetheless, the negative stereotypes of blindness were not so potent as to disqualify blind individuals from roles of leadership. Among blind rulers in the Middle Ages, one of the best known was John I of Bohemia (1296–1346). An energetic warrior, John met his death on the battlefield determined, though blind, to have the satisfaction of striking one last blow (Tuchman 1978: 64). Another noted blind ruler was the Byzantine emperor Isaac II Angelus. Isaac II Angelus was deposed and blinded by his brother, but then restored to power in 1203 by another blind ruler, the Doge of Venice, Enrico Dandolo. Even Magnus IV of Norway, though blinded, crippled, and castrated, was able to regain his throne. Such cases make it evident that exchanging a reliance on sight for a reliance on touch was not thought to result in mental incapacitation and that the possession of royal blood was of greater importance to kingship than the possession of eyesight.

Among the poorer blind, some managed to turn their disability to monetary advantage by making a living as beggars and fortune tellers. For most people, nonetheless, the loss of sight would have been a grievous one. Perhaps many would have sympathized with Milton's lines in "Samson Agonistes" in which the blind and enslaved Samson wishes that sight might have the ability of touch to perceive through any part of the body:

> Why was the sight
> To such a tender ball as the eye confined
> So obvious and so easy to be quench'd?
> And not, as feeling, through all parts diffused,
> That she might look at will through every pore.

Physicians often could not do much for the visually impaired. Even the renowned medieval surgeon Guy de Chauliac could do nothing to stop King John of Bohemia from going blind. (Chauliac was running a serious risk in treating John, as the hot-tempered king had had an earlier physician who failed to cure him sewn into a sack and thrown in a river.) Thus it was that the saints seemed to offer sufferers from eye ailments the best, and perhaps only, hope for recovery.

However strong their faith in the power of the saints, people were not unaware that miraculous healings, and particularly such a dramatic event as the restoration of sight, might be faked for the purpose of acquiring fame or profit. One "blind" man supposedly cured by Saint Thomas Becket around 1290, for example, was later seen being "miraculously" cured again at another saint's shrine. In a case from the fifteenth century, which would later be retold by Shakespeare, the Duke of Gloucester was suspicious of the miraculous recovery of a man who claimed to have been blind from birth. The man was asked to name the colors the duke had on his clothing, which he promptly did, no doubt thinking in this way to verify his newfound power of sight. The duke, however, found this ability to suddenly name colors the man would never have known when blind proof of fraudulence and had the trickster whipped (Finucane 1995: 70–71).

To reduce the chances of fraud, persons claiming to be cured by a saint were usually asked to provide witnesses who could testify to their former disabilities. Tales warned of the terrible punishments that befell those who falsely claimed miraculous cures. Nonetheless, the temptation to stage a dramatic healing must have been great, both for the monks in charge of a shrine—the reputation of which would thereby be vastly enhanced—and for individuals, who could expect to receive charitable donations from awed witnesses to their supposed cure.

LEPROSY, THE BLACK DEATH,
AND DANCING MANIA

The most stigmatized illness of the Middle Ages, and one that was incurable as well, was leprosy (now called Hansen's disease). Leprosy had a particularly close association with the sense of touch. While it could produce painful sores, it could also result in the loss of the sense of pain, together with a general deterioration of the sense of touch. The leprosy of King Baldwin IV of Jerusalem was discovered when, as a boy, he and a group of friends were playing at pinching each other to see who could endure the most pain. Baldwin, ominously, felt no pain at all (Hamilton 2000: 27). Leprosy could also produce thick, lumpy skin, erosion of the nose, muscle weakness, and lead to the loss of fingers and toes. As a final blow, another potential consequence of leprosy was blindness, which left lepers reliant precisely on that sense of touch that their disease had debilitated.

To many, such graphic signs of corporeal disintegration strongly suggested a physical manifestation of moral corruption. Transgressive sexual activity was, in fact, singled out as a likely cause of leprosy (P. L. Allen 2000: 34). The medieval tale of Odo de Beaumont, for example, told of how Odo had contracted leprosy after visiting a prostitute, but was subsequently cured on confessing his sins and undertaking a pilgrimage to the shrine of Thomas Becket (Rawcliffe 2006: 81–85).

Fear of contamination as well as feelings of revulsion made lepers the untouchables of the medieval world (255–73). They were obliged to wear special clothing and gloves and to carry a bell or clapper to warn others of their approach. One characteristic set of medieval regulations regarding lepers ran as follows:

> I forbid you to ever leave your house without your leper's costume. . . . I forbid you to touch anything you bargain for or buy, until it is yours. I forbid you to enter a tavern. If you want wine, whether you buy it or someone gives it to you, have it put in your cask. I forbid you to live with any woman other than your own. I forbid you, if you go on the road and meet some person who speaks to you, to fail to put yourself downwind before you answer. I forbid you to go in a narrow lane, so that should you meet any person, he should not be able to catch the affliction from you. I forbid you, if you go along any thoroughfare, to ever touch a well or the cord unless you have put on your gloves. I forbid you to ever touch children or to give them anything. I forbid you to eat or drink from any dishes other than your own. I forbid you drinking or eating in company, unless with lepers (Brody 1974: 66).

The outcast leper was cut off from all the rites of fellowship fundamental to everyday sociality: eating together out of common plates, sitting companionably around a hearth, sharing a warm bed or a hot bath, kissing and holding hands.

From the twelfth century on lepers were increasingly kept isolated from the community in leper houses. Their exclusion from society was in some places signaled by a ritual burial in which the expelled leper was required to stand in a grave while a priest threw a handful of earth over him (66–67). For reasons unknown the incidence of leprosy declined in the later Middle Ages. However, the horror it inspired in the popular imagination remained (Hays 2003: 24–25).

The other side of leprosy in the Middle Ages was the leper's symbolic association with Christ, who had likewise been reviled and cast out of society and who had cured leprosy with the touch of his hand (Mark 1: 40–41). This association could make caring for lepers a sign of great piety. In 1105 when King David of Scotland visited his sister Queen Matilda of England, he found her washing and kissing the feet of lepers. David protested that if her royal spouse knew about it "he would never deign to kiss you with his lips after you have been polluted by the putrefied feet of lepers!" Matilda, who apparently modeled her actions on the biblical washing of Jesus's feet, replied with a smile that "the feet of the eternal King are to be preferred over the lips of a king who is going to die" (cited in Huneycutt 2003: 104). A pious touch reclaimed the outcast leper and enabled the toucher to feel united with Christ.

Hugh of Lincoln, who similarly practiced "leper-kissing," was once chided with being unable to heal lepers with his kiss, as Saint Martin had reputedly done. To this Hugh modestly replied, "The kisses of St. Martin healed the bodies of lep-

ers: but with me it is the other way, the kisses of the lepers heal my sick soul"
(Thurston 1898: 203). Here again the leper served as a symbol of the crucified
Christ. Francis of Assisi, in turn, began his religious life by kissing a leper, thus
conquering his former abhorrence of the disease and liberating himself from
worldly preoccupations (see also Le Goff 2009: 720).

While kissing a leper was a dramatic sign of one's commitment to Christian
charity, it did not necessarily entail great personal risk as leprosy is not very
contagious. It was a different matter with the plague, which spread so rapidly and
had such high rates of mortality that it seemed to kill at a touch. One firsthand
account described the sequence of corporeal onslaughts experienced by plague
sufferers: "First of all it would hit us as if with a lance, choking, and then swelling
would appear, or spitting of blood with shivering, and fire would burn one in
all the joints of the body; and then the illness would overwhelm one, and many
after lying in that illness died" (cited by Byrne 2006: 79).

While holding God's wrath to be the ultimate cause of the plague, European
physicians looked for more immediate causes as well. Putrid vapors, emanating
from the planets or from earthly sites of decay such as swamps and cemeteries,
were commonly said to convey the disease. Aromatic substances that could supposedly counter such vapors were therefore employed to purify and ward off
"bad" air. A number of physicians, however, proposed what seemed apparent to
those witnessing the spread of the disease, that the plague was communicated
by bodily contact. Boccaccio wrote of the situation in Florence: "Touching the
clothes of the sick or anything touched or used by them seemed to communicate
this very disease to the person involved (1977: 4). Even a glance from a plague
victim, it was suggested, might carry the disease with it, a notion based on the
theory that the eyes transmit rays that touch the objects they view.

The plague was indeed so contagious that whole households often died of
it. Though many selflessly nursed the sick, many others abandoned even their
closest relatives if they showed signs of the dreaded disease. From one day to the
next, anyone might become a plague "leper," shunned by society (Byrne 2006). A
factor that made the plague all the more devastating was that animals, as well as
humans, suffered from it. Boccaccio wrote about the transmission of the plague
to domestic animals: "When the rags of a poor man who had died of this disease
were thrown into the public street, two pigs came upon them, as they are wont
to do, and first with their snouts and then with their teeth, they took the rags and
shook them round, and within a short time, after a number of convulsions, both
pigs fell dead upon the ill-fated rags, as if they had been poisoned" (1977: 5). When
the plague entered a home it often left nothing living, not even the household
cats and dogs.

The disease had no effective remedy and at times it seemed that everyone was doomed to perish from it. An Irish monk, John Clynne, wrote at the end of his account of the plague, "I leave parchment for continuing the work, in case anyone should still be alive in the future and any son of Adam can escape this pestilence and continue the work thus begun" (cited in Horrox 1994: 83). However, while the plague would continue to harass Europe for centuries, by the fifteenth century the worst was over.

The plague had hardly receded in Europe when a strange new ailment appeared on the scene—dancing mania, sometimes also called St. Vitus's Dance due to that saint's supposed power to cure those afflicted with it. For no obvious reason—though demoniacal possession was suspected by the authorities—men, women and children gathered in towns all over Europe to dance and leap together in the streets. "They formed circles hand and hand, and appearing to have lost all control over their senses, continued dancing, regardless of the by-standers, for hours together in wild delirium, until at last they fell to the ground in a state of exhaustion" (Hecker 1970: 1). A drawing from 1564 by Brueghel the Elder shows a group of distracted peasant women affected by the mania, each woman restrained by a man on either side.

The thousands affected by this phenomenon, later deemed to be largely hysterical in nature, were predominantly poor and perhaps represented that segment of the population that found it most difficult to face a seemingly bleak future after the harrowing events of the past. Perhaps it was impossible for many to return to the slow-paced routine of ordinary life after the fast-paced turmoil of the plague years. The wild, exorbitant movements of the dancers would certainly have presented a forceful contrast with the customary, controlled movements normally required within society.

The dancing mania would have called to mind legends that told of how certain persons who had profaned the Sabbath or the churchyard by dancing were condemned to dance unceasingly until they dropped or died. In keeping with the sinful associations of unbridled dancing, exorcisms and pilgrimages were frequently recommended as treatments for the mania. More worldly remedies included cold baths, beatings, and forcible confinement. The sixteenth-century physician and alchemist Paracelsus suggested that afflicted persons make a wax image of themselves, mentally transfer all their evil thoughts and sins to it, and then burn it. One means employed to shorten the duration of an attack was to hire musicians to play fast music and send athletic dancers to mingle among those affected so that these would be the more quickly exhausted. Conversely, soft, slow music was sometimes played to calm the dancers' agitation. Whatever the efficacy of such treatments, the mania followed its own course, generally subsiding by the mid-sixteenth century, but reappearing in subsequent centuries in times of social stress (Hecker 1970; Midelfort 1999: 32–49).

Along with the dancing mania were three other premodern dance-related phenomena: St. Anthony's Fire, Tarantism, and the Danse Macabre. St. Anthony's Fire (erysipelas), named after the saint whom sufferers invoked for relief, was a disease predominantly caused by eating bread made with rye infected by a poisonous fungus. It reddened the skin and produced a sensation of burning heat, hence its characterization as fire. (A woodcut of 1504 by Hans Weiditz shows a sufferer from the disease coming to Saint Anthony with his hands literally on fire.) It could also cause hallucinations, convulsions, and wild behavior, and thus may have been a contributing factor in some of the occurrences of dancing mania. (Another disease that may have contributed to the dancing mania was Sydenham's chorea, which causes jerking movements.) St. Anthony's fire was much feared for, not only was it intensely painful, it could result in the loss of limbs and death. In fact, a popular curse in the Middle Ages was "may St. Anthony's fire burn you!"

Tarantism was a dancing fit that first manifested itself in fourteenth-century Italy and was believed to be caused by the bite of the tarantula. Some sufferers found that being rocked in a cradle or swing allayed the irritability caused by tarantism; others relied on beatings—but most found their only relief in dancing. A particular style of lively folk song, called the tarantella, was the music of preference for this purpose and bands of musicians would traverse Italy to play therapeutic tarantellas for their dancing patients.

The Danse Macabre or Dance of Death appeared for the first time in the early fifteenth century in Paris, though it was suggestive of old folk practices that used dance as a form of mourning the dead. Rather than an actual dance the Danse Macabre was a pictorial and literary theme expressing the power of death over the living. Pictures of the Danse Macabre show the skeletal figure of Death leading a chain of dancers—young and old, rich and poor, noble and common—into the grave. This image would have expressed a perception, which must have been common in those traumatic times, of being whirled away to one's death, ready or not. Literary expositions of the theme warned people not to be "harde-hettid as a stone" but to correct their ways before Death came to take them too by the hand (Pearsall 1999: 354).

THE USES OF PAIN

Pain and illness have clearly been a profound and often unavoidable part of human experience for most of history. However, if people could not hope to master pain in the centuries before the development of modern medicine, they could and did become masters of the uses of pain. And the uses of pain were many: instruction, discipline, domination, exorcism, purification, redemption, transcendence, subversion, stimulation, diversion, punishment, and deterrence, among others.

The common motif of the schoolmaster striking a pupil exemplifies the instructional and disciplinary role of pain. This role extended outside the schoolroom to encompass a good part of social life. Parents used pain to instruct and discipline their children. Masters used it to control their serfs, servants, and apprentices. Husbands might inflict pain on their wives for similar reasons, and wives, though in contravention of the social norms, sometimes did the same with their husbands (i.e., Kettle 1995: 25).

As in the schoolroom, the infliction of pain was ideally intended to make a lesson—whether it concerned intellectual attainments or good behavior—memorable. Another motive for a beating might be to drive out the demons held to be causing disruptive or mad behavior in an individual (Woolgar 2006: 37). This does not mean, however, that beatings were always informed by such intentions nor that pain was always meted out in just measure. Many a child or wife or servant would have endured severe beatings at the hands of their correctors, and in many cases, a beating would have been prompted more by a fit of anger, a desire for self-assertion—or perhaps mere habit—than by any explicit intention to instruct or exorcise. In theory, excessive beatings were out of line and even illegal: conventional morality decreed that one should only strike an "inferior" with moderate force "in order to train him in good deeds and virtue" (Osterberg and Lindström 1988: 51). In practice, they may well have been frequent. The records do not provide us with much information on this account for the persons so beaten only rarely complained. However, certain collateral evidence—a French account that considers a prior exceptionally courteous for not striking his servants, a London bylaw forbidding wife-beating after nine P.M. (for the sake of the neighbors, not the wives)—indicates that the physical chastisement of inferiors was a commonplace of premodern life (Coulton 1989: 52; K. Jones 2006: 86).

Contemporary accounts, suggest, moreover, that people came to blows easily, whether in the heat of an argument or as a means of settling old scores. Serious crimes of violence were almost exclusively the domain of men. Statistics show that the vast majority of murderers and their victims in the Middle Ages were male. The records indicate that it need not have taken more than an insult or two or an argument over a game for two men to take out their knives (the usual weapon of assault) and attack each other. In such cases angry impulses found expression in customary acts of violence that were deemed to both punish the offender and safeguard the assailant's honor. Significantly, murderous attacks were usually carried out on social equals. Social inferiors, it was thought, did not have the status to impugn a superior's honor and did not merit so high an attention as murder; in their case a simple beating sufficed (Spierenburg 2008: 34–36).

The highest uses to which pain could be put traditionally concerned purification, redemption, and transcendence. At times pain might appear to be directly inflicted by God, as in the case of illness. It might then be seen as an occasion to purify the soul of sin through suffering. This was the argument made by Bernard of Clairvaux. Similarly, the *Ancrene Wisse* advised its readers that "nothing cleanses the soul like illness" (Rawcliffe 2006: 55–56). Pain and disease, therefore, far from requiring treatment, could be seen as treatments themselves. This is clearly the case with Lydwine of Schiedam (1380–1433) who prayed that her twelve-year-old nephew might be afflicted with illness for the good of his soul (Classen 1998: 39).

It was widely believed that whatever personal pain was in excess of what was required to cleanse one's own soul might be put to use cleansing the souls of others. Hence Alice of Schaerbeek, a thirteenth-century nun afflicted with leprosy, believed that her ordeal might help ransom souls suffering the torments of Purgatory (Rawcliffe 2006: 64). God had, in effect, singled her out as a sacrificial victim. Such beliefs helped make exceptional suffering comprehensible and meritorious.

At the same time the experience of pain, by divorcing one from everyday realities, could enable the mystically minded to experience a transcendence of the body and a corresponding exaltation of the spirit. On a more prosaic level, it could result in the sufferer leading a wretched existence dependent on poor or unsympathetic relatives. In some cases, however, such as that of Lydwine of Schiedam, chronic pain might well have seemed an acceptable price to pay for an extraordinary life of visionary experiences.

Pain might also be considered an inexpensive and commendable way to take one's mind off one's troubles. Saint Francis de Sales found it "surprising how much good" giving oneself fifty lashes a day did. "There is no doubt that the outer sensation generated by the practice will drive away inner troubles and sadness" (Largier 2007: 47). The very heat generated by whipping was thought to be useful for counteracting the coldness of melancholy. The experience of pain had medical, as well as moral, uses.

Suffering inflicted by the State could be understood as necessary to the treatment of an ailing social body. In many cases judicial penalties were tangibly linked to offenses in the Middle Ages. Thus, heretics were burnt to purify—and signal—their corrupting effects on society, thieves often had a hand cut off to punish and prevent stealing, and slanderers might have their lying tongues cut out. A baker who had sold adulterated bread might be paraded through the streets with a loaf of his bread around his neck (Gies and Gies 1969: 49). Such penalties helped to identify criminals with their crimes and also ensured that offenders would have a direct bodily experience of the specific nature of their offense. The public enactment of a penalty not only served as a warning and as a demonstration of justice in action, it also added humiliation to the suffering endured by the offender.

Amputating a hand was a common punishment not only for stealing but also for making a false oath. (An oathtaker would lay his right hand on a Bible or relic.) After Protestant reformer Thomas Cranmer signed a recantation of his religious views under duress he decided that he himself would punish his offending hand: "Forasmuch as my hand offended, writing contrary to my heart, my hand shall first be punished therefore; for, may I come to the fire, it shall be first burned." When Cranmer was indeed burnt as a heretic he dramatically and courageously "put his right hand into the flame, which he held so steadfast and immovable . . . that all men might see his hand burned before his body was touched" (cited in Hutchinson 1965: 157–58). Cranmer thus turned what was meant by the authorities to be a fiery condemnation of Protestantism into a scorching denunciation of a politically expedient Catholicism.

It was in the late Middle Ages that torture became important to the judicial procedure, both as a means of extracting information and as a form of punishment. This development occurred in response to anxieties about growing social and religious unrest. The new importance of torture could also have been influenced by recent torturous experiences of plagues and famines that stamped the power of pain onto the premodern psyche.

Torture was used as an interrogative tool to uncover subversive elements within society and to extract the confessions that made convictions straightforward. (In England, where convictions were based on the verdicts of juries, confessions— and therefore judicial torture—were of much less importance [Langbein 2004: 99–100].) Torture was also used as a form of punishment, often preceding the execution itself (Cohen 2003: 214). In this situation it manifested the absolute power of the authorities to injure and destroy those bodies that supposedly threatened the integrity of the social body.

While judicial torture and execution may have ultimately had as their target the purification and subjugation of the whole social body, they were very much experienced by the individuals concerned. The extent to which fear of the pangs of torture affected sensitive minds is well seen in the reflections of Thomas More as he awaited execution for refusing to recognize Henry VIII as the supreme head of the Church of England. Contemplating his doleful fate, More found himself "much more shrinking from pain and from death, than methought it the part of a faithful Christian man" (2000: 101). Death, for More, meant experiencing "pains in every part of your body, breaking your veins and nerves with so much suffering and distress," feeling "your heart panting, your throat rattling, your flesh trembling, your mouth gaping, your nose narrowing, your legs cooling" with the departure of life (2002: 23–24). It must have come as a considerable relief to More when the manner of his execution was changed from being hanged, drawn, and quartered—the customary penalty for treason—to a relatively simple beheading.

THE TORMENTS OF HELL

The death of a condemned sinner did not constitute the end of one's suffering in traditional Christian thought. It was, indeed, only the prelude to the worse and unending pains awaiting sinners in Hell. The notion that the seriously sinful would be subjected to an eternity of pain in the afterlife may have even seemed to justify giving them a foretaste of Hell on Earth. If God took no pity on such wretches, why should humans? It could certainly be used to justify the torturous interrogation and execution of those persons who might, through their corrupting influence, condemn not only themselves but also others to this horrendous fate.

Hell was the sensory opposite of Heaven. Where Heaven, at the outermost edge of the cosmos, was all light, fragrance, music, and spiritual delight, Hell, in the center of the Earth was all darkness, stench, din, and physical torment. So as to leave no pain unsuffered, all the senses were tormented in Hell:

> The eyes will shout out their demand for light and yet they will be always constrained to gaze on terrors, shadows and smoke. . . . The ears will shout out their demand for the pleasure of harmony and yet they will hear nothing but groans, shrieks, uproar, oaths, and curses. . . . The sense of taste will long to assuage its burning thirst and hunger and yet there is no way of satisfying it, not even with the refuse of the sewers. . . . The sense of smell will demand perfumes and yet it will not be able to smell anything except such putrid air, such a stinking fetor that a single whiff would infect the entire earth. (cited by Camporesi 1991: 56)

As the sense most particularly linked to both sin and suffering, touch came in for the greatest share of infernal pain. The traditional seven scourges of Hell—smoke, stench, cold, heat, hunger, thirst, and serpents—were predominantly tactile in nature (8). Similar torments could be found in pre-Christian European mythologies that described otherworldly places of punishment with giant, boiling cauldrons; icy, knife-filled rivers; and dens of venomous serpents (Turner 1993: 105–8). The general preference in descriptions of the underworld was for punishments of brutal intensity—burnings and freezings, beatings and piercings—calculated to make a strong impact on the dullest imagination.

While the torments of Hell were described in terms of earthly pains, it was emphasized that they were, in fact, far fiercer than anything one could experience on Earth. Indeed, compared to the sufferings of Hell, earthly pains were said to be positive pleasures: "Love your darkness, oh [sic] blind persons; lepers, cherish your sores; epileptics, love your falls; paralytics, your tremors; sufferers from gout, your stabbing pains . . . condemned prisoners love the ropes which strangle you, the wheels which break you to pieces and the pincers which tear you" (cited by Camporesi 1991: 56). An even more important difference between earthly and hellish torments was that, while the former were temporary, the latter were unending. The bodies of the damned could never be destroyed: no matter if they were chewed or dismembered or burnt to cinders, they always came back for more.

While fire was usually viewed as a good all-purpose medium of punishment, particular infernal torments were sometimes linked to particular sins. Just as on Earth slanderers might be punished by having their tongues cut off, their punishment in Hell might be to have their tongues eternally ablaze. A common torment for the greedy and lustful was to be eaten, either by demons or by each other (see C. Bynum 1995: 293, 299).

The biblical basis for theological reflections on Hell consisted of scriptural references to "unquenchable fire" (Matt. 3: 12), "eternal destruction" (2 Thess.: 1–9), and a "place of torments" (Luke 16: 28). Biblical exegesis prompted but could not always provide answers for the questions that vexed theologians about the afterlife of sinners. How was it that damned souls suffered physical torments *now,* when they would not be reunited with their resurrected bodies until the Day of Judgment? The dilemma was solved by concluding that the souls of the dead were allotted temporary spiritual bodies that could feel and act much like physical bodies but that were imperishable. Another question concerned how large this place of torments need be to accommodate all of its denizens. In early Christianity Hell was imagined to be vast in its dimensions, a bottomless pit into which any number of sinners could be thrown. Medieval meditations on Hell similarly had no difficulty in multiplying burning valleys and fiery rivers in their expansive infernal geographies. Later theologians, trained to think quantitatively, preferred a smaller and more precisely bounded underworld. If Hell were to fit in the center of the Earth, it was argued, an area four miles in diameter would be about right. So long as the damned were piled on top of each other "in the same way as wood in a pile," a space of this size would suffice for many millions. Such a cramped infernal territory did not suit the traditionalists, however, who required more ample dimensions to elaborate a proper landscape of pain for Heaven's antithesis (Camporesi 1991: 30–31).

Information about the nature of Hell came not only from theological dissertations but also from descriptions of visionary voyages. Such reputedly firsthand accounts of the infernal realms gave a strong touch of realism to Hell. Bede recorded having known a man who had heard the seventh-century monk Furseus tell of his visionary tour of Hell. The man recounted that, though it was winter,

Furseus, still hot from Hell, had sweated during the telling of his journey as though it were midsummer (Turner 1993: 95). When writing his own literary exposition of Heaven, Hell, and Purgatory in the fourteenth century, Dante would appropriate this tradition of visionary voyages to present himself as a traveler through otherworldly realms.

One of the most popular accounts of visionary voyages was the twelfth-century *Vision of Tundale* that reputedly related the experiences of a high-living and hard-hearted nobleman whose soul went on a tour of the afterworld while his body lay in a coma for three days. In this account an angel shows Tundale's spiritual self the hellish future that awaits if he does not mend his worldly ways. First Tundale is shown a valley of burning coals on which murderers are being grilled, then a half-frozen, half-fiery mountain where deceivers are being driven from one side to the other. Tundale finds himself facing a plank a thousand feet long and only one foot wide. Those who stumble fall into a smoking abyss in which the damnably proud languish. Taking him by the hand, the angel enables the knight to cross.

He then finds that he must make his way through the belly of the Great Beast of Hell (named Acheron after the river of pain in the Greek underworld). This is the place of punishment for the greedy, and here the angel leaves Tundale to have a direct experience of the burnings, bitings, and beatings they suffer. This touch of Hell leaves Tundale so weak that he requires a heavenly touch from his angel to continue. The nobleman's next ordeal is to cross a lake filled with ravenous, fire-breathing creatures by means of a bridge that is studded with nails and only a palm's width across. This is the bridge that robbers must cross and, as he once stole a cow, Tundale must cross it leading a cow. He almost falls when meeting a soul coming the other way, but miraculously reaches the other end. His torn feet are healed by another angelic touch and he is led through a new series of torments into the very bowels of Hell where Lucifer ceaselessly chews up and spits out sinners. After this follows a tour of the way stations between Hell and Heaven and a glimpse of Heaven itself, where all is beauty and harmony and joy. Tundale then reenters his earthly body determined to lead a reformed life (Mearns 1985).

A feature that greatly adds to the effectiveness of this account is that Tundale not only sees the torments of Hell, he also feels them: the journey is a tactile experience and not just a visionary voyage. That Tundale is a nobleman also adds interest, for the tale then becomes a kind of knightly quest with personal salvation as the goal. The skills that Tundale requires to complete the journey are not the traditional knightly ones of combat, however, but skills of balance and endurance. Tundale must cross narrow bridges, climb infernal mountains, and endure devastating pains. Whereas as a nobleman Tundale would have needed to know how to ride well, now he has to learn how to walk well. (In this work the medieval device of dividing up a narrative poem into "passus," or paces, takes on an extra meaning.) It is, indeed, humorous to read of this arrogant knight pussyfooting his way along a narrow bridge and breaking down in tears when he finds his path blocked by a poor sinner coming the other way. Ultimately, Tundale's walk through Hell can only be accomplished with the support of his guardian angel. Visiting Heaven afterwards, Tundale sees something of which there is no sign in Hell—seats, on which the blessed can rest at their ease.

The theme of keeping one's balance that we find in the *Vision of Tundale* can also be found in many other premodern accounts of the afterworld. The twelfth-century *Vision of Alberic,* for example, has not only a hellish bridge—which shrinks to the width of a thread at its midpoint—but also a burning ladder (derived from the scriptural Jacob's ladder). The eighth-century *Vision of the Monk of Wenlock* describes an otherworldly ordeal in which sinners try to keep their balance on a slippery log placed over a river of fire (Zaleski 1987: 67- 68).

Presenting a counternarrative to secular tales of knightly heroics, the *Vision of Tundale* emphasized that it was not grand gestures and bold deeds that saved souls from damnation. Only a careful consideration of each step along the path of life could keep one (with God's help) from falling into sin. However, just as practice enables acrobats to walk a tightrope with confidence, habitual acts of virtue would eventually enable one to walk the narrow path of righteousness without stumbling. In Tundale's vision, a pilgrim priest, accustomed to virtuous ambulation and carrying a steadying palm branch, makes it across the one-foot-wide bridge without a problem (and presumably goes on to a more pleasant place). Tundale himself, it is suggested, becomes a pilgrim on returning to the world, showing that he has learnt the importance of right-minded walking.

Dante would make use of similar motifs of walking, balance, and endurance in his account of Hell. At the start of his great poem Dante describes himself as halfway along the path of life. His tour of the underworld begins when he loses his way in a dark forest. On his visit through the Underworld Dante learns that each sinful step taken on Earth results in a punitive "counterstep" (contrapasso) in Hell. This is illustrated literally in certain cases: men guilty of simony stand upside down with their feet on fire (Canto XIX); fortune tellers walk backwards because their heads have been twisted around (Canto XX), while hypocrites plod slowly around a circular track, weighed down by gilt cloaks lined with lead (Canto XXIII).

The conclusion of the *Divine Comedy* does not tell us whether the fictional Dante, like Tundale, recovers his way and henceforth walks aright. We do know, however, that the historical Dante, exiled from Florence by his enemies, refused to perform a humiliating penitential walk through the city to receive a pardon: "Not by this path will I return to my native city. If some other can be found . . .

which does not derogate from the fame and honour of Dante, that I will tread
with no lagging footsteps. But if by no such path Florence may be entered, then I
will enter Florence never again" (B. Reynolds 2006: 380–81). In the real world,
right-walking evidently had political and social, as well as religious, dimensions.

Accounts of journeys to Hell strove to make the point that Hell is not just for
other people: it might be for oneself if one did not watch one's step. Along with
their moral messages, however, such accounts might also be used for very worldly
purposes. By locating certain individuals in Hell and others in Heaven a writer
could make a powerful statement about on whose side justice lay. Moreover, it
must have been very satisfying to be able to place, as Dante did, one's enemies
among the damned in Hell, and one's heroes among the saints in Heaven.

It is hard to estimate the extent to which people, hearing such tales, trembled
at the thought of Hell's torments. Many, no doubt, like the old woman (the poet's
mother) in Villon's "Testament," were terrified by the image of a "Hell wherein the
damned are boiled" and uttered heartfelt prayers for deliverance (Villon 1994:
115). In the Middle Ages few publicly doubted the existence of a real, physical
Hell, though some remained skeptical. (One who did, Johannes Scotus Erigena,
was said to have been stabbed to death by his students with their pens—a death
doubtless deemed suitable for a writer of "false" doctrines [Turner 1993: 89].) That
unorthodox notions about the afterlife did indeed circulate is attested to by the
twelfth-century romance *Aucassin & Nicolette*. When Aucassin is threatened with
Hell for courting Nicolette he declares that he'd rather go to Hell and be with
the goodly knights who die in jousts and wars and the gracious ladies "that have
two lovers or three" than go to Paradise and mingle with old priests, cripples,
and beggars "who all day and night cower continually before the altars" (*Aucassin
and Nicolette* 1887: 112). This overtly humorous view of the afterlife suggests a
populace that was less than overwhelmed by the terrors of Hell, despite all the
efforts of the preachers (Turner 1993: 112).

SORROW AND COMPASSION

Frequently exposed to pain as they were, did people of earlier eras become
inured to it? The expectation that this would happen was certainly behind many
traditional practices, such as the blows and beatings that formed a customary part
of military training. Was suffering indeed so commonplace that only exceptional
pains could make an impact on the imagination? To what extent did the mass of
people reflect on the pains they or others were feeling? The harshness of life, it
could be argued, demanded continual unreflective effort, with little time for or
training in the cultivation of feelings of pity—even perhaps of self-pity.

A strong sense of empathy might have made the beatings, badgerings, and burnings that were part and parcel of premodern life too emotionally harrowing to bear. Rather than occasioning pained avoidance on the part of the public, however, acts of violence and aggression—from bear-baiting to executions—were frequently popular social diversions. Mandrou writes: "If a joust or tournament resulted in death, this was no cause for lamentation. Such an event received only the briefest mention in the journal of a bourgeois of Paris (in 1515). . . . A century later Moncoys crossed Holland and greatly admired . . . '[the] many magnificent gibbets' [erected for displaying hanged criminals]. . . . At Metz in 1500, three thousand people gathered on the ice of a lake in midwinter to see the drowning of two women." "In such instances," Mandrou concludes, "cruelty came very close to utter insensitivity" (1976: 57, 58).

Few people ever had the experience of being publicly tortured or burnt at the stake but many, particularly in the later Middle Ages when such punishments became more commonplace, would have witnessed such events. Bernardino of Siena, the fifteenth-century organizer of bonfires of "vanities," or objects of worldly pleasure, described the differing perceptions of the participants and the spectators at a burning at the stake of a "sodomite": "The sodomite felt the smoke and the fire, and he burned to death; the executioner felt only the smoke, and whoever was standing around watching saw nothing but smoke and fire" (cited by Mormando 1999: 152). Bernardino makes no mention of the sensations of sound or smell that would also have been an integral part of the experience. These would have blurred the distinction he wishes to make between participants and spectators, as hearing and smell would have drawn everyone together in a common experience. In his description there is only tactile experience at one end and visual perception at the other.

The moral lesson Bernardino drew from his sensory analysis was that "in hell the sodomites will burn with smoke and fire [while] their torturers down there will get the smoke. . . . Those who stand watching [represent] the blessed spirits in paradise who see the punishment of the sodomites and rejoice over it because they see the justice of God shining forth from it" (ibid.). The sight of the destruction of the ungodly was hence expected to arouse a godly joy in devout spectators, who themselves remained untouched and unpitying.

In actual fact, however, crowds might be moved to tears by the painful death of what seemed to them to be an innocent victim. When the fourteenth-century mystic Marguerite Porete was burned for her unorthodox writings—which would later become classics of medieval mysticism—"the [entrails] of the crowd were moved toward pious, even tearful compassion with her" (cited in Sells 1994: 141). Here, through the interior touch of empathy, spectators not only watched

Marguerite suffer, they suffered alongside her. This example indicates that the simple presence of a crowd at an execution cannot necessarily be taken as a sign of insensitivity to the suffering of others.

It would, in fact, be a mistake to think of compassion as an alien experience in premodernity (see McNamer 2010). As in all times and places, however, it was modulated by cultural factors. The medieval emphasis on group solidarity, for example, prompted individuals to experience sorrow at pains suffered by members of their own group. We see this expressed in the twelfth-century *Song of Roland* when Charlemagne and his "noble knights" shed "embittered tears of grief" upon discovering that some of their companions have been killed in a Saracen attack (*Song of Roland* 2002: 131). Yet, when those afflicted belonged to an alien group, such as an enemy army or a Jewish community, the degree of compassion felt was likely quite low. No pity is shown in *The Song of Roland* when the Saracens, chased by the pursuing Franks into the river Ebro, "are drowned in dreadful agony" (132). Charlemagne is simply shown collecting the spoils and giving thanks to God. The experience of empathy in such situations, indeed, would have worked to erode the protective boundaries and special status of one's own group, as it would have suggested that outsiders be accorded the same treatment as insiders.

Sorrow, whether for one's own pains or those of others, was recognized as a valid and even praiseworthy response to a number of situations. Sorrowful weeping was taken to be a mark of sincerity, the wordless speech of the heart. Within religious culture, crying was esteemed as a sign of contrition and devotion. Numerous saints, from Francis of Assisi to Catherine of Siena to Ignatius of Loyola, were said to have been dedicated weepers: Saint Francis was even said to have gone blind from his copious shedding of tears (Lutz 1999: 44–47). Saint Louis, for his part, bitterly lamented the stubborn dryness of his eyes, which seemed to signal a dry and stubborn heart. When he was occasionally granted a few tears in his prayers, and "felt them softly flowing down his cheeks into his mouth, he would very sweetly savor them not only in his heart but also on his tongue" (Le Goff 2009: 716).

When it came to real suffering, however, most people were inclined to think pangs of sorrow no match for physical agonies. As we have seen, medieval accounts of Hell—the place of supreme suffering—vividly described sinners being roasted, frozen, pierced, and eaten for their sins. Whatever grief the damned might suffer at their separation from God (the *poeni damni* of the theologians) was definitely made secondary to their physical tribulations, when alluded to at all. Similarly, no matter how incorporeal the sins of the dammed may have been, they are almost invariably punished in Hell with direct corporeal pain. In an era desirous of physical signs and not yet fully aware of the power of psychological torment, true pain was tangible pain.

CHAPTER FOUR

A Woman's Touch

MALE AND FEMALE BODIES

Hot, dry, cold, and moist. The same qualities thought to shape the cosmos in pre-modernity were also believed to shape the bodies of men and women. The creation of a human being involved the union of cold matter, provided by the mother, with hot seminal spirit, contributed by the father. If the father's semen had been sufficiently "cooked" or concocted the newborn would be male. If the amount of heat was insufficient to fully concoct the semen, a female child would result. The conclusion was that women were imperfect, "half-baked" men (P. Allen 1985).

According to received wisdom, a superior endowment of heat accounted for many of the characteristics of the male body. Heat pushed the male body upwards, giving men narrow hips and broad shoulders and extending their height. Heat also pushed the male organs of generation outwards. Heat could even account for male baldness: rising to the head, it was said to "burn up" the hair that grew there. A lack of rising heat, by contrast, made the female body broad at the bottom and narrow at the top, as well as relatively short in height. With insufficient heat to impel them outwards, the female organs of generation remained ensconced within the body.   Furthermore, while a greater endowment of heat supposedly gave men greater vitality, their relative coldness made women inactive. Hot men used up most of the food they consumed in activities, cold women, it was thought, stored their food as fat, menstrual blood, and milk, enabling them to carry and nourish children (Allen 1985; Maclean 1980).

Once made, bodies, particularly female bodies, might still change their sexual characteristics. It was considered possible for an overheated woman—one who, for example, raised her body temperature by engaging in vigorous activity—to acquire male corporeal traits. The increase in heat could burn up feminine fat and menstrual blood and even possibly cause women's internal organs of generation to externalize and be transformed into male genitals (Laqueur 1990: 140–42). The opposite circumstance of a male body taking on female characteristics could occur in the case of men who had been "cooled down" by castration.

Along with being hotter than women's bodies, men's bodies were considered to be drier and hence harder and stronger. Women's cold moist bodies, in comparison, were thought to be like uncooked dough, soft and malleable. Scriptural authority for the notion of men being harder than women was found in Genesis: whereas Adam was created from hard ground, Eve was made out of soft flesh—Adam's rib. Thus Hildegard of Bingen wrote in the twelfth century that "through the vital powers of the earth, Adam was manly. . . . Eve, however, remained soft in her marrow" (cited by Allen 1985: 296). The very words for man and woman in Latin—*vir* and *mulier*—were understood to express this difference, for *vir* could also mean strong while *mulier* was similar to *mollier*, meaning soft (Isidore of Seville 2006: 144).

The dryness that accompanied masculine heat additionally gave to male bodies qualities of incorruption and inodor. Excessive moisture, by contrast, was said to predispose female bodies to corruption and malodor—of which menstrual blood was taken to be a prime example. Along with being a source of odor, the womb was considered to be sensitive to odor, to the extent that physicians occasionally used incense to induce a displaced womb to return to its proper position within the body (Maclean 1980: 40; Jacquart and Thomasset 1988: 131).

Further support for linking thermal qualities to sexual differences was found in the stars. The Sun—the foremost astral body—was associated with masculinity and typed as hot and dry. The female Moon, by contrast, was deemed to be cold (like the nighttime in which it appeared) and wet (like the tides it governed). Hence the medieval theologian and astrologer Pierre d'Ailly proclaimed: "The Moon is cold and wet and the mother of waters" (cited Grant 1996: 466). The unchanging nature of the Sun was taken to be a sign of masculine constancy while the changeable nature of the Moon signified feminine inconstancy. Feminine menstrual cycles, of the same duration as lunar cycles, seemed to provide conclusive evidence of women's physical connection with the cold, wet, mutable Moon.

The different qualities that shaped male and female bodies were also considered to shape male and female characters. Hence, the superior heat that made men active and forceful was thought to also make them courageous and forthright. Their relative coldness, by contrast, was said to make women retiring in nature. Rather than attaining their ends through direct means—the assertive method of the hot male—women preferred cold techniques of guile and deceit.

Masculine dryness, in turn, supposedly made for clear thinking, while hardness resulted in firmness of character. Feminine wetness led to muddy thinking and a fickle nature. Softness made women both soft-hearted (compassionate) and soft-minded (incapable of forceful thinking). Their malleable natures meant that strong impressions were easily made on women, but just as easily washed away due to women's fluid mutability.

Internal heat had the power to strengthen whichever part of the body it most affected. In the case of men, the forceful heat that rose to their heads was imagined to endow them with superior intellectual faculties. What heat there was in female bodies was thought to remain concentrated around the waist. This was presumed to give women a powerful appetite and, as Isidore of Seville put it, "lusty, fiery thighs." Women hence were thought to be predisposed to indulge in carnal pleasures, which men, with their greater rationality, were better able to resist.

In fact, men were generally associated with the mind and soul and women with the body and senses. Even in the curse God laid on Adam and Eve this distinction seemed to be made: men were to suffer through their toil—understood to potentially involve intellectual as well as physical effort—while women were to suffer through childbirth, a purely corporeal form of labor. Men were above all rational beings, while women were, under it all, sensual beings. "Woman is a symbol of sense, and man, of mind," Philo instructed readers in the first century (Philo 1961: 22). And there was no doubt in his mind as to which was superior. "Most profitless is it that Mind should listen to Sense-perception, and not Sense-perception to Mind, for it is always right that the superior should rule and the inferior be ruled" (see Lloyd 1984: 22–25; Baer 1970).

This is an example of the train of logic that justified the subordinate position of women in society. That the superior should rule over the inferior seemed eminently sensible. Few would have disputed, likewise, that the body and the senses should be governed by reason. That women were less rational and more sensuous than men was an assertion grounded in the highest authorities and, as it appeared, evident in the very nature of female and male bodies. Therefore, the almost irrefutable conclusion seemed to be that women should be ruled by men.

While negative typologies of women were woven into the fabric of Western culture, there were nonetheless, particularly from the Renaissance on, attempts to arrive at more positive valuations of female nature. It was difficult in premodernity, given the weight of the authorities behind these assertions, to argue that women were not cold, wet, and soft. However, these characteristics could be turned from liabilities into assets. One woman who undertook such a reevaluation was the Italian humanist Lucrezia Marinelli. In 1600 Marinelli wrote an essay titled "The Nobility and Excellence of Women" in which she cleverly poured new values into the old ideological skins of the female body.

In response to the common characterization of women as imperfect men, Marinelli stated that Genesis indicated that women were physically superior to men "because a woman is made of a man's rib and a man made of mud, she is nobler than he because the rib is nobler than mud." She further contradicted the notion of the greater perfection of men by using a variation of the Aristotelian thesis that nature always tends towards perfection: "Nature, knowing the perfection of the feminine sex, produces women more abundantly than men, for nature always generates more of those things that are better and perfect" (cited in Allen and Salvatore 1992: 19).

With respect to women's coldness, Marinelli argued that in matters of judgment a cool head is better than a hot one, for excessive warmth results in immoderation. A man who acts wisely does so because "he comes closest to the nature and temperature of women, for there is a placid and non-exceeding warmth in him." For this reason, according to Marinelli, the tepid middle-aged man "acts more wisely and maturely"—and in a more womanly fashion—than the hot-headed youth. Wetness of temperament had similar advantages to coolness in that it dampened irrational passions. Indeed, women's cooler temperature and humidity ensured that "their senses are ruled by reason," rather than being opposed to reason (25–27).

Feminine softness was likewise presented as a highly desirable trait in "The Nobility and Excellence of Women." Following Aristotle, Marinelli argued that "a soft and delicate flesh reveals that the intellect of such a person understands more quickly than that of someone who has tough and hard flesh" (18). As for the idea that women are malodorous, Marinelli adamantly denied it, saying that women "hate messiness which renders their pretty bodies ugly, and all those things that emanate stinky odor." Men, on the other hand, "being rougher creatures, are much more frequently untidy and dirty." In fact, the champion of women declares, in some cases "such a stench comes forth from [men] that women who stand by them are obliged to plug their nose." All in all, according to Marinelli, the physical characteristics of the female sex "denote and signify all the wonderful perfections that are to be found in this world" (28, 25).

Marinelli's challenge to contemporary gender paradigms demonstrates that women were not always accepting of the prevalent characterizations of their physical and moral natures, supported by eminent authorities as such characterizations might be. It also reveals an acute awareness of the fact that sensory models of male and female nature were inflected with gender ideologies that—far from being immutable—could be manipulated with a skillful touch.

A WOMAN'S TOUCH

While the senses were typically considered feminine in nature when opposed to male rationality, when considered on their own they could be assigned feminine or masculine connotations. Touch, taste and smell were generally held to be the lower senses and thus were readily linked to the lower sex—women. Similar associations were made between touch, taste, and smell and the lower classes, the lower (non-European) races, and (as we shall see) the lower species. All of these groups were imagined to dedicate themselves to the corporeal comforts of the lower senses—whether these comforts were seen as the plowman's lunch and rough bedding of a farm worker or the rich spices and silks of an Oriental potentate. The European male elite, by contrast, was deemed to find its fulfillment in more rational satisfactions—such as reading and discoursing—associated with the higher senses of sight and hearing. In the case of women, their association with the senses of touch, taste, and smell reinforced the cultural link between femininity and the body, for these senses were closely tied to intimate bodily experience. The distance senses of sight and hearing, by contrast, were associated with the perception of the external, masculine world.

Women's connection with the lower senses was grounded in the scriptural account of the Fall. In that story, it was Eve who first disobeyed God's injunction not to eat or even touch the fruit of the tree of the knowledge of good and evil. This act of disobedience was taken by many as a sign of woman's inability to restrain her covetous touch and her greedy appetite. Hence, when in the medieval play *Jeu d'Adam* the serpent tells Eve that the forbidden fruit contains "all knowledge," the first woman only asks in response, "What does it taste like?" (Burns 1993: 81). Unable to comprehend the intellectual or spiritual significance of the fruit, all sensual Eve can think about are its gustatory attractions.

One popular source of information about the gendered nature of perception was provided by the premodern "bestiary of the senses." In this system the animals traditionally associated with touch (the tortoise and the spider) were typed as feminine, while the animals associated with sight (the eagle and the stag) were thought of as masculine. Forever encased in a shell, the tortoise suggested the quintessential homebody, the woman who never leaves the walls of her house. The tortoise further symbolized wet sensuality and was linked to the planet Venus (held, like the Moon, to be cold and moist in nature). The spider represented woman as housewife, spinning and homemaking, and as temptress, trapping her (male) prey in a silken web of seduction. The former occupation made an approved use of a woman's touch. The latter employment was viewed with suspicion, when not condemned outright.

A woman did not have to actively employ her sense of touch for her body to constitute a tactile threat to men—the mere fact of its being pleasurably touchable made it seem a peril. In one of Ben Jonson's plays a "feast of sense" is described in which there are melodies for the ear, perfumes for the nose, and so on, but "for the touch, a ladies waste; which does all the rest excel!" (cited in Kermode 1971: 89). However, if the touch of a woman's body excelled all other attractions, it also constituted the supreme enticement to sin, "the greatest of all obstacles in the way of salvation" (Power 1995: 8). Evidently, it was a danger requiring formidable safeguards and warnings. Church authorities proclaimed that if only "men could see beneath [women's skin]" then they would be safe from the temptations of touch, since "how can we desire to embrace such a sack of dung?" (cited by Dalarun 1992: 20).

Feminine touch could be seen as constituting a serious threat to masculine dominance—as the image of woman as a deadly spider indicated. The seductive touch of a woman was considered to rob men of their rational powers and even, it was thought, of their sight, the sense most closely allied with reason. The biblical tale that provided an iconic example of the supposed opposition between feminine tactility and masculine visuality was that of Samson and Delilah. In this story Delilah seduces the mighty Samson and, while he is asleep in her lap, disempowers him by having his head shaved and then delivers him to the Philistines, who blind and enslave him (Judg. 13–16). Succumbing to a woman's touch, this tale was taken to say, changes a man from a clear-sighted leader to a blind slave.

The threat a woman's touch posed to a man's vision was held to be physical, as well as metaphorical. The brain, the male organs of generation, and the eyes were all held to make use of seminal fluid in their operations. Women, it was believed, also had a kind of seminal fluid, but one that was weaker than men's and that resulted in a correspondingly weaker sense of sight and a weaker intellect. Castrated men were also thought to have a poor sense of sight due to the reduced amount of seminal fluid in their bodies. Similarly, when an man engaged in excessive sexual activity the subsequent depletion of seminal fluid was believed to harm both his sight and his brain. Albertus Magnus related an account of a monk who died after satisfying his lust "seventy times before matins was rung." A subsequent autopsy found that the monk's brain had shrunk and his eyes were destroyed. This was taken as proof that semen was shared with both the brain and eyes (Jacquart and Thomasset 1988: 52–56). A woman's seductive touch, hence, was understood to literally have the power to rob a man of his sight and his reason.

The danger of a woman's touch extended beyond the purely tactile into other domains. One of these was speech. According to the gender norms of the time, speech, as a form of self-assertion, was masculine in character. It was, however, a faculty deemed to often be usurped by women. The attribution of talkativeness to women was supported by an association made between speech and the feminine quality of fluidity. Speech was imagined to flow like water, and, in the case of women, like an unending stream. Women gushed with words the way they gushed with body fluids. In fact, feminine volubility was held by some to result from uterine vapors rising to the brain and stimulating women into an unnatural loquacity (Maclean 1980: 41).

The speech that poured out of women could be either soft or "as sharp as a thystyll / as rugh as a brere [briar]" ("Segunda Pastorum" 1897: 119). It was frequently said that the transition from one state to the other occurred after marriage. "Soft, modest, meek, demure, / Once joined, the contrary she proves, a thorn," wrote Milton of women before and after wedlock in *Samson Agonistes*. Responding to the frequent characterization of women as viragoes, Lucrezia Marinelli claimed that men who slandered women with their falsehoods proved themselves to possess the sharp tongues they attributed to women (Allen and Salvatore 1992: 21). Whether soft or sharp, however, any use of speech by women could be considered a travesty of rational male discourse and a transgression of the truly womanly condition of silence.

WOMEN'S WORK

Women's work was understood to be above all housework. The very bodies of women were said to be made for the job. The inherent coldness of the female body seemed to make it advisable for women to stay warm indoors. Their soft flesh, broad hips, and narrow shoulders were taken as further evidence that women were designed to stay at home, leaving hardened, broad-shouldered men to brave the rigors of the world outside. Martin Luther confirmed this view: "Women ought to stay at home; the way they were created indicates this, for they have broad hips and a wide fundament to sit upon" (Luther 1967: 8).

The female function of childbearing was thought to definitively commit women to homely caretaking duties. The one seemed to follow from the other. A visual depiction of this can be found in a medieval text employed to teach zoology at the University of Oxford. One illustration shows a man and woman in the act of procreation while underneath a woman is depicted rocking a cradle. In the bottom margin the same woman is shown nursing the baby before a fire. On either side a rabbit, one blue representing the cold female principle of procreation, the other red, representing the hot male principle, face each other (Camille 1999: 370). It all seemed inevitable. From the point a woman wed, her future was laid out. At its inception was the union of the tactile values of hot and cold, and from then on followed a series of predominantly tactile tasks.

If the woman were poor, the household tasks expected of her could be arduous indeed, as William Langland described so movingly in *Piers Plowman:*

> What they may spare in spinning they spend on rental,
> On milk, or on meal to make porridge
> To still the sobbing of the children at meal time.
> Also they themselves suffer much hunger.
> They have woe in winter time, and wake at midnight
> To rise and to rock the cradle at the bedside,
> To card and to comb, to darn clouts and to wash them,
> To rub and to reel and to put rushes on the paving,
> The woe of these women who dwell in hovels
> Is too sad to speak of or to say in rhyme. (Langland 1935: 92)

In a seventeenth-century satire by John Taylor, a better-off but still busy housewife complains to her husband that, while he spends the day outside the home, she is forced to remain inside undertaking an endless round of chores:

> A woman's work is never at an end and never done, but like a wheel, still running round and hath no end. I am forced as soon as I rise in the Morning to make a fire, sweep the house, and get the children's and your servants' Breakfast; no sooner that done and they out of the way, think upon Dinner; then no sooner Dinner eaten, than I must make all the dishes clean again and sweep the House. Then, because I would be thought a good Housewife, I sit me down to spin, then think upon your Supper and study what will please your dainty chops (Taylor 1985: 193).

Even a woman wealthy enough to have servants to take care of the basic household chores was still expected to be confined to the domestic sphere: sewing, caring for children, planning meals, and attending to the comforts of home. This is made clear in the subtitle of a seventeenth-century housekeeping manual that lists the "virtues which ought to be in a complete woman": "skill in physic [healing], cookery, banqueting-stuff, distillation, perfumes, wool, hemp, flax, dairies, brewing, baking, and all other things belonging to a household" (Markham 1986). No one would have suggested that such an array of housekeeping skills could make for a complete man, who would have been expected to engage with worldly matters outside the home. Yet it was evidently considered possible for a woman to complete herself without ever setting a foot outside her house—except to go to church. As Ruth Kelso noted in *Doctrine for the Lady of the Renaissance,* "Occupations which filled books especially addressed to gentlemen encompassed government, war, the learned professions, agriculture, and commerce; but for women only one occupation was recommended—housewifery" (Kelso 1956: 3).

A woman out of her home, in fact, might be considered a woman dangerously out of place. It was not for women to leave behind their tactile labors and go out to see the world. In the sixteenth-century "Rule for Women to Brynge Up Their Daughters," mothers were advised to forcibly prevent their daughters from transgressing the bounds of their physical and visual confinement:

> If they wyll go or gad abrode,
> Their legges let broken bee:
> Put out their eyes if they wyll looke
> Or gase undecentyle. (cited by Hull 1982: 76)

The woman who did not restrict herself to the bounds of her home and restrain her sense of sight, this poem suggested, should have her body violently remade so that it conformed to a more appropriate model of feminine sensory and social behavior.

Within the range of skills that formed part of women's work was one, healing, that would later largely be taken out of the hands of women. Women's skill in healing was traditionally taken to be a point in their favor. Hence in the fourteenth century Christine de Pisan asked rhetorically, "What profit comes from thus defaming women . . . from whom many deeds are designed / To nurse the body of man tenderly?" (cited by Hughes 1968: 42). The curative power of a woman's touch indeed might be taken to compensate for their supposed ill uses of the sense.

The healing tasks undertaken by women were not slight. Medieval romances, for example, tell of women competently cutting away dead flesh from a wound and setting a dislocated shoulder (50–60). In a seventeenth-century collection of culinary and medicinal recipes, Hannah Woolley exhorted women to be their "own Chirugiens and Physicians, unless the case be desperate," noting that her "Mother and Elder Sisters were very skilled in Physick and Chirugery" (Woolley 1684: 6).

Healing was considered women's work not only among those classes that couldn't afford physicians, but within the upper classes as well. Many upper-class women kept notes on the preparation of medicaments together with culinary recipes, for the two endeavors were held to be similar in nature (Nagy 1988: 67–68). Among the Paston Letters is one in which Sir John Paston asks his wife Margery to prepare a special medicinal plaster for the "Kynges Attorney" and to send it along with instructions as to how "it shold be leyd to and takyn from his knee" (Hughes 1968: 42). Sir John obviously set great store by his wife's homemade remedies.

As the medical profession grew and competition for patients increased, action was taken that curtailed the medical practice of women, along with that of folk healers in general. One early example of this comes from the fourteenth century when a charge was brought against Jacoba de Almania in Paris for illegally practicing medicine. The female healer's methods and treatments—pulse-reading, prescribing hot baths and herbal remedies—did not differ substantially from those of male physicians, for at the time the distinctions between folk and professional medical practice were not always great. However, certain aspects of Jacoba's practice allied her more with housewife practitioners than with professional physicians. First, she collected fees only from those patients she cured (an example that surely must have seemed threatening to the doctors). Most housewife-healers, similarly, charged little or nothing for their services. Second, she prepared her own medicines and bandages (rather than purchasing them from specialists) and personally tended to her patients during their recovery—another customary practice of housewife-healers. Third, and most critical in the eyes of the law, she was not accredited to practice medicine by a university, and not, according to the charges against her, even able to read and write (Hughes 1968: 89–92).

Hands-on methods were deemed no match for the visual and auditory expertise acquired through university schooling and Jacoba lost her case (though her patients testified fervently on her behalf). "It is certain," the court decreed, "that a man approved in [medicine] could cure the sick people better than such a woman" (Minowski 1994: 92). As women were prohibited from attending university, the possibility of acquiring medical authority was thereby closed to them.

Women who healed as part of their housewifely duties posed less of a threat to the medical profession than healers such as Jacoba de Almania, who made a trade of their medical abilities. Yet they, too, as the centuries progressed, were encouraged to leave the practice of medicine to the doctors. Thus the housekeeping manual discussed above, which included "physic" among the virtues to be possessed by a complete woman, nonetheless qualified and excused this inclusion: "[The] most excellent art of physic is far beyond the capacity of the most skilful woman, . . . lodging only in the breast of the learned professors; yet that our housewife may from them receive some ordinary rules and medicines that may avail for the benefit of her family, is in our common experience no derogation at all to that worthy art" (Markham 1986: 56).

In the eighteenth century, the practice of medicine moved further out of the grasp of women. For one thing, the traditional field of medicinal cookery developed into pharmacology and began making use of ingredients unavailable to the housewife. The determination of disease, furthermore, became less dependent on sensory acuity and more reliant on diagnostic instruments available only to specialists. For another, the academic basis of medicine increased substantially. In an essay attacking amateur healers, physician James Adair overwhelmed "the good lady of the family" with all the fields of knowledge requisite for the proper practice of medicine: anatomy, physiology, pathology, nosology, chemistry, botany, and pharmacy, "beside a knowledge of the dead languages, geometry, and natural and experimental philosophy" (1812: 136).

Some women tried to hold on to at least midwifery as an acceptably feminine branch of medicine. The English midwife Elizabeth Nihell argued that men should not "spin, make beds, pickle and preserve, or officiate as a midwife," thereby locating midwifery within the homely sensory domain of women (Nihell 1760).

Women's presumed competence to care for—or detect—pregnant bodies was based on their own intimate experience of reproduction. In one seventeenth-century investigation of a supposed illegitimate pregnancy, a Yorkshire woman who had examined the accused declared: "If you all say she is with child, she is not, for I have born nine children and I can tell who is with bairn and who is not" (cited by Gowing 2003: 45). However, even the care of women in childbirth would come to be the preserve of male doctors in many urban centers. The authority of the doctor concerning the female body did not come from direct embodied experience but rather rested on knowledge gained from more highly regarded sources: medical practice, texts, and anatomical dissection (48). It bears noting that women themselves often preferred being attended by a male doctor, for, aside from his scientific authority, a physician had a higher prestige-value than a midwife (see further Keller 2003).

Women could still act as nurses, performing simple, everyday tasks of patient care as long as their manual labors were supervised by the watchful eye of a trained physician. After summing up his case against amateur doctors James Adair wrote, "I therefore offer this serious and urgent admonition, that as health and life are at stake, my worthy countrywomen would quit this dangerous medical department and confine themselves *solely* to the amiable and most worthy office of exercising their humanity and goodness, in taking care that the sick be regularly supplied with foods or medicine, as directed by the medical men, and thereby avoid the hazard of committing *a breach of the sixth commandment* [thou shalt not kill]" (1812: 139). Hannah Wooley would have been dismayed to hear that her mother and sisters, whom she so greatly admired for their skill in "Physick and Chirurgery," had in fact been *femmes fatales,* threatening their victims with a killer touch.

TEXTS AND TEXTILES

One skill that a number of women plied contrary to convention was that of writing. Writing had the social advantage for women that it could be undertaken within the feminine domain of the home. When contrasted with the quintessential male instrument of power, the sword, the pen might even seem demurely feminine.

Thus, in an open letter to her husband, the Duke of Newcastle, seventeenth-century writer Margaret Cavendish contrasted his manly deeds on the battlefield with her own lady-like penwomanship: "[Your actions] have been of war and fighting, mine of contemplating and writing: yours were performed publicly in the field, mine privately in my closet: yours had many thousand eye-witnesses, mine none but my waiting-maids" (Cavendish n.d.: xxxviii). Cavendish here made writing seem a very modest, homey endeavor compared to the aggressive, public, and highly visual act of warfare.

Writing, furthermore, arguably bore some manual and metaphorical similarity to the quintessential feminine occupations of spinning and sewing. It was a work of the hand and, if it used words rather than threads, it could still be conceptualized as a kind of weaving. Why could not writing therefore be an approved occupation for women? Provided, of course, that it did not lead them to neglect their housework. Catherine des Roches wrote on this point in the sixteenth century:

> But spindle, my dearest, I do not believe
> That much as I love you, I will come to grief
> If I do not quite let that good practice dwindle
> Of writing sometimes, if I give you fair share,
> If I write of your merit, my friend and my care,
> And hold in my hand both my pen and my spindle.
> (in Sankovitch 1988: 52)

However, while certain kinds of writing—letters, recipes—were approved for elite women, the practice did not form a socially acceptable counterpart to the unquestioned feminine occupation of needlework. For one thing, while needlework had important visual dimensions, it was quintessentially tactile in nature, centered on the creation of items that contributed to the bodily comfort of the family. Writing, however, was done solely to be seen. It could not dress anyone or warm anyone, be used to carry anything or to cushion anything.

Writing, furthermore, partook of a public nature. It might be that a woman's written work was meant solely for her own eyes or for those of her family and hence remained appropriately confined, like her needlework, to the domestic space of the home. The poet Katherine Fowler Phillips ("Orinda") declared that she "never writ any line . . . with any intention to have it printed" for she did not wish to seem "bold and masculine enough to send her writings into the world" (M. Reynolds 1964: 57–58). However, writing was imagined to be produced above all for public view and many woman wrote with this aim in mind—which in itself made writing a questionable practice for women. Women's work was so closely associated with women's bodies that for a woman to put her writing on public display seemed disturbingly close to putting her body on public display.

We come here to another reason writing was not thought of as appropriate women's work: it was considered brain work—and hence masculine in nature— rather than feminine body work. Margaret Cavendish brought out this essential cultural difference between spinning and writing at the same time as she tried to liken the latter to the former: "True it is, Spinning with Fingers is more proper to our Sexe, then [sic] studying or writing Poetry, which is the Spinning with the braine: but I having no skill in the Art of the first (and if I had, I had no hopes of gaining so much as to make me a Garment to keep me from the cold) made me delight in the latter . . . which made me endeavour to Spin a Garment of Memory" (Cavendish 1972: Dedication).

In fact, Cavendish and many other female writers found themselves continually obliged to explain and justify their practice of creating texts instead of textiles, garments of memory instead of garments to keep out the cold. Margaret Cavendish stated that she wrote because nature had made her "a spinster in poetry" rather than "a spinster in huswifry": "I cannot Work, I mean such Works as Ladies use to pass their Time . . . Needle-works, Spinning-works, Preserving-works, as also Baking, and Cooking-works . . . I am Ignorant in these Imployments" (1969: Dedication, 311–12). Cavendish further suggested that writing was actually morally superior to needlework as a feminine activity. Whereas needlework was primarily a manual task that left the mind dangerously free to wander, writing employed all of a woman's faculties (313–14). This point had also been made by Margaret More Roper who argued that "in all handiworks that men say be more meet for a woman the body may be busy in one place and the mind walking in another: and while they sit sewing and spinning with their fingers, may cast and compass many peevish fantasies in their minds" (cited in Wilson 1987: 465–66). Given that women were not all body, all touch, according to this view, something more intellectually stimulating than handiwork was necessary to keep them fully occupied.

The consensus of opinion, however, was against penwork being considered acceptable women's work. In *The Necessarie, Fit, and Convenient Education of aYoung Gentlewoman,* Giovanni Bruto presented the acts of writing and reading not only as unsuitable for women, but also potentially highly injurious: "Let the small profit got by learning, be compared with the great hurt that may happen to [women], and they shall be shewed . . . how much more convenient the needle, the wheele, the distaffe, and the spindle . . . then [sic] the book and pen" (cited by Hull 1982: 155). Other authors implied that "the great hurt" that might come from women's writing would be felt more particularly by men. Women's writing could be likened to women's speech: it was a chaotic and fluid form of self-expression that threatened male social dominance and thus would be better staunched.

Needlework, on the other hand, not only kept women busy within the traditionally feminine sphere, it also, supposedly, kept them quiet. This view was expressed in 1624 by John Taylor in "The Praise of the Needle":

> And for my countries quiet, I should like,
> That woman-kinde should use no other Pike,
> It will increase their peace, enlarge their store,
> To use their tonges less, and their needles more.
> The Needles sharpness, profit yields, and pleasure
> But sharpness of the tongue, bites out of measure.
> (cited by R. Parker, 1984: 86)

While a housewife's sharp needle could create useful garments, this poem suggests that a woman's sharp tongue—or, by extension, sharp pen—might tear the social fabric.

One cutting response to Taylor's writings on women came in the form of a pamphlet titled "The Women's Sharp Revenge" written under the pen names of Mary Tattlewell and Joan Hit-Him-Home: "We, whom they style by the name of weaker Vessels, though of a more delicate, fine, soft, and more pliant flesh and therefore of a temper most capable of the best Impression, have not . . . [been allowed] Education, lest we should be made able to vindicate our own injuries, we are set only to the Needle, to prick our fingers, or else to the Wheel to spin a fair thread for our own undoing" (1985: 313). Sharp words indeed, and ones that cut right to the heart of the matter. The softness of the female body, the tract argued, fit women for the acquisition of knowledge rather than manual labor. However, women were kept in bondage to their needlework and thus prevented from acquiring the skills that would enable them to avenge their wrongs. As Madeleine Fredonnoit Des Roches had complained a century earlier:

> Our parents have the praiseworthy custom
> Of making us unused to reason,
> Of keeping us shut up in the house
> And giving us a distaff for a pen. (cited by Jordan 1990: 181–82)

If traditional women's work might be seen as a way to keep women silent and subordinate, however, it could nonetheless also serve as a field for feminine empowerment and self-expression. One means by which this could be undertaken was through the creative elaboration of traditional feminine craftwork, as will be seen in chapter 6. Another way in which women's work might be considered empowering concerned its basis in fundamental processes of life and nature.

Out in the public sphere, studying, discoursing, politicking men seemed more powerful than stay-at-home women. But within the home, giving birth, cooking, healing women appeared to be more in touch with the elemental forces of the cosmos. This cosmic power of femininity would find two basic forms of cultural expression: the figure of the female saint and that of the witch.

MYSTICAL RAPTURES AND PAIN CRAFT

In Catholic countries the religious life offered women the one socially acceptable alternative to housekeeping. Women certainly did not have all the possibilities for religious vocations available to men: they could not be priests nor preachers nor hold office in the Church. What made a religious life socially acceptable for women was that it was a cloistered life. The convent was considered an appropriate, sheltered repository for well-to-do women who had few prospects of marrying and acquiring their own homes and family duties. While there were exceptions, such as Catherine of Siena (who said she was instructed by Jesus to work in the world), a nun was generally even more confined to a life indoors, even more separated from the masculine public sphere, than a housewife. The most enclosed of such women were the anchoresses who were ceremonially locked within their cells to lead lives of contemplation and prayer.

After the social and religious upheaval of the Protestant Reformation, the enclosure of nuns was even more strictly regulated. Not only were nuns not permitted to set foot outside their convents, they were not permitted even to look outside: "All existing windows, gates, grilles, or holes facing the public street were to be walled up" (Evangelisti 2007: 48). The sense of touch was also guarded from any contact with the outside world, as the grilles through which the nuns communicated with visitors in the convent parlor did not allow a hand to pass through. The visual and tactile world of enclosed nuns was the world within the monastic compound. Only sounds could pass through the barriers. This was enough in some cases, however, to give nuns a public voice when they were consulted on social and political matters by influential relatives and patrons.

While convents severely restricted the activities of their inmates, they might at the same time offer women exceptional opportunities for reading and writing. Formal Christian culture was very much a culture of literacy and, though they lived on the margins of that culture, nuns still partook of it. A book, provided it were devotional, was considered a highly proper object for a nun to hold in her hands. A pen was acceptable as well, provided what was written with it concerned matters of the spirit. Furthermore, the texts of a holy woman might well be viewed with worldly approbation if they seemed divinely inspired and dogmatically orthodox. (Though they might also be censured—Teresa of Avila was ordered to burn a commentary she wrote on the Song of Solomon on the grounds that it was an improper subject for a woman [Ahlgren 1998: 153]). It is not to be wondered at then, that a great deal of premodern women's writing came from women in orders.

When a woman left home to enter a convent, however, she did not necessarily escape the traditional sphere of women's work. Floors needed to be swept and washed, meals to be cooked, clothes to be mended, wherever one lived—though in wealthier convents much of this menial labor would be undertaken by servants or lay sisters. Many nuns spent long hours spinning, laboring over the sewing of their habits or embroidering liturgical garments. Convents helped support themselves by selling (or giving in exchange for a donation) samples of the nuns' handiwork to relatives or the public. Certain convents specialized in particular crafts, such as lace, confectionaries, perfumes, or medicines. Customarily these would all be products associated with the feminine domain of the lower senses.

The missing family component of religious life could be supplied not only by the sisters and the mother superior of the convent, but by a mystical integration into the Holy Family. In some cases a nun might see herself as Mary, tenderly mothering a baby Jesus, in others as a loving bride embracing an adult Jesus. More than just metaphors or meditational techniques, these mystical relationships were often experienced in terms of tactile, corporeal encounters. Saint Ida of Louvain, for example, enjoyed bathing the infant Jesus in her visions: "Taking him, she squeezes him hard with hugs and kisses, . . . [and lowers] the child ever so carefully into the warm water. When he was sitting, this most chosen of children, after the manner of playing infants, clapped with both hands in the water, and in childlike fashion stirred and splashed the water. He thus soaked his surroundings. . . . After the bath, she again lifted the baby from the water, wrapped him again in his swaddling cloths, enfolded him on her breast, playing intently with him as mothers do" (cited by Herlithy 1995: 171). Saint Catherine of Ricci reportedly held a visionary baby Jesus dressed in swaddling clothes made from her prayers (Klapisch-Zuber 1985: 326; see further Bynum 1987: 246).

A number of nuns, such as Catherine of Ricci and Catherine of Siena, felt themselves to be united with Christ in a spiritual marriage. The same woman, indeed, could have both the mystical experience of holding Jesus the child and that of embracing Jesus the man—perhaps even on the same day. Margaret of Oignt wrote how on a Christmas morning she kissed and held Jesus as a baby, in the afternoon she took Christ down from the cross and "put Him in the arms of my heart," and in the evening "in my spirit I put him down on my bed, and I kissed His tender hands and those blessed feet which were so cruelly pierced for our sins" (Milhaven 1993: 102).

Those nuns who did not have mystical contact with Jesus might still have the physical substitute of holding, rocking, and dressing Christ child dolls made of wood, wax, plaster, or papier-mâché. (One should keep in mind here that many women became nuns while still in their teens). Alternatively, an image of the crucified Christ might become a focus for tactile devotion. "Every cross I came upon," wrote the German nun Margaret Ebner, "I kissed ardently and as frequently as possible" (Ebner 1993: 96). Such contact in itself might lead to a mystical rapture. Margaret Ebner told of an experience in which a wooden Christ child came alive and asked to be held in her arms: "So, with desire and joy I took him out of the crib and placed him on my lap. . . . I said 'Kiss me, then I will forget that you have awakened me.' Then he fell upon me with his little arms and kissed me" (Ebner 1993: 134; see further Hale 1995).

It should not be presumed that these visions were more visual or intellectual than tactile in nature, for the women who experienced them, whether cloistered nuns or devout laywomen, often emphasized their physicality. When Margery Kempe held Jesus's toes in a vision, "to her feeling it was as if they had been very flesh and bone" (Kempe 1936: 296). Such visions reaffirmed the fleshly, human nature of Jesus. There were theologians who dismissed the value of this kind of visionary experience. When Albertus Magnus heard of a woman who claimed to have nursed the infant Jesus in a visionary trance he deemed it a typical feminine "idiocy" (Caciola 2003: 146). At the same time, however, a number of spiritual manuals advised the devout to cultivate just such a mystical physical connection with Jesus. "Touch him with as much love as you would a man" urged the guide for anchoresses, *Ancrene Wisse*. There was, then, significant external support for such visionary experiences.

The dominant position that women—who occupied a very subordinate position within the Church—often assumed in these visions is striking. Jesus customarily appears to them either in the form of a helpless baby or in that of a helpless victim on a cross. Margaret of Oignt wrote that after she had taken her visionary Jesus down from the cross she "carried him as easily as if He had been one year old" (cited by Milhaven 1993: 102). The sense of love felt by these mystics must have been combined with a delightful sense of power. It is also striking how these women, through their mystical contact with Christ, are able to bypass all the male-dominated structures of mediation between the soul and God (78). After her spiritual union with Jesus, Angela of Foligno felt that there was "no intermediary between me and Him" (Angela of Foligno 1999: 70). The female mystic, disqualified by her sex from becoming a priest, played the anthropological role of the shaman, having direct, trance-induced encounters with the Divine.

While critics from Albertus Magnus to twentieth-century theologians might find the physicality of such encounters indicative of a low-minded feminine obsession with sensuality (Milhaven 1993: 87), it was by no means absent from the experiences of male mystics. Gazing on a crucifix, the German monk Rupert of

Deutz saw the image of Jesus come to life. Compelling as this vision was, Rupert declared that mere looking "was not enough for me, unless I could grasp him with my hands, and embracing him, kiss him." This Rupert proceeded to do "for a long time" (Vilaudesau 2006: 77).

Nonetheless, in part because of the association of women with carnality, as well as because of the greater predominance of physical imagery in the visions of female mystics, the experience of concrete, tactile union with God was (and is) seen as a particularly feminine phenomenon (Milhaven 1993: 79). The masculine approach to a visionary experience was to move as quickly as possible from the senses to the intellect. Feminine mysticism, however, at times seemed to find visionary contact with Christ an end in itself, a form of bodily knowing that did not require or benefit from a cognitive extraction of the spiritual message wrapped in the sensory experience. Indeed, Angela of Foligno said that it made her feel sick to try to put her mystical experience into words for "brother scribe" (Angela of Foligno 1999: 69). Margaret Cavendish would write in support of the notion of corporeal knowledge in the seventeenth century that each part of the body is as knowing as any other for "The Heads Braines cannot ingross all knowledge to themselves" (Cavendish 1972: 122). Yet, however satisfied they may have felt with what they learned from the language of the senses, female mystics well knew that the proper thing was to transform visionary experience into theological discourse, and many, such as the anchoress Julian of Norwich, spent long years laboring to do so.

The close association of women with the body, along with the exclusion of nuns from worldly activities, resulted in a good part of women's religious work being body work. One important dimension of this concerned what could be called pain craft—the transformation of the raw material of suffering into the finished product of a sacrificial offering. Christ was seen as the supreme master of this form of body work and many devout women, particularly from the late Middle Ages on, took his salvational suffering as a model to be emulated. For some mystics, including Angela of Foligno, Catherine of Siena, and Catherine of Ricci, this emulation, or co-suffering, included manifesting the wounds of the crucified Christ on their own bodies—the so-called stigmata.

Both holy women and holy men engaged in practices of pain. In the case of women, however, such practices were seen as both more central, given the limited possibilities for women to achieve and demonstrate sanctity, and more necessary, given the assumed sinful proclivities of the female body. An examination of the lives of saints indicates that while male saints tended to imagine sin as besetting them from outside, female saints often saw sin as internal to themselves and therefore requiring self-castigation (Weinstein and Bell 1982: 235–36).

Physical illness provided a valued means for devout women to attain holiness through bodily suffering (235). One greatly suffering female saint was the medieval Lydwine of Schiedam who, although not in orders, was effectively cloistered in her home. After a skating accident at the age of fifteen Lydwine remained ill to the end of her life with a grab bag of agonizing ailments including (apparently) tumors, ulcers, dropsy, plague, gangrene, paralysis, and toothache. Her biographers wrote that in 1412 she vomited "little pieces of her lung and liver, with several intestines": "The same virgin [Lydwine] was corrupt in the lower part of the body with a permanent and large wound; and that her holy bowels might not altogether fall out, they closed the opening with some soft bandage" (Thomas a Kempis 1912: 66–67). While other women might labor over the making of embroidered roses or rose perfume, Lydwine, through her paincraft, made "roses" that were fragrant tears of blood that had hardened on her cheeks overnight. These were reverentially collected and kept in a casket (198).

Even the great sixteenth-century "Doctor of the Church," Teresa of Avila, theologian and reformer of the Carmelite Order, conformed at least in part to a conventional model of suffering female sanctity. She asked God to be afflicted with illness, for she was "determined to gain [salvation] by any and by every means" and subsequently suffered paralysis for three years (2007: 93). After her recovery from paralysis she still experienced recurrent seizures and malarial fevers. "Doctors have told me," she wrote, "that the excruciating pain I have endured is the worst a human being can bear here on earth" (251). When in better health she made up for her diminished suffering through painful penances: "the austerities that my illnesses had prevented now became irresistible to me" (179). Another exemplary mistress of pain craft, it would seem, except that Teresa ended up believing religious obedience to be of more value than any amount of self-inflicted pain (Teresa of Avila 2002: 345).

However painful and confined the lives of many holy women might seem, the women who led them often did not see themselves as disadvantaged by their circumstances. If physically confined to a convent or a sick bed, saintly women such as Lydwine and Teresa might have the compensation of undertaking visionary voyages. If isolated from ordinary social life, they could enter into ecstatic communion with God. If wracked by pain and illness, they could dedicate their suffering to the salvation of souls. "I would willingly suffer a thousand deaths," Teresa wrote, "if it meant I could set even one such soul free from [the] terrible torture [of hell]" (2007: 253). To this end Catherine of Ricci was said to have suffered such elevated fevers that her cell seemed to be on fire. However, while her body blistered with heat the saint asserted that "I long to suffer all imaginable pains, that souls may quickly see and praise their Redeemer" (Butler 1956: 70).

Far from leading marginalized lives, therefore, saintly women might well have been understood by themselves and others to be playing a vital role in the cosmic drama of salvation. Mystical raptures and pain craft, moreover, could give women social power in the form of influence over their contemporaries. And no matter how "otherworldly" such women might seem, they often had worldly goals they wished to pursue, whether avoiding a forced marriage or promoting ecclesiastical reform.

In the process of carrying out their particular forms of body work, many holy women actually remade their own bodies, becoming less like cold, wet feminine matter and more like hot, dry masculine spirit. *Virtus,* the supernatural power attributed to saints, was associated with manliness and often conceptualized as fire (i.e., Barton 2001: ch. 3). One of the core values of *virtus* in antiquity was a willingness to endure pain and death (McDonnell 2006: 25). In Christian culture the concept of *virtus* was expanded to include other values, such as those of piety and chastity; however, the classical influence that emphasized self-sacrifice remained strong. By increasing their amount of hot *virtus* through devotion, celibacy, and especially through the endurance of pain, female saints were able to burn up some of their cold, wet femininity. In certain cases holy women even ceased to menstruate (Bynum 1987: 122–23, 138, 200). Instead of giving off the putrid, cold, and wet odors associated with female bodies, they began to emit a pure, hot, and dry odor of sanctity (see Classen 1998: ch. 2). Holy women hence were able to retain the tender, nurturing aspects of femininity while transforming the female body from a supposed source of corruption and sin into an acknowledged force for purification and redemption.

THE WITCH'S TOUCH

The female witch was the symbolic inverse of the female saint. Whereas female saints counteracted or spiritualized all the qualities associated with women, witches (generally thought of as female) put those qualities to demonic ends. Women were said to be gluttonous by nature. Female saints, by contrast, often starved themselves as part of their quest for holiness (Bynum 1987). At the other end of the moral scale, witches gorged themselves at demonic feasts and transgressed the greatest of food taboos by eating human flesh. While holy women had visions in which they spurned devils offering them food (147), witches accepted the Devil and took the food. One Italian woman accused of witchcraft in 1432 confessed that "she had invoked the devil at noonday . . . [and] begged him for food, when he spread a quantity of food on the grass . . . she ate some and carried the rest home" (Lea 1957: 232–33). (This account says much about the scarcity and consequent power of food in premodernity.)

Women were said to be seductresses. Female saints were celibate spouses of God. Witches not only seduced and bewitched ordinary men but also engaged in unnatural acts with demons. The fifteenth-century witch-hunting manual the *Malleus Maleficarum* described how readily a lustful woman might become the Devil's lover: "[A witch] met the devil in human form on the road where she herself was going to visit her lover for the purpose of fornication . . . , 'I am the devil [he said], and if you wish, I will always be at your pleasure, and will not fail you in any necessity.' And when she had consented, she continued for eighteen years, up to the end of her life, to practice diabolical filthiness with him, together with a moral abnegation of the Faith as a necessary condition" (Kramer and Sprenger 1971: 64). This was no isolated example, according to the same work, which asserted that "all witchcraft comes from carnal lust" (Kramer and Sprenger 1971: 47).

Women were supposed to nourish and nurture. Female saints nourished and nurtured through their acts of devotion and self-sacrifice. Witches subverted this most basic of the traditional duties of womanhood by poisoning instead of feeding and injuring instead of nurturing. Eve, the first woman, was the prototype of the poisonous witch, for she handed Adam the forbidden fruit that would cause the downfall of all humanity. Women, indeed, were thought by some to have a special vocation for poisoning, just as they had for witchcraft. Reginald Scot wrote in *The Discoverie of Witchcraft*: "As women in all ages have beene counted most apt to conceive witchcraft . . . so also it appeareth, that they have been the first inventers, and principal practisers of poisoning" (Scot 1964: 112; see also Hallisey 1987). Unlike ordinary women who nursed their children with milk, or holy women who might mystically nurse the infant Jesus, the witch fed her demonic familiars blood from special nipples on her body—"witch's teats."

The mere touch of a witch was held to be harmful, in opposition to the healing touch of a saint. Nicholas Rémy wrote in *Demonolatry* that "[the] touch of a witch is noxious and fatal . . . to those whom the witch wishes to injure" (1930: 244). If such noxious touching did not happen directly, it might be effected indirectly through an evil glance, for a witch's eyes were imagined to emit venomous vapors—a sorcerous refinement of the turbid mists thought to cloud the vision of menstruous women (Maxwell-Stuart 2003: 23).

George Sinclair wrote in *Satan's Invisible World Discovered*: "Men and Women have been wronged by the touch of a Witches hand, by the breath and kiss of their mouth. . . . By their looks . . . as when a Witch sendeth forth from her heart thorow her eyes venemous and poysonful Spirits as Rayes" (cited by Lea 1957: 1326). Not surprisingly, given the multisensory peril posed by the witch, it was suggested that witches be conveyed to prison blindfolded, gagged, and wheeled in a barrow (257).

Another way the witch manifested her aberrant femininity was by refusing to play the role of the silent sufferer, exalted by so many holy women. Their pain craft was of an entirely different sort. While saints mystically suffered for others, witches magically inflicted suffering on others. The body of the witch was not the soft, easily wounded, female body of tradition. "Witches' bodies were hard and intractable, like an inversion of female openness. In one trial a magistrate tried to cut a witch's hair, only to have the scissors bend in his hand; in others, victims and accusers tried, and failed, to draw the witch's blood, a recipe to destroy her power" (Gowing 2003: 74). When they were tortured or burnt the Devil was believed to render witches impervious to pain. In fact, one identifying mark of a witch was supposed to be her inability to feel pain in certain spots on her body when pricked with a pin.

In terms of class background, female saints had the advantage over witches, for they often came from wealthy families (convents usually required dowries). The women who were singled out as witches, by contrast, were often poor and socially marginal. From a mythic perspective, however, both female saints and female witches stood out as supernaturally powerful women. It is likely no coincidence that Protestant Europe, which by abolishing monasteries removed women's one legitimate possibility for a sacred vocation, showed the greatest zeal in persecuting witches.

One of the most disturbing characteristics of witchcraft from a social perspective was that its supernatural challenge to the established order was based on ordinary women's work: the homey, manual tasks of cooking, cleaning, and caretaking. With a sorcerous touch a witch could brew up spells in the very cauldron she used to cook dinner, suckle demons along with children at her breast, and fly out at night on the same broom she used to sweep the house. Women, apparently, not only had to be excluded from masculine exercises of power, they also had to be prevented from empowering themselves through the traditional tactile practices of women's work. Burning at the stake was a way to vanquish the cold, corrupt femininity of the witch with hot, pure masculine fire. Later, in modernity, the witch would be even more effectively vanquished by a denial of her existence. If the supernatural threat posed by a woman's touch diminished in an age of reason, however, feminine tactility would continue to hold a powerful sway over the Western imagination as a source of both comfort and chaos, pleasure and danger.

CHAPTER FIVE

Animal Skins

ANIMAL BODIES

Intimate contact with animals was part of daily life in the premodern world. Animals were everywhere. Outdoors, oxen plowed fields, cattle and sheep grazed, horses and donkeys transported people and their possessions, hawks and hounds accompanied hunters, and pigs and dogs roamed farmyards and streets. Indoors, birds and squirrels clambered in cages, cats chased mice, and dogs warmed laps or turned spits. In many regions farm animals were lodged under the same roof as farmers. Even within urban centers people often kept their own chickens, pigs, and cows in their cellars and backyards (K. Thomas 1983: 95). On cold nights a household dog or cat or even piglet might join the human family in bed. In such an environment one did not have to go far out of one's way to reach out a hand and touch an animal.

According to the zoological symbolism of the senses, the animals particularly associated with touch were the tortoise and the spider, both said to be sensitive to the slightest contact. All animals, however, had a general association with touch. This was due to touch being considered the primary sense of the body and animals being considered virtually all body. Furthermore, many familiar animals were eminently touchable (furry, sleek and warm)—and their speechlessness made touch an essential medium for human-animal interaction. Humans pulled and prodded and patted animals; animals bit or nuzzled, kicked or carried humans. A whole system of tactile acts, each with associated meanings, animated the network of human-animal relationships. Touch was not only the sense linked with the Earth in medieval philosophy, it was also the common medium of communication of all the inhabitants of the Earth.

An important part of people's involvement with animals concerned using them as a work force. Unlike the native civilizations of the Americas, which relied almost entirely on human labor, European civilization was heavily dependent on the labor of animals. From farming crops to building cathedrals, the West was created and sustained by animal muscles. As Keith Thomas writes, "The civilization of medieval Europe would have been inconceivable without the ox and the horse" (1983: 25).

The most frequent contact humans had with animals, however, was not with their living bodies but with their body parts. Not only did animals' bodies serve humans as food, they were fundamental to the creation of innumerable material goods. Clothing came from wool, fur, and skins; soap and candles were commonly made of animal fat; pillows and mattresses were stuffed with feathers; and a multitude of objects, from combs to dice, made use of bones in their fabrication.

The following sixteenth-century poem titled "A Praise of Sheep" gives an idea of the perceived material usefulness of one of the more common domestic animals:

> No harmful beast, nor hurt at all,
> His fleece of wooll doth cloth us all:
> Which keepes us from the extreme colde:
> His flesh doth feed both young and olde.
> His tallow makes the candles white
> To burne and serve us day and night.
> His skinne doth pleasure divers wayes,
> To write, to wear at all assayes.
> His guts, thereof we make wheele strings,
> They use his bones to other things. (cited in Fudge 2002: 127–28)

It is significant that the value of sheep as presented here rests entirely on their nonaggressive nature and the usefulness of their body parts. Nothing that they might do is considered worthy of note.

Christianity, as it was conventionally presented, helped support the view that the prime, and indeed only, purpose for the existence of animals was to serve humans. The world and everything in it, according to this way of thinking, was created for humans to use as they deemed fit. Some commentators understood the process of utilizing the natural world for human benefit to be inherently violent. As the Italian essayist Giovanni Bonardo put it in the sixteenth century, "We live by force, as we eat by force the food which the earth gives us as a result of sweating and ploughing. We dress as a result of the force we use in stripping the animals of their wool and skins, almost stealing from them their own clothing . . . nor can we live except by the death of other things" (cited in Camporesi 1989: 30). Others preferred to represent the Earth's creatures as willing collaborators in their domination and consumption by humans. Thus an early seventeenth-century poem by Thomas Carew depicts animals as complicit in their slaughter by the lordly master of a country estate:

> The pheasant, partridge and the lark
> Flew to thy house, as to the Ark.
> The willing ox, of himself came
> Home to the slaughter, with the lamb;
> And every beast did thither bring
> Himself, to be an offering.
> The scaly herd more pleasure took,
> Bathed in thy dish than in the brook. (1899: 36–38)

By offering their lives to humans, the poem declares that animals are fulfilling their proper role in the world and thus "coming home" to their true destinies. This way of representing the matter had the advantage of absolving humans of any guilt they might feel over their appropriation of animals' lives and bodies for their own ends. It can be seen in a more popular form in stories of the mythical land of Cockaigne in which deer let themselves be caught by humans and precooked birds fly into hungry mouths (although in this case the emphasis would seem to be more on the ease of life for humans than on the happy complicity of animals in their consumption). Perhaps playing into this myth, it was popular prior to the eighteenth century to display a cooked animal looking as it did in life: leaving the head on, redressing it in its skin, and arranging the body in a lifelike position (Scully 2005: 106) In this way the illusion was fostered that animals, like fruit, came prêt à manger.

The reality behind the myth was that many animals raised for food lived in miserable conditions and died slow, painful deaths. A good number of methods for supposedly rendering animal flesh more palatable were based on beating or bleeding the living animal. An example of this was the practice of bull-baiting, in which a tethered bull was attacked by trained bull dogs. The notion was that this practice, a popular public entertainment as well as a perceived culinary requirement, would tenderize the otherwise tough flesh of the bull. (Nineteenth-century opponents of such practices worked hard to convince traditionalists that "beasts killed at one blow are tenderest" [K. Thomas 1983: 189]). Seventeenth-century physician Thomas Muffet wrote of harshly treated domestic animals that "they feed in pain, lie in pain and sleep in pain" (K. Thomas 1983:94). And die in pain, one could add.

Such callous treatment of animals suggests a considerable degree of detachment from them. Yet, as noted above, people lived in close intimacy with their animals. Such intimacy, together with the relatively small numbers of domestic animals, meant that cows and pigs and sheep were often known as individuals, with their own physical and character traits, and perhaps given personal names as well. As Keith Thomas writes: "Shepherds knew the faces of their sheep as well as those of their neighbours" (95). When slaughter time came, farmers knew just whom they were killing.

The slaughter of animals was not considered to be completely without pathos. Shakespeare (who reputedly worked as a butcher's boy in his youth), poignantly described the scene of a calf being taken away to be slaughtered:

> And as the butcher takes away the calf,
> And binds the wretch and beats it when it strays.
> Beating it to the bloody slaughter house . . .
> And as his dam runs lowing up and down,
> Looking the way her harmless young one went,
> And can do naught but wail her darling's loss. (Henry VI.iii)

Few, however, were not prepared to accept the situation, painful though it might be. The prevention of animal pain, it was believed, could not take precedence over the promotion of human pleasure. If calves provided humans with a tasty, filling meal then there was no better end to which they could be put.

The strong tendency to relate to animals first as potential food is evident in European accounts of the animals of the New World. Rarely is an animal, whether an iguana or a tapir, mentioned without a remark on its edibility and flavor (Asua and French 2005: 8). Indeed many of the New World animals brought back to Europe by ship arrived only as skins because the sailors had eaten them along the way (George 1985: 184). It was a hungry age.

Hungry sailors apart, not all potentially edible animals were considered good for the pot. In general, land animals that were either too dissimilar or too similar to humans fell into this category. Few wished to dine on such "alien" species as ants or snakes, while eating monkeys and apes seemed to smack of cannibalism: "There is something extremely disgusting," the naturalist William Bingley would write of the consumption of monkeys, "in the idea of eating what appears, when skinned and dressed, so like a child" (cited by K. Thomas 1983: 54). Carnivorous animals, whose bloody diet seemed to render them unpalatable, also rarely appeared on the dinner table. There was, as well, a widespread taboo against eating horses and donkeys. Their consumption was tainted by a vague association with heathenism; there may also have been a disinclination to encounter the animal on whose back one rode served up at the table.

On the other side of the issue of diet, humans might provide a meal for animals. The fear of being eaten by ravening wolves loomed particularly large in the popular imagination through the ages. So awful, indeed, was the thought of becoming a mere meal for a hungry carnivore that being consumed by wild beasts figured prominently among the torments of Hell. On a more prosaic level, a variety of insects avidly fed on the blood of lords and laborers alike. This was so commonplace as to be virtually unavoidable: people of all ranks lived a bitten existence.

Within the body itself, worms might consume the very food that humans intended for their own nourishment. After death the whole human body became available for animal nourishment. As George Gascoigne noted in the sixteenth century: "The hungry fleas which frisk so fresh, to worms I can compare / Which greedily shall gnaw my flesh and leave the bones full bare" (1870: 59). While highly disturbing, it was considered salutary for one's spiritual health to be confronted with such graphic, tangible reminders of human mortality.

However necessary it was considered, it may have been partly the intimation of human mortality that led to the slaughter of animals being regarded by many with repugnance. Butchers were socially tainted by their trade and it was commonly assumed that the "repeated strokes of violence" they carried out in the course of their work imprinted their minds with cruel tendencies (see Tryon 1691). In Thomas More's *Utopia,* butchery is considered such a base occupation that it is relegated to slaves (2008: 58).

Distaste for the butchery of animals increased in the eighteenth and nineteenth centuries without, however, the taste for meat declining (K. Thomas 1983: 294–95). This created a contradictory situation in which people who would shudder to slit a lamb's throat nonetheless contentedly consumed its flesh. A number of contemporary writers pointedly remarked that the mouths of flesh-eaters must be at least as tainted with blood as the hands of the butchers they despised (see Plumptre 1816: 23; K. Thomas 1983: 299). Diners, no doubt, did not see it quite this way, for by the time the lifeless flesh was served up for dinner it had undergone a culinary and ritual transformation into food.

Yet the touch of death still lurked within the food bowl, as one seventeenth-century Protestant theologian made clear: "Let us put our hand into the dish, and what doe we take, but the foode of a dead thing, which is either the flesh of beasts, or of birds, or of fishes." Not only in the grave then, but even on the dinner table did one find evidence of human mortality: "We taste [death] daily . . . we feele it betwixt our teeth." (cited in Fudge 2004: 131). Meat here has gone from being a pleasure to being a horror. Yet it still has a crucial function for it provides humans with a sobering daily contact with death—shoving it, as it were, down their throats.

ANIMAL COMPANIONS

Not everyone was unsympathetic to animals in premodernity. Some, like the prioress in *The Canterbury Tales,* who "would weep if she saw a mouse caught in a trap," had a strong sense of empathy for the animals who lived in their midst. Many others had affectionate relationships with at least some animals—at times, no doubt, even with animals who might otherwise be harshly treated. In her history of hunting Emma Griffin writes that prior to the twentieth century, "people's lives and homes were shared with animals, and there was little room for sensitivity and compassion in this world, and ample scope for cruelty and ill use" (Griffin 2007: 149). By substituting "people" for "animals," however, one sees that this statement is one-sided. While closeness to other beings, whether human or animal, can provide "ample scope for cruelty," it can also enable the expression of tender intimacy and compassion. Many instances of the latter within human-animal relationships can be found throughout Western history.

Although a range of animals, from birds to rabbits to donkeys, might serve as objects of human affection, dogs were a particular favorite. The fifteenth-century *Morte D'Arthur* provides a number of examples of the attachment felt by the no-bility for their hunting hounds. When Sir Dinas's lady leaves him and takes two of his favorite hounds with her, he feels the loss of the dogs more than that of the lady. Sir Gawain, in turn, is ready to fight to the death with a knight who has slain two of his greyhounds. "Thou shalt die," said Sir Gawain, "for the slaying of my hounds" (Malory 1998: 55).

A choice, well-trained hound added considerably to the prestige of his owner, as well as to the owner's success in hunting. An indication of how highly such dogs were valued can be found in a Burgundian law that decreed that whoever stole a hunting dog be punished by having to kiss the dog's posterior (J. Salisbury 1994: 39). The thief was thus obliged to ritually humiliate himself in what was deemed to be a doglike fashion. Hunting dogs' high status brought them privileges. The dogs were given names, were cared for by their own "servants" (hunt attendants), and might even be taken to a shrine to be healed when ill (Yamamoto 2000: 117).

Even the all-important fellowship of the table was often shared by hunting and household dogs. A number of contemporary paintings, including depictions of the Last Supper, commemorate the presence of dogs at (or under) the table. A banquet scene from the *Book of Hours* of the Duke of Berry (a renowned dog-fancier) shows two small dogs actually on the table, licking at the dishes. However much the writers of etiquette manuals may have disapproved of feeding dogs from the table, there was a biblical precedent for it: in the Gospel of Matthew a Gentile woman is able to enlist Jesus's aid by reminding him that "even the dogs eat the crumbs that fall from their masters' table" (Matt. 15:22).

In 1599 Ben Jonson satirized the medieval passion for hounds in his play "Every Man Out of His Humour."The main character in this play is a knight who, like the knights in Malory's *Morte D'Arthur,* is passionately fond of his greyhound. When the dog dies, a buffoon responds to the knight's grief by suggesting that he have the dead dog flayed and purchase another dog to place inside the skin (T. Grant 2007: 98–105).This coarse jest indicates that the knight's affection is misguided, for all dogs are alike under the skin. The knight's sorrow, however, testifies to the unique significance of one particular dog and one particular human-animal relationship.

While most domestic dogs, even prized hunting hounds, were essentially working animals, some were kept solely as pets. Chaucer's prioress was among those who engaged in this practice.

> Of small hounds had she, that she fed
> With roasted flesh, and milk, and wastel-bread [white bread],
> But sore wept she if one of them were dead,
> Or if men smote it. (Prologue)

Judging from the repeated (and apparently futile) injunctions prohibiting nuns and monks from owning pets, the prioress was not alone among those of her profession in enjoying the company of a friendly animal. Indeed, William of Wykeham felt obligated in 1387 to warn nuns to "presume henceforth to bring to church no birds, hounds, rabbits or other frivolous things that promote indiscipline" (cited in Davis and Demello 2003: 63).

Part of the appeal of pet dogs lay in the physical warmth they provided. Having a dog in one's lap was a good way to keep warm on a cold day. Soft, strokable hair added to the pleasure of the tactile encounter. Thus the medieval tale of *Tristan and Isolde* describes a little dog given as a gift as having hair softer than silk (Yamamoto 2000: 121).The very word "pet" reminds us that one of the key functions of the pet was to be "petted."The sixteenth-century treatise "Of Englische Dogges" notes that the spaniel is "otherwise called the comforter": its presence on the lap is said to be soothing while its "moderate heat" is attributed the power of alleviating stomach and chest ailments (Caius 1576: 22). Although not strictly "working" animals, therefore, lap dogs did have an important functional role as "living heaters" (Dickenson 2007: 190).

From the late Middle Ages on, lap dogs were especially associated with women, who were said to delight in such sensuous playmates. "Englische Dogges" disapprovingly calls such dogs "play fellows for mincing mistrisses to beare in their bosoms, . . . to lay in their lappes, and lick their lippes as they ryde in their waggons" (Caius 1576: 21). Evidently, according to the critics at least, dogs might overstep the bounds in their role as comforters.

While suitably lap-sized and pleasantly warm and soft, cats were generally regarded more as useful exterminators of household mice than as pets. However, throughout the centuries there were those who had a soft spot for them. A number of apparent cat-lovers are reported among monastics—perhaps because cats, as pest exterminators, were permissible cohabitants of a monastic cell (see "Pangur Ban" 1987: 22–23). It was said of Gregory the Great in the sixth century that "he possessed nothing in the world except a cat, which he carried in his bosom, frequently caressing it, as his sole companion" (Dudden 1905: 250). The sixteenth-century saint Philip Neri was so fond of his cat that, when he himself was no longer able to personally care for her, he would send one of his disciples to feed her and report on how she was doing.

Indeed, in the lives of the saints it is not uncommon to hear of companion animals of various sorts—Saint Jerome and the lion, Saint Roch and the dog, Saint Giles and the deer. An association with a companion animal, recounted in stories and depicted in paintings, likely added to the popular appeal of a saint. A saint removing a thorn from a lion's paw, receiving food from a friendly dog, or sheltering a deer, might well seem a more interesting (and full-bodied) figure than one whose fame for sanctity lay solely in ascetic feats and holy discourse. That there existed a widespread interest in animal stories is attested to by the popularity of fables and folk tales concerning animals in the Middle Ages and long afterwards.

Many of the animals associated with saints were not pets in any ordinary sense, but rather allies. Saint Jerome plucks a thorn out of a lion's paw and the lion repays him with labor (an account reminiscent of the ancient tale of Androcles and the lion). Saint Giles is suckled by a deer and later saves the deer from being killed by hunters. Saint Roch befriends a dog and the dog (described as a hunting hound accustomed to helping himself from the table) brings him loaves of bread. The saint who would become best known for his friendly interactions with animals was Francis of Assisi. Accounts tell of Saint Francis cuddling a hare, preaching to birds, sealing a pact with a wolf (with a good medieval hand-clasp), and generally referring to animals as his brothers and sisters.

Insofar as any of the stories of animal-loving saints were true, however, there might be a significant difference between the personal feelings of saints about their animal companions and the ways in which such relationships were interpreted by others. Some saints (although they could hardly help being influenced by the prevalent ideologies about the moral status of animals) would seem to have had a genuine concern for animal welfare. Among these are the vegetarian Saint Richard of Chichester who decried the slaughter of animals for food, and Saint Philip Neri who once rebuked a member of his congregation for treading on a lizard, saying: "Cruel fellow, what has that poor little animal done to you?" (Bacci 1902: 242).

(It would have been no use, one feels, for the guilty party to argue in the fashion of the bestiaries that the lizard was a palpable emblem of sin.)

Many hearers of such stories, however, would not have interpreted them as promoting compassion for animals. Indeed it would not have seemed appropriate to conventional minds for a man of God to have busied himself with the well-being of animals. A vivid example of how little impact apparent messages of saintly concern for birds and beasts might have on underlying attitudes toward animals can be found in the fourteenth-century collection of anecdotes concerning Francis of Assisi titled *The Little Flowers of Saint Francis.* In one tale a Franciscan monk, Juniper, cuts the leg off a live pig to satisfy a sick man's desire to eat a pig's trotter. Saint Francis rebukes the monk—not for mistreating "brother pig"—but for neglecting to ask permission of the pig's owner before cutting off a leg. Seeking out the angry owner, Juniper "embraced him and kissed him, and told him how it had been done wholly for charity's sake." Such tactile and verbal effusion moved the man to kill and cook the pig and present it to the gathered monks. A pleased Saint Francis is then reported as quipping that he wished he had a whole forest of such Junipers (*Little Flowers* 1907: 133). It may be that pigs were considered such marginal creatures that they merited no consideration whatsoever, yet this story throws into doubt whether any of the animals mentioned in the accounts of Saint Francis's life were considered worthy of humane treatment.

If the apparently tender behavior of many saints toward animals was not taken to signify an actual concern for real feeling beings, what was it understood to signify? The general opinion among theologians was that kindness to animals, while directed toward unworthy objects, had the merit of fostering kindness to humans. The real value of saintly kindness to animals, therefore, might be found in the way it could serve as a model for greater kindliness among humans.

There was, however, more to it. From a theological perspective, the cooperative relationships saints had with animals indicated that the saints had, in a sense, returned to the Garden of Eden. As all attentive readers of Scripture knew, God initially decreed that humans be vegetarian and live in a state of harmony with animals. Only after Adam and Eve's expulsion from the Garden was this primordial peace disrupted (and only after the biblical flood was the practice of meat eating explicitly conceded to a corrupt humanity).

Friendship between a saint and an animal, therefore, was a potent sign of prelapsarian purity. Given this symbolic context, it is difficult to assert that the numerous accounts describing ostensibly caring relationships between saints and animals manifest that the saints deemed animals "worthy of their healing and protective powers" (Hobgood-Oster 2008: 75). The stories may rather have been intended to demonstrate the spiritual purity and supernatural power of God's servants, who are able to mediate among human, divine, and animal worlds.

Such a conventional interpretation, however, would not have suited everyone. Some people doubtless took the stories of saints' friendship with animals at face value and understood them to promote extending the bounds of Christian charity to include at least some animals some of the time. Others could use the examples of the saints to justify what might otherwise seem an inappropriate fondness for the "brute creation." Many an aspiring holy man or woman must have attempted to imitate Francis of Assisi or other revered saints by extending a benevolent hand to a fellow creature.

However, even Franciscans, with the model of their saintly founder as a justification, might incur criticism for wasting their time on mere beasts. Salimbene di Adam, a Franciscan himself, criticized members of his order in the thirteenth century who, although "of excellent learning and great sanctity" had a "foul blemish" of one kind or another. One such foul blemish was that "they love to play with a cat or whelp or with some small fowl" (Armstrong 1973: 103). Evidently it was hard for some to imagine that one could embrace God and caress an animal at the same time.

While the practice of keeping animals as companions extended back to antiquity, it grew in popularity from the seventeenth century on. Among the different features often said to make a pet of an animal—living indoors, having a name, not being used for food or work—one not usually mentioned, but which seems virtually essential (except in the case of fish), is receiving a caring touch. Whether a dog, a rabbit, or a bird, an animal was not really a pet until a willing and trusting skin-to-skin contact had taken place between human and animal. This trusting touch was a key feature of the human-pet relationship.

Some scholars have linked the rise in pet-keeping with the growth of an urban middle class that was supposedly out of contact with rural life and so tended to romanticize animals (K. Thomas 1983). However it has been pointed out that the density of animals (few of which were pets) was, in fact, much greater in cities than in the countryside (Kete 2007: 6). Daily encounters with horses pulling urban vehicles, pigs rooting through urban garbage, cattle being driven to urban slaughterhouses, dogs fighting on urban streets, and mice scampering through urban houses can hardly have encouraged city dwellers to develop a romantic view of animals. A number of more plausible factors suggest themselves. One is that more families during this period could afford the luxury of maintaining an animal that was not needed for work or for food. Another is that the greater social mobility of the time, which allowed many people to move up a class, may have suggested that animals' station in life need not be fixed either. A third possible factor is that, as society became more individualistic, people grew more disposed to relate to animals as individuals, rather than simply as exemplars of their kind. It is furthermore likely that the greater opportunities for social intercourse available in cities stimulated people to think in new ways about many things, including animals, and enabled these new notions to be quickly and widely disseminated.

Learning to relate to animals as individuals through pet-keeping led some people to look on whole species with greater benevolence. For example, dog owners went from caring about their dog to caring about dogs in general through the realization that every dog could be an individual with sympathetic personal traits. We can observe this process happening in the case of the eighteenth-century poet William Cowper, who made pets of three young hares. One of these, named Puss, "would leap into my lap, raise himself upon his hinder feet and bite the hair from my temples. He would suffer me to take him up, and to carry him about in my arms, and has more than once fallen fast asleep upon my knee." How could Cowper fail to feel gratified by such signal tokens of affection? His experience with the three hares led him to write a letter to the *Gentlemen's Magazine* condemning the hunting of hares. "You will not wonder, Sir, that my intimate acquaintance with these specimens of the kind has taught me to hold the sportsman's amusements in abhorence; he little knows what amiable creatures he persecutes" (cited by Davis and Demello 2003: 66). It is hard to shoot a being who has lain asleep cuddled in one's lap.

While affection for animals has been typed as a phenomenon peculiar to the middle and upper classes and virtually limited to privileged pets, it would be mistaken to think that ordinary working animals never inspired affection in their ordinary, working-class owners. As anthropological research has shown time and again, what is eminently utilitarian may still have great sentimental and symbolic value. We see a case of this in an eighteenth-century account of a reunion between a poor man and his stolen donkey. The man asserted that he would not part with his beloved donkey again for "a King's Ransome." "Poor Duke!" the man exclaimed, "Thou hast had many an empty Meal since I saw thee, and so has thy Master too for want of thee." After this there "followed a scene of tenderness between the man and the ass, in which it is difficult to say, whether the beast or its master gave tokens of the higher affection" (cited in Battestin and Battestin 1993: 553; see similarly Bingley 1805: 117). Although the donkey was evidently essential to the man's livelihood, the reverse was also the case and this interdependence heightened, rather than reduced, the sense of fellowship between the two. Affection and necessity were combined. Such sentiments cannot have been very unusual, considering that an animal was many a worker's closest companion during long days of toil.

BEASTS, WILD MEN, AND SLAVES

Given the very different roles of animals and humans in the Christian world order it was important to establish clear distinctions between the two groups. Many of the distinctions employed dealt with perceived physical differences between animals and humans. One of the most apparent differences was that humans had hands, while land animals had paws or hooves or some variation thereof. (Water dwellers were usually deemed too alien to be compared to humans). The hand, with its special abilities to grasp and manipulate, was seen as a clear indication of human superiority (Lynch 1988 39–40). It was through their hands that humans were able to transform the world around them, whereas "handless" animals, it was believed, must live with the world more or less as they found it. The importance of maintaining this special distinction between humans and animals can be seen in the fact that even monkeys' very handlike appendages were usually termed "paws."

Aside from not having hands, animals were characterized as hairy beings who walked on all fours and had their heads oriented toward the ground. Humans, by contrast were (relatively) hairless, walked upright, and turned their faces to the sky. The physiological reason for these differences was held to lie in the different elementary natures of animals and humans. Animals were said to have an affinity with the cold, heavy element of earth, which made them colder in nature—and hence hairier—and also drew their bodies toward the ground. Humans' presumed superior spirituality, by contrast, gave them a certain affinity with the higher and lighter elements of air and fire, an affinity that drew human bodies upwards and reduced their amount of body hair.

Closeness to the ground was strongly indicative of inferiority in Western culture. Slithering animals, such as snakes and worms, were deemed to be particularly lowly from a moral perspective due to their full bodily contact with the Earth. Birds, on the other hand, were something of a conundrum, for their ability to fly associated them with the air and the spiritual beings thought to inhabit that element. Fundamentally, however, birds were still base animals and merited no special consideration from humans.

The association of the ground with animality made people uncomfortable with the crawling stage of infancy. Premodern parents discouraged their children from crawling and employed various devices to enable them to stand upright and walk as soon as possible (C. Heywood 2001: 89). A crawling baby seemed too much like an animal. In numerous ways, human bodies were trained in premodernity to be *human* bodies.

Just as walking upright was deemed vastly superior to crawling or walking on all fours, riding on horseback was considered greatly superior to walking. Indeed, it is hard to overestimate the symbolic importance of riding in premodernity. Traveling on the back of a horse enabled one to remove oneself completely from the base earth. At the same time it showed one's dominance of the animal kingdom—and, by extension, of those lowly humans who were obliged to use their own legs for locomotion. Walking on foot did have the one merit of being associated with humility and penitence, and thus was considered a suitable mode of travel for pilgrims and monks. (Hence it was said of Francis of Assisi that he rode a horse only "in the greatest and strictest necessity" [Armstrong 1973: 123].) In secular society, however, the physical elevation that one acquired on horseback translated into social elevation, while the mastery one displayed by obliging another being to do one's walking for one translated into social mastery. The most salient characteristic of the medieval knight was his position on the back of a warhorse.

Clothing provided another means of distinguishing between humans and animals: the former used it and the latter didn't. However, as most human clothing was made from animal skin or hair, wearing clothing also involved a close physical contact with animals. Furthermore, by putting on animal skins humans symbolically took on something of their identity. In pre-Christian Europe this did not necessarily have a negative connotation. Norse warriors believed that wearing wolf skins and bear skins in battle would give them the fierceness and courage of wolves and bears. Though there were times within Christian culture when an animal skin might be used to promote an association with a certain animal—as when Jews were obliged to swear oaths standing barefoot on a sow's skin (Cohen 1993: 92)—generally such identifications with animals through their skins were discouraged. On a practical level, techniques of processing helped to remove some of the animal from animal skins before they were transformed into human clothing.

Food practices marked another important area for differentiating between humans and animals. The use of fire to cook food created an essential mark of distinction, as did other culinary practices. To further distinguish human modes of eating from animal modes of eating, the Church enjoined its members to eat in an upright position (Salisbury 1994: 63). The consumption of meat by humans had particular significance. On the one hand, eating meat signified human dominion over animals. On the other hand, eating meat associated humans with savage beasts of prey, and brought the very flesh and blood of animals into human bodies. While ritual periods of fasting from meat helped to humanize humans by showing their ability to abstain from bloody feasts, this dilemma was never really resolved.

Meat eating also formed an important mark of distinction between the wealthier classes, who could afford to eat meat on a regular basis, and the peasants, who could not. Thus the French tale "Le Despit au Villein" complains about socially presumptuous meat-eating serfs: "Should they eat meat? Rather should they chew grass on the heath with the horned cattle and go naked on all fours" (Tuchman 1978: 175). Attitudes such as this help explain why, in an infamous act during the fourteenth-century Jacquerie rebellion in France, peasants roasted a knight on a spit (177). Now it was the turn of the high and mighty nobility, this extraordinary act implied, to be transformed into lowly, despised animals..

That both humans and animals were motivated to eat by hunger and that what was food for one could be food for the other produced an uncomfortable area of overlap between the two groups. Rules forbidding eating food that had already been partially eaten by an animal were intended to keep human and animal meals separate. (Presumably eating food that had merely been carried in an animal's mouth was acceptable, for a number of saints were said to have been fed by animals.) One concern was that sharing in the fellowship of eating would bind humans and animals too closely together. A greater concern was that, by eating animals' "leftovers," humans might seem to be subordinate to animals. Apparently the notion of being subservient to a dog—the archetypal animal servant of humans—was particularly disturbing, for a whole year of penance was the prescribed penalty for eating food that had first been tasted by a dog (Salisbury 1994: 67–68). How seriously ordinary people took these rules is another matter. Judging by the common presence of dogs and cats around or under or even on the table at meals it must often have been a question as to who got to the food first.

One of the most frightening aspects of periods of famine was that they blurred all the carefully instituted distinctions between what and how humans and animals ate. As a thirteenth-century writer noted, famine "turned everything into food and compelled human teeth to chew things that were not even customarily eaten by animals" (cited by Sorrell 1988: 53). During the Great Famine of the fourteenth century it was said that people "gnawed, just like dogs, the raw dead bodies of cattle" and "grazed like cows on the growing grasses of the fields" (W. Jordan 1996: 115). Lurking under the "civilized" human exterior, such famine experiences suggested, was a simple, hungry beast.

There was one food which humans did their best to reserve for their species alone and one meal to which animals were definitely not invited. The Duke of Berry might have dogs sharing the food at his table but no animals at all were allowed a share of the bread and wine served at the Lord's Supper. Much ink was expended by theologians on the subject of the consequences of an animal eating Christ's flesh in its eucharistic form. How could the body of Christ be integrated into the body of a animal? While many rules tried to ensure that animals did not partake of the Eucharist, the awareness existed that they sometimes did. (Church mice, apparently, were particularly likely to surreptitiously partake of the Holy Feast.) The omnipresence of animals meant there was no practical way of ensuring their complete separation from humans, even during those rites that were the most definitive of humans' special status in the world.

On a more worldly level, the greatest threat to maintaining humans and animals separate and unequal involved human-animal matings. While an accepted part of classical mythology, from a Christian perspective such an intimate union between humans and animals was almost too abhorrent to be contemplated. Reported instances of bestiality were thus often treated with great severity, especially in the later Middle Ages when concern about the blurring of the boundaries between humans and animals increased.

Not only did the coupling of a human with an animal confuse the distinctions between man and beast, it was also believed to enable the birth of hybrid offspring. The existence of such semi-human beings was widely reported in the Middle Ages and afterwards, if not universally credited. Also widely reported were accounts of races of apemen and dog-headed humans (of whom Saint Christopher was sometimes said to be one) inhabiting exotic lands. Closer to home were occasional stories of werewolves or of wild men—men who lived an animalistic existence in the forests.

Supposed human-animal hybrids were not just the stuff of legend, they were also a popular fairground attraction from the Middle Ages to the nineteenth century. A survey of the shows on offer in eighteenth-century London offers ample evidence of this. "When a man is tired of London," Samuel Johnson once declared, "he is tired of life; for there is in London all that life can afford" (Boswell 1873: 342). It certainly would appear that almost every life form the popular imagination could envisage was on display in London in Johnson's day. One of the most popular sights was a "learned pig" who "would spell any word or Number from the Letters and Figures that were placed before him" (Bondeson 1999: 25). At various times one could also have seen a card-playing horse, "Two Wood Monsters from the East Indies," and a "Wild Hairy Man" from Bengal. Of this last Joseph Addison remarked, "He is by birth a Monkey; but swings upon a Rope, takes a pipe of Tobacco, and drinks a glass of Ale, like any reasonable Creature" (cited in Ashton 1882: 272). (From the number of times reputed animal-men are described as being able to drink a glass of ale, this would appear to have been one of the distinguishing marks of human status in eighteenth-century England.) Addison's remark that the Wild Hairy Man was "by birth a monkey" even seems to offer the startling possibility of an animal-human metamorphosis.

More alarming perhaps than the above spectacles were the "Child with a Bear growing on its back alive," and the Wild Man from Spain, who due to his "Estrangement from human Conversation," had a monkey for a companion and "licked his nose with his tongue like a cow." Those looking for something more exciting were invited to see a "Bull to be turned loose with Fire Works all over him; also a Mad Ass to be baited; with a variety of Bull Baiting and Bear Baiting, and a Dog to be drawn up with Fireworks" ("Sight-seeing" 1881: 421–25). One can scarcely be surprised if, confronted with this panoply of corporeal diversions, many people were confused about the distinction between humans and animals and about the just usage of each: Could a learned pig avoid the slaughterhouse? Could a wild man who had been born a monkey attend church? Could a bear growing on a child's back be baited?

The imprecision about where animality ended and humanity began found expression in a number of social practices. For example, apart from the practice of slaughtering animals for food and body parts, much of the treatment meted out to domestic animals could also be meted out to humans in subordinate positions. Moreover, both animals and humans might be regarded as property. The Puritan Samuel Gott's proclamation that animals "have no right or propriety in anything, no, not in themselves" (K. Thomas 1983: 21) might have applied almost equally well to countless humans. Slavery was practiced throughout most of Europe in greater or lesser degree from antiquity to modernity. Both human slaves and domestic animals were considered chattel and in stock inventories it was not uncommon to find human and animal stock mixed together.

As there was little notion of any general human rights, the enslavement of humans was not usually deemed any more unjust or amoral than the enslavement of animals. (Church institutions, in fact, were often major slave owners.) Aristotle himself had declared that, just as animals were the natural slaves of humans, inferior humans were the natural slaves of superior ones. Thomas Aquinas and his followers accepted Aristotle's notion of the human slave as fitted by nature to be a "living tool" and explained it from a Christian perspective as one of the consequences of the original fall from grace (Freedman 1999: 63).

While not technically slavery, medieval serfdom often came to much the same thing in actual practice. In the most complete state of serfdom, that of the so-called "body man," the serf's very body was said to belong to his lord. Serfs were hence often treated as little more—and sometimes as a little less—than laboring animals (Coulton 1989: 19; Freedman 1999: 140–42). No doubt many knights would have considered a good warhorse of more value than a serf. In any case, troublesome peasants were held to require the same handling as troublesome horses: "to bridle them, and to make them feel the spur too, when they begin to play their tricks and kick" (cited in K. Thomas 1983: 45).

The encounter of Europeans with the inhabitants of the Americas in the sixteenth century raised its own questions about the boundaries between humans and animals. Were Indians part of humankind—true children of Adam and Eve—or did they constitute another species? While certain missionaries and theologians, most notably Bartolomé de Las Casas, argued strongly for the former position, many Europeans (particularly those who wished to use Indians as beasts of burden) supported the latter viewpoint. A papal proclamation asserted that Indians were "truly human" and laws were passed to protect them from brutal treatment, but these measures by no means ended the controversy over the status of Native Americans.

It was only in the early nineteenth century that notions of human-animal crosses, werewolves, and apemen were generally discounted and a firm line drawn between humans and animals on scientific as well as religious grounds. "How slender so ever it may sometimes appear," confidently declared the naturalist William Bingley, "the barrier which separates men from brutes is fixed and immutable" (cited in K. Thomas 1983: 35). The hand and the paw could never join. Only humans were human and only animals were bestial.

It would not be long, however, before evolutionary theory would forge a new bond between the two groups by claiming that, far from being separate creations, humans had evolved from animals. The human hand, it seemed, had once been a paw, human skin had once been animal skin, and human behavior was merely an offshoot of animal behavior. This new bond between humans and animals made it harder to assert any absolute distinction between the two groups or produce any categorical justification for the domination of the latter by the former. In 1837 a young Charles Darwin wrote that animals are "our fellow brethren in pain, disease, death, suffering, and famine—our slaves in the most laborious works, our companions in our amusements—they may partake of our origin in one common ancestor—we may all be melted together" (1958: 179).

The perceived connection between the enslavement of humans and the enslavement of animals led a number of individuals involved in the anti-slavery movements of the eighteenth and nineteenth centuries to also concern themselves with the welfare of animals. William Wilberforce, for example, both campaigned for the abolition of the slave trade in the British Empire and helped to found the Royal Society for the Prevention of Cruelty to Animals. However, when institutions of human bondage were attacked by social egalitarians it was almost always at least partly on the grounds that humans should not be treated as animals (Freedman 1999: 55; see also K. Thomas 1983: 48). This argument, employed through the centuries and most particularly in the anti-slavery movement of the 1800s, took for granted that animals *should* be treated like beasts, that is, forcibly dominated and even deprived of their lives. And so, while the human workforce had its bonds loosened by the modern politics of egalitarianism, the animal workforce remained as enslaved as ever.

ANIMAL SOULS

The most significant difference between humans and animals was not held to be based on the possession of hands or paws, fur or hair, nor on any physical or social distinction. It was based on the possession of the faculty of reason. Humans were said to be rational, animals were said to be irrational. This was the ultimate dividing line between the two groups. Thus, when the question arose of whether the inhabitants of the Americas were human or not, the basic issue to be resolved (and eventually settled in their favor) was whether they were rational beings. To be deemed irrational meant that one's existence was held to be of use only insofar as it might serve one's rational superiors. As the possession of an immortal soul was tied to rationality, it also meant that a being deemed to be irrational was excluded from any of the benefits of religion and any chance of an afterlife according to Christian theology.

Reason was customarily conceptualized as a kind of internalized speech. Consequently, the most important criteria for judging whether a being was rational was usually taken to be the use of spoken language. (It might seem that the use of language by Native Americans would have immediately indicated their rationality, but to European ears native speech often seemed mere gibberish.) Animals' lack of speech hence became the key outward sign of their presumed inward irrationality (Osborne 2007: 64).

For some, the fact that animals could not speak out indicated that humans should be particularly protective toward them (or, at least, toward some of them). The fourteenth-century *Goodman of Paris,* for example, bade housewives to "diligently take thought for your chamber animals . . . for they cannot speak, and therefore must you speak and think for them" (2006: 139). Generally, however, the opposite conclusion was reached: little thought need be given to those who could not speak or think for themselves. Furthermore, since animals could not tell of their ill treatment, there was little reason to fear retribution for any acts committed against them. When encountering animals being led to slaughter Saint Richard of Chichester was said to have exclaimed, "If you were reasoning beings and could speak how you would curse us!" (Linzey 1995: 136). In fact, no one had to worry about being cursed by an animal for, howsoever they were treated, animals never—in so many words—complained.

The more language-centered society became over the course of the Middle Ages, the more the linguistic model of reason and agency tended to dominate over notions of selfhood and social integration derived from nonverbal modes of communication, such as might be employed by animals. As described in previous chapters, body language (based on position, gesture, and touch) was key to the social life of the early Middle Ages. By the late Middle Ages, stimulated in part by the growth of universities and the spread of literacy, verbal, and particularly written, statements were displacing some of the older nonverbal customs.

Modes of communication potentially shared, at least in part, by humans and animals hence decreased in social value at the same time as there occurred a rise in the importance of a means of communication completely foreign to animals: writing. Indeed, up until the nineteenth century many texts were written or printed on the very skins of animals, transformed into parchment or vellum. (The forty-some copies of the Gutenberg Bible that were printed on vellum required skins from nearly six thousand calves [Salisbury 1994: 23].)

Imprinting the codes of human authority on animal skins was a potent symbol of the forcible human domination of animals. It might also, by analogy, be taken as a potent symbol of the upper-class domination of the lower, largely illiterate, classes. In *Henry VI, Part 2,* Shakespeare has the leader of a peasant rebellion say, "Is not this a lamentable thing, that of the skin of an innocent lamb should be made parchment? that parchment, being scribbled o'er, should undo a man?" (ii). Evidently, a sequence of oppressive acts, of undoings, is outlined here, with writing serving as the alien and deplorable motive for their performance. Nonetheless, while writing and reading helped to alienate their practitioners from the lower orders and species, these practices would also contribute to a critical reevaluation of the status of both groups by encouraging habits of reflection and revision.

The first written work people turned to for guidance on the treatment of animals was Holy Scripture. Beyond granting humans dominion over them, however, the Bible was not entirely clear on the nature and status of animals. While generally animals seemed to be depicted as purely utilitarian, subservient beings with no cognitive capacities, a few passages suggested there might be something more to them. There were strong intimations, that God, who "satisf[ies] the desires of every living thing" (Psalm 145: 16), cared for animals and expected humans to do the same: "Six days do your work, but on the seventh day do not work, so that your ox and your donkey may rest" (Ex. 23: 12). Furthermore, readers wondered, might not the commandment to "love thy neighbor" extend to animal neighbors, whose lives were interwoven with human lives?

Potentially even more unsettling were passages that suggested animals were endowed with selfhood. In Genesis 9, for example, God speaks of making a covenant with "all living creatures of every kind" (see also Hosea 2: 18). If animals, however, have no rational capacities, what kind of covenant could be made with them?

Moreover, there was the startling story of Balaam's ass, ever popular with medieval audiences. This told of a donkey who rebuked her master for beating her when she stopped on the road three times upon seeing an angel in her path.

> When the donkey saw the angel of the Lord, she lay down under Balaam, and he was angry and beat her with his staff. Then the Lord opened the donkey's mouth, and she said to Balaam, "What have I done to you to make you beat me these three times?" Balaam answered the donkey, "You have made a fool of me! If I had a sword in my hand I would kill you right now." The donkey said to Balaam, "Am I not your own donkey, which you have always ridden to this day? Have I been in the habit of doing this to you?" "No," he said. Then the Lord opened Balaam's eyes, and he saw the angel

of the Lord standing in the road with his sword drawn. So he bowed low and fell face down. The angel of the Lord asked him, "Why have you beaten your donkey these three times? I have come here to oppose you because your path is a reckless one. The donkey saw me and turned away from me these three times. If she had not turned away, I would certainly have killed you by now, but I would have spared her. (Num. 22: 21–32)

This morality tale of sight and touch, of humans, animals, and angels, seemed to confuse all the distinctions between human beings and beasts. The soulless donkey, and not the soul-endowed man, is the one who is able to see the angel. The donkey is furthermore presented as the more rational being of the two. While the man wishes to kill the donkey for her insubordination, it turns out that it is the man instead who should be killed for his insubordination. Finally, the angel preserves the life of the errant man only for the sake of the faithful donkey.

Mainstream theologians dealt with such challenging passages in the only way they could without threatening the unique status of humans in Christian theology: they discounted their apparent meaning. Animals, they asserted, could not enter into covenants or contracts. Neither could they think or talk, and if an animal appeared to speak in the Bible it only showed what God could do, not what animals could do. Furthermore, while animals might be everywhere, they were not neighbors, for no amount of physical intimacy could make up for an absence of a meeting of minds. Thomas Aquinas was clear on the matter: "The word neighbour cannot be extended to irrational creatures, since they have no fellowship with man in the rational life" (cited by Linzey 1995: 14). Hence, there was no requirement to love animals as neighbours.

In fact, whatever Scripture implied, the standard theological view was that animals did not merit kind treatment of any sort, a view that must be taken into account when considering the rough handling animals often received in premodernity. Thomas Aquinas bluntly stated that "if any passage in Holy Scripture seems to forbid us to be cruel to brute animals . . . that is either . . . lest through being cruel to animals one becomes cruel to humans or because injury to an animal leads to the temporal hurt of man" (cited in K. Thomas 1983: 151). In other words, whatever the Bible seemed to say, the only good reasons for not being cruel to animals were that doing so might encourage cruelty among humans or result in humans being harmed. Animals could not matter in themselves. With a clarity of logic that would elude many later thinkers on this issue, Aquinas saw that if animals were good in themselves—and therefore worthy of kind treatment— then it would appear unjust of God to ultimately consign them to nothingness. If animals were only good insofar as they served earthly human needs, however, there would be no injustice in putting an end to their existence once humans had no more need of them in Heaven.

What then, was one to make of these beings with faces but no souls? If they were only, as one writer put it, devices for keeping meat fresh until needed, what was the point in their being much different from plants? One answer to this question was that animals, through their diverse traits, provided humans with living symbols of moral truths. Hibernating dormice might be said to signify sluggards, and blind moles, heretics. Sheep, due to their docility, could "represent the innocent and simple among Christians" for "the Lord Himself exhibited the mildness and patience of a sheep" (*Bestiary* 1993: 111, 78). Animals, according to this paradigm, were simply symbols of good and bad morality, created for the edification of humans and possessing no moral agency themselves.

While the irrationality of animals was a generally accepted doctrine in pre-modernity, it was not entirely unchallenged. In many cases personal experience led people to attribute rational or pseudo-rational traits to animals. The fifteenth-century author of *The Master of Game* wrote from his experience with hunting dogs that "An hounde is of greet vnderstondynge and of greet knowynge" (Yamamoto 2000: 117). Strictly speaking, one could attribute a certain amount of sagacity to animals and still remain true to an Aristotelian notion of animals lacking higher rational faculties. Still, allowing animals the possession of any degree of intellectual ability seemed to transform them from mere animated bodies to self-directed individuals.

One widespread and long lasting practice that seemed to attribute rational capacities to animals was the custom of trying and executing animals for criminal offenses. From a modern perspective there would be no sense in trying irrational creatures, for they could not understand the nature of their crimes nor the reason for their punishment. However, in premodern justice the interior disposition of the alleged criminal was of limited importance; what mattered most was the physical act itself. Therefore, if someone was murdered, whether by a human or a pig, what counted was proving that the murder had been committed, not delving into what the human or pig thought about it. Regardless of what the mind intended, the murderous body required punishment. Indeed, the law of "deodand" ("given to God") allowed retribution to be exacted in the case of "any beast animate or movable thing inanimate" that contributed to the death of a person, as when a person died by falling off a horse or by being hit by a falling object. The argument was that the horse or the object had "moved to" the death of the person and thus must be "given over to God"—which in practice meant being forfeited to the Crown. In the case of an animal, the customary practice was to kill the animal and require the owner to pay the value in money to the Crown.

Actual trials of animals, however, not only exacted retribution for violent deaths, they formally tried and executed animals according to the same methods used for human offenders. While rationality was not a necessary prerequisite for standing trial in premodernity, animal trials must still have suggested to many that the accused animals had acted with at least a glimmer of rational intent. Supporting this idea is the fact that the perceived rationality of the accused was sometimes taken into account in criminal trials. For example, by the fourteenth century it was generally held that children under age seven were not mentally competent to commit crimes. Curiously, this judgment did not affect the prosecution of animals whom, one might conclude, were therefore considered to be mentally competent—unless they were under age. In 1457 a sow was found guilty of murder but her piglet accomplices were deemed too young to stand trial (Evans 2006: 153–54). This decision may well have been made with the intent of minimizing the loss of valuable assets (the pigs). However, the implication certainly would have been that mature animals, like adult humans, knew what they were doing when they committed crimes.

Moreover, while theologians might assert that there was no fellowship between humans and animals, domestic animals might still be informally regarded as part of the household, and therefore partake of a certain common identity. (C. S. Lewis presented a modern version of this concept when he suggested that domestic animals might enter Heaven as part of the extended family group [1946: 127].) A member of the household could not simply be removed and executed without certain formalities being observed. Therefore, even a cow or a pig or a dog, when accused of a criminal offense, might seem to require a trial. In line with this thinking, the trial and execution would not simply be directed toward a single guilty individual but at the individual's whole social group, serving to warn, shame, and admonish everyone connected with the crime.

Even more fundamentally, trials and executions of animals sought to reassert the principle of human dominion over animals, a principle that animal assaults on humans appeared to challenge (see Bergman 2007:67). (Animals were never tried for offenses against other animals.) Cases of domestic animals killing humans would have been particularly unsettling, as domestic animals were expressly intended to serve humans. Animal trials and executions could hence have functioned as extraordinary shows of condemnation for acts considered particularly disturbing.

Furthermore, the human victim of an animal murderer might well be seen as having been violently incorporated into the animal world. In this case, the trial of an animal accused of killing a human would seek to reassert the human status of the victim by symbolically transforming the victim's killer into a human. This would help explain why in 1366 a sow convicted of killing a child was dressed in man's clothing for her execution (E. Evans 2006: 140): the clothing publicly signaled the sow's status as a usurper of (male) human authority while at the same time it declared the infant she mauled to be the human victim of a bad man, and not merely animal fodder. Similarly, the customary ban on eating the flesh of an animal executed for murder was likely not only because the flesh had been contaminated by the blood of the human victim, but also because the murderer had symbolically acquired human status and therefore could no longer be considered a food source.

Although domestic animals were tried by secular courts, wild animals accused of offenses against humans were tried by ecclesiastical courts. The logic here was that, while domestic animals were under human management, wild animals were the province of God, and therefore of the Church. In the case of wild animals, a whole group—a colony of rats or a swarm of insects—was usually indicted. Another difference with the trials of domestic animals was that the alleged crime usually concerned the destruction of human property or crops. While not so dramatic an assault on human authority as murder, the destruction of human property by animals could similarly be seen as a case of animals competing with humans for dominion. The problem was not usually brought before the court until the people concerned found the animal invasion overwhelming. Such trials customarily ended with the judge ordering the accused to leave the site of their predations or else be excommunicated.

Excommunication, or being deprived of the sacraments of the Church, may seem like a strange penalty to apply to "soulless" animals. However, beyond its specific purpose, excommunication was regarded as a generally powerful supernatural weapon. The death penalty, aside from being difficult to apply to large groups of animals, was not available to ecclesiastical courts, which were required to abstain from the shedding of blood. As with criminal trials of animals, one of the purposes of ecclesiastical animal trials would seem to have been to symbolically transform threatening animals into humans to reinforce the human status of their victims and to more powerfully and dramatically remove the offenders from the community.

An explanation commonly put forward for bad behavior or seemingly unnatural acts by unreasoning animals was that they were possessed by demons. The supposed spiritual vacancy within animals was thought to leave them prone to be inhabited by evil spirits. A biblical instance of this occurs in the Gospels where demons are described as entering the bodies of pigs (Mark 5: 11–12). Any animal, but particularly one deemed unusually harmful or intelligent, might hence be viewed as a devil in disguise. Indeed, as late as the eighteenth century there are accounts of suspiciously clever horses being brought before the Inquisition (Cook 2007: 228).

Presumably, animal bodies might also be possessed by angels, but this scenario was posited much less frequently. As subhuman beings, animals hardly seemed suitable vehicles for angelic spirits. In representations of angels and demons, wings are the only attribute that angels customarily took from animals, which helped associate them with the airy upper regions and distinguish them from earth-bound humans. Demons and devils, on the other hand, were often depicted with horns and claws and hairy bodies, all particularly bestial characteristics that gave them a symbolic feel of base otherness.

Despite the frequent association of animals with demons, folklore provided an abundance of accounts of nondemonic animals acting in a humanlike fashion, as did the lore of saints. Indeed, such stories not only presented animals as rational beings, they also often presented them as morally worthy beings. One example was the widespread story of Saint Florentius, who made friends with a bear. When the bear was killed by four jealous monks, the grieving Florentius cursed the evildoers whereupon they all perished miserably. While Florentius is said to have regretted his vindictive act, the story still seems to point to the life of one good bear being worth more than those of four bad men. In the fourteenth century a Dominican came across a case in which a good dog, unjustly killed by his master, was reverenced as a saint (Saint Guinefort) in France (Hobgood-Oster 2008: 103–4). While the Church tried to stamp out the practice, it continued for centuries in the French countryside.

Such cases indicate how far popular Christianity might deviate from official Christianity on the subject of the moral potential of animals. The notion of animal selfhood is often stated to have been a modern bourgeois idea imposed by an educated elite on the working classes. However, it may well be that the common people preserved a folk notion of animal spirituality long after it was suppressed in high culture.

One of the strongest medieval challenges to the conventional view of animals as mindless and soulless came from the Franciscans. While, as previously noted, it was possible to position Francis of Assisi's acts of inclusion toward animals within an orthodox theological framework, they also stimulated some quite unorthodox interpretations. One of these, developed within the Franciscan community, presented the saint as the recipient of a new revelation according to which the Gospel message of God's love was to be extended to all creatures. An example of this apparently occurred in one of Francis' sermons to birds. In Matthew 6: 26, Jesus says: "Look at the birds of the air: they neither sow nor reap nor gather into barns, and yet your heavenly Father feeds them. Are you not of more value than they?" Francis used the first part of this quotation in his sermon to the birds but he omitted the second part in which humans are presented as being worth more to God than birds. Instead he reputedly discussed the particular nobility God has granted birds by allotting them "a habitation in the purity of the air" (the air being a nobler element than the earth). Jesus's words were directed at humans and refer to birds primarily to make a point about humans. Francis's words, by contrast, appear to be addressed primarily to birds. (Armstrong 1973: 57). This is a radical moment in the history of Christianity.

While some Franciscans may have hoped that Francis's engagement with the totality of creation would form part of a new Christian age ushered in by the saint, it was not to be (38). The more radical Franciscans were suppressed by the Church and the Dominican Thomas Aquinas, born around the time of Francis's death, took over the job of interpreting the place of animals in the cosmic order.

The conflict in ideas about the nature of animals in premodernity often makes it difficult to know just what is being communicated in statements concerning animals. In the fifteenth century, for example, Saint Bernardino of Siena told his listeners to "look at the pigs who have so much compassion for each other that when one of them squeals, the others will run to help him. . . . And you children when you steal the baby swallows, what do the other swallows do? They all gather together to help the fledglings" (127). Was the renowned preacher being a radical Franciscan here, challenging the orthodox view of animals by insisting on their moral capacities? Or was he simply using animals as moral exemplars for humans in the time-honored fashion of the bestiaries, without intending that the animals themselves be given any credit for their actions? Perhaps it was not a point on which he himself was certain.

In the end it was the Protestant reformers who would have the greatest influence in reshaping the Christian attitude toward animals. Relying more on Scripture than on classical philosophy or Church doctrine, a number of reformers were cautiously ready to extend some moral consideration to animals. According to John Calvin, although God placed animals under human dominion, "he did it with the condition that we should handle them gently" (K. Thomas 1983: 154). When Martin Luther was asked if dogs would have a place in heaven he replied "Certainly, for . . . [Scripture] said that the last day would be the restitution of all things" (Ickert 1998: 91).

In the following centuries certain Protestant theologians would finally go all the way and concede animals to have souls. Among these were the founder of Methodism, John Wesley, and his bitter opponent, the Calvinist Augustus Toplady (K. Thomas 1983: 140). While the belief in the immortality of animals would not become part of any mainstream Protestant doctrines, it did influence people to think of animals as "fellow beings" to be "handled gently" and not simply "useful things," which could be put "to any kind of death" humans deemed necessary (21).

EXPERIMENTATION AND THE
CAMPAIGN AGAINST CRUELTY

While there might be considerable divergence as to the rational capacities of animals, it was generally accepted that animals, as sentient beings, could suffer. Touch, the common medium of all the inhabitants of the Earth, was also the medium of pain. Conventional theology held that animal pain was not a subject for human concern. According to Augustine, animals' lack of a rational soul meant that while "we see and perceive from their cries that animals die in pain," this is "something, of course, on which a human being places little value" (Augustine, 2005b: 95 [59]; see also Clark 1998).

However, while Augustine and his followers might have been able to write off animal pain as inconsequential, to many it seemed that God had not really played fair with animals: they suffered in this world though innocent of sin and yet were denied any recompense for their sufferings in an afterworld. After all, if it had not been for human sinfulness, animals would presumably have continued to enjoy their peaceful, pleasant existence in Paradise. As things now stood they were condemned to a painful life on Earth followed by complete annihilation. Elaborating on this issue, Richard Overton argued in the seventeenth century that if animals do not share in the Resurrection then the original curse by which death came into the world is not entirely lifted: "If the other Creatures do not rise againe, then Christ shall not *conquer death,* but when it is said, *O Death where is thy sting, O grave where is thy victory?* it will be answered in Beasts, because they are still captivated under its bondage" (cited in Fudge 2002: 151, emphasis in original).

In the same century René Descartes provided a possible solution to the theological dilemma of animal pain by asserting (or seeming to assert) that animals, despite all appearances, did not suffer. Influenced by new theories about the nature of life and encounters with ingenious mechanical automata, Descartes envisioned animals as organic machines, responding to stimuli in an automatic, unthinking, and unfeeling manner (Steiner 2005: ch. 6). One of Descartes's followers, Nicolas Malebranche, stated bluntly that animals "eat without pleasure, they cry without pain, they grow without knowing it, they desire nothing, they know nothing" (Jolley 2000: 42)—an image of animals completely out of touch with themselves.

Many were happy to take up Descartes's idea for, not only did it absolve God of the charge of injustice toward animals, it also opened up a world of guilt-free possibilities for scientific investigation. In the Garden of Eden, it was said, Adam had enjoyed a knowledge of animals' inner dispositions that allowed him to name and interact with them appropriately. After the Fall, however, humans lost their knowledge of animals' interior natures and could only perceive and relate to their external forms. Thus, Thomas Adams wrote that when Adam interacted with animals he "saw all their insides," whereas "we his posterity ever since, with all our experience, can see but their skinnes" (Fudge 2002: 103–4). The seventeenth-century proto-scientists had a hands-on remedy for the human inability to understand the inner nature of animals in a fallen world: vivisection. The notion that animals were unfeeling automata seemed to remove any objections to cutting through their living skins in the quest to regain the Adamic mastery of nature.

The theory of the mechanistic nature of animals did not perhaps have many adherents outside of the broader scientific community, but there it exerted a major impact. Vivisectionists did occasionally wonder whether such convincing demonstrations of distress as were evinced by the animals they experimented on could truly be solely mechanical simulations of pain. Seventeenth-century anatomist Niels Stensen, for example, wrote to a former teacher that he "could not feel convinced that . . . there was no difference between touching, cutting or burning the nerves of a living animal and doing the same thing to the strings of a moving automaton" (Elliot 1990: 27). On the whole, however, the perceived importance of furthering scientific knowledge overrode such concerns. In coming centuries, the notion of animals as organic automata would also contribute to their reconceptualization as so many faceless products to be processed by the machinery of industrial agriculture.

The new scientists, however, were not the only ones interested in rethinking the nature of animals. Already in the sixteenth century Michel de Montaigne had picked apart some of the traditional markers of human and animal difference in an essay provocatively titled "Man is No Better than the Beasts." Montaigne scoffed, for example, at the oft-repeated notion that lowly animals incline their heads toward the earth while high-minded humans lift their faces to the sky: "What animals fail to have their face above and at the front, to look at one another as we do, and to discover in their proper posture as much of the sky and the earth as man does?" (2003: 45). As for the denial of animal subjectivity, Montaigne found all the dogma on the matter mere moonshine, for how can humans "know the internal movements and secrets of animals?" (15).

On the political front, class conflicts in the sixteenth and seventeenth centuries led many to rethink the validity of social hierarchies including, in a few cases, the lordship of humans over animals. (One of the most radical thinkers in this regard was the revolutionary Leveller, Richard Overton.) The political philosopher Thomas Hobbes argued that it was injust to grant a predatory species dominion over its prey and that granting humans dominion over animals amounted to the same thing as granting lions dominion over sheep (K. Thomas 1983: 123, 171). As for the argument that animals were created expressly for the use of man, from the seventeenth century on an increasing conviction among scholars was that certain species of animals had lived and become extinct without ever having come in contact with humans. How could this be reconciled with the belief that the purpose of animals was to serve humans?

One of the foremost of Descartes's critics was the French philosopher-priest Pierre Gassendi who boldly proclaimed "I RESTORE REASON TO THE ANIMALS"

(Preece 2002: 112 [capital letters mine]). Gassendi argued that while animals lacked human reason, "they do not lack their own kind of reason" and that "the difference seems to be merely one of degree" (Steiner 2005: 144). Reuniting body and mind, sense and intellect, Gassendi claimed knowledge to be derived from the senses. Animals, as well as humans, he stated, could learn from their sensory experiences and acquire knowledge—though animal knowledge might take a different form from human knowledge (Preece 2002: 112). As Margaret Cavendish put it, "Man may have one way of knowledge . . . and other creatures another way, and yet other creatures' manner or way may be [as] intelligible and instructive to each other as Man's" (cited by K. Thomas 1983: 128). Not even a lack of language could be taken as an infallible sign of animals' irrationality, for by this time it had been noted by many that deaf persons who lacked language nonetheless appeared to be rational beings. Due to the ongoing influence of such argumentation, in the nineteenth century Charles Darwin could write optimistically that "only a few persons now dispute that animals possess some power of reasoning" (Preece 2002: 112; see also Darwin 1958: 305).

Perhaps the writer who best refuted the Cartesian theory of the animal-machine in terms the public could understand was the eighteenth-century Jesuit Guillaume-Hyacinthe Bougeant. Bougeant wrote a book in which he argued so forcefully for animal sentience and intelligence that he found himself obliged to assert that animals were possessed by demons in order to absolve God from the charge of cruelty toward them (an assertion quite possibly made to appease his heresy sniffing ecclesiastical superiors). In response to the Cartesians, Bougeant claimed that if animals were simply machines then one should have no more feeling for a dog than one has for a clock. However, as Edward Evans summarized Bougeant's argument, "even the strictest Cartesian would never think of petting his chronometer as he pets his poodle, or would expect the former to respond to his caresses as the latter does (E. P. Evans 2006: 66; Bougeant 1739: 8). On a practical level therefore, the point was made that the ways in which humans touch and are touched by animals establishes a community of feeling only possible between sentient and conscious beings.

The issue of animal sentience became especially important in the eighteenth century when the debate over the status of animals shifted from being based on rational capacities to being based on feelings. As Jeremy Bentham put it: "The question is not, Can they *reason*?, nor, Can they *talk*? but, Can they *suffer*? (1779: 311, emphasis in original). If they could, then, the Anglican priest Humphrey Primatt argued, "Pain is pain, whether it is inflicted on man or on beast" (cited in K. Thomas 1983: 176). In certain cases, it was asserted, pain might even be felt more strongly by an animal than by a human. In the opinion of the physician George Cheyne: "I believe some [humans] would suffer less in being butchered than a strong Ox or red Deer." "And," Cheyne added, "in natural morality and justice, the degree of pain here makes the essential difference" (cited in Preece 2008: 178). The age of reason was also the age of sensibility—an age in which feelings, even those of animals, might merit respect.

While animals were unable to put their sufferings into words, from the six-teenth century on there were humans ready to do it for them. Balaam's ass spoke again, as it were, in the works of such voices for the animals. One example of this is the sixteenth-century poem by George Gascoigne entitled "The Hare to the Hunter."

> Are mindes of men become so voyde of sense,
> That they can joye to hurte a harmelesse thing? . . .
> If that be so, I thanke my Maker than
> For making me a Beast and not a Man. (1870: 316)

This tradition culminated in the nineteenth century with Anna Sewell's *Black Beauty,* a novel that told of the sufferings of cab horses from the perspective of one of them. In *Black Beauty,* as in a number of other animal autobiographies, the reader is taught to interpret the signals of animals as emanating from self-aware beings. This opens up the possibility of engaging in person-to-person communica-tion with animals through nonverbal means, such as those reported by the horse Black Beauty: "He put out his hand, and gave me a kind pat on the neck. I put out my nose in answer to his kindness. The boy stroked my face" (Sewell 1922: 243).

Since at least the nineteenth century some argued that campaigns to better the condition of animals had as their ulterior motive the repression and reform of the working class. In 1809, on the occasion of the presentation of an animal welfare bill in the House of Lords, the British politician William Windham asserted that "the Bill for preventing Cruelty to Animals should be entitled, A Bill for harass-ing and oppressing certain Classes amongst the lower Orders of His Majesty's Subjects" (Windham 1841: 221). In 1848 Karl Marx and Friedrich Engels claimed in the "Manifesto of the Communist Party" that "animal welfare enthusiasts" were among those who promoted "the maintenance of bourgeois society" (1996: 25). This view of the animal welfare movement continues to be presented in a number of contemporary publications (i.e., Griffin 2007; Kete 2007: 2).

In many cases the campaign for animal welfare was, indeed, part of a larger project of social reform that included the moral "improvement" of the work-ing class. However, it is far too simplistic to reduce the whole issue to one of a bourgeois assault on working-class lifestyles. For one thing this view assumes monolithic identities for both the middle and the working classes. However, many members of the middle classes were strongly against the concept of animals requiring protection from humans, and campaigners for animal welfare were frequently publicly ridiculed. Catholics of all classes continued to be instructed in the doctrine that humans owed no duties to animals (see Rickaby 1888: 249–50). Many members of the working classes, on the other hand, joined animal protection societies (Lansbury 1985).

The reluctance of many campaigners to place the more genteel pastime of hunting on the anti-cruelty agenda, while popular practices of animal-baiting were strongly attacked, has been taken as an example of a one-sided persecution of working-class blood sports (Griffin, 2007: 150). It is true that baiting seemed to many more reprehensible than hunting. However, it would have been poor politics in the nineteenth century to have attacked hunting, for that would have alienated many powerful supporters and perhaps have prevented any anti-cruelty laws from being passed.

Additionally, one of the major targets of animal welfare societies was bourgeois vivisectors. Indeed, far from solely wishing to tame the working man, the animal welfare campaigners almost welcomed his rage if it might be used against the vivisecting man of science. "If vivisection were practiced in Trafalgar Square," pronounced one clergyman, "it would be the last experiment of the kind in England inasmuch as when the public saw what was being done they would not keep their hands from the vivisectors" ("Home Intelligence" 1888: 29).

Despite the popularity of the literature asserting the subjectivity of animals in the nineteenth century, change in the actual status and treatment of animals came slowly, when at all. Many viewed the animal advocates as mere sentimentalists who erroneously attributed feelings to mindless beasts and then attempted to burden humans with groundless responsibilities toward them. "We have . . . no duties of charity, nor duties of any kind, to the lower animals, as neither to sticks and stones," Jesuit moral philosopher Joseph Rickaby bluntly asserted (1888: 249). This viewpoint was, of course, backed by enormous, not-so-hidden, interests. The *New CatholicWorld* of 1875 published a response to those "infidels" who "most stupidly confer" souls and rights to animals that went to the heart of the matter. "If beasts have the same rights as men, it is a crime to kill them; or, if this is no crime, it must be as lawful to kill and devour men! Are you ready to accept this doctrine?" ("Discussion with an Infidel," 1874–75: 414).

Most people were not. However, neither were many people ready to deny animals any moral consideration. Animals in the modern age, it seemed, could be endowed with just enough personhood as to merit kind handling when convenient, but not so much as to prevent them from being served up for dinner.

"A medieval missionary told of having found the place where the sky touches the earth."
(In Camille Flammarion, *L'atmosphère: météorologie populaire*, 1888.)

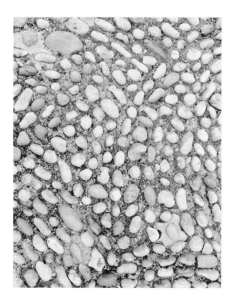

A textured world: cobblestones in Oxford.
(Photograph: Constance Classen)

Close quarters:
A narrow medieval
street in Oxford.
(Photograph:
Constance Classen)

The insistent pull of Death. (Hans
Holbein, "Danse Macabre XXXVII.
The Pedlar," 1538.)

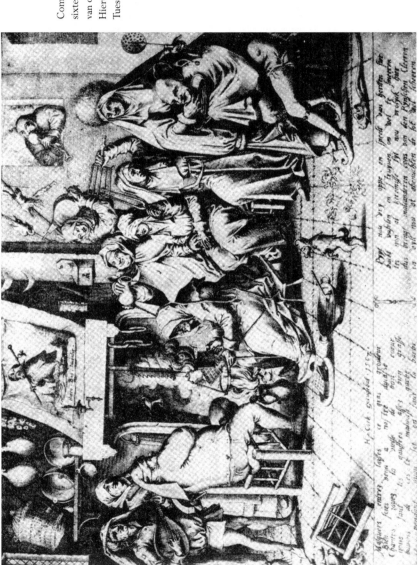

Communal intimacy in the sixteenth century. (Pieter van der Heyden, after Hieronymous Bosch, "Shrove Tuesday," 1567.)

A hands-on investigation of a museum. (George Cruikshank, "A Scene at the London Museum, Piccadilly," 1816.)

Disciplining Victorian bodies: prisoners picking oakum. "Large Oakum-Room (under the silent system) at the Middlesex House of Correction, Coldbath Fields." (In Henry Mayhew and John Binny, *The Criminal Prisons of London and Scenes of Prison Life*, 1862.)

The tactile seductions of the department store. (Félix Vallotton, "Le bon marché," 1893.)

CHAPTER SIX

Tactile Arts

THE AESTHETICS OF TOUCH

Medieval literature evidences a keen appreciation of the tactile world. In Chaucer's "The Legend of Good Women," the narrator kneels upon the meadow with its "small, soft, sweet grass." In *Sir Gawain and the Green Knight,* Gawain enters the deep forest where "hazel and hawthorn were densely entangled, thickly festooned with coarse, shaggy moss" (1992: 43). Indeed, both literature and art disdained distant views in favor of intimate, close-up depictions of a world within hand's reach. As C. S. Lewis wrote in *The Discarded Image*, "Medieval art was deficient in perspective, and poetry followed suit. Nature, for Chaucer, is all foreground" (1964: 102).

A number of practical factors might have encouraged an intimate approach to the world. Long, dark nights spent in close contact with others or engaged in such work as could be undertaken in low light, together with a significant percentage of people with impaired vision, could have helped stimulate the development of a tactile sensibility. Philippe Braunstein writes of the absence of landscapes in medieval literature: "Since defects of vision were not commonly corrected by eyeglasses, it is hardly surprising that the panoramic landscape does not appear in descriptive literature until quite late, and then only symbolically" (1988: 610–11).

Whether or not such material factors influenced the aesthetic life of premodernity, there can be no doubt that the people of the time delighted in aesthetic forms with strong tactile components, from embroideries and tapestries to carvings and metalwork. Such craftwork was highly valued, so much so that an inventory of a collection might well provide a detailed description of an intricately carved frame while dismissing the painting in the frame in a few vague words.

Even the seemingly intangible art of poetry directly engaged the sense of touch through the tactile and kinesthetic dimensions of speech. It was a time when the feel of words was important. Louis IX, for one, is known to have valued words that had a good mouth-feel and disliked those that did not. Among the latter Louis felt a particular aversion to *rendre,* which scratched his throat with its two r's—"devil's rakes," he called them (Le Goff 2009: 705).

The alliterative style of verse that was popular across Europe in the Middle Ages has been described as displaying "a firm grasp on the material world" through its sonic and kinesthetic evocations of material objects (Spearing 1987: 141–42). It has been noted of *Sir Gawain and the Green Knight,* for example, that it makes use of "words whose abrasive quality evokes a world of gnarled weather-worn shapes" (Winny 1992: viii).

Alliteration might be employed both for rhythmic effect and to convey a sense of the action or object being described. Take the line from *Sir Gawain:* "Mist muged on the mor, malt on the mountes" ("mists merged damply with the moors and melted on the mountains"). The rhythm of the words suggests the uneven step of a person stumbling in the mist (xvi). The lines "The King coveris the cragge wyth cloughes full hye / To the creste of the clyffe he clymbez on lofte" from *Morte D'Arthur* similarly evoke the labor of climbing—afterwards followed by the refreshment of "colde wynde to comforthe hym selven" (Spearing 1987: 142). A tongue-twister from *Sir Gawain:* "Sythen thrawen wyth a thwong a thwrde knot alofte" ("Then tightly bound with a thong topped by an intricate knot") not only describes but enacts the intricate decorations on the Green Knight's horse, "forc[ing] the mouth to mimic the involved and tightly knotted decoration" (Winny 1992: xv).

This emphasis on the material qualities of speech is in keeping with the pre-modern view of words as quasi-material objects with power and substance. Thus in *Beowulf* a man about to begin a speech is said to "unlock his treasury of words" (Spearing 1987: 141–42), while medieval medical texts describe "herbes, wordes and stones" as all similarly imbued with healing virtues (Bishop 2007: 99). Words are presented as partaking of some of the physicality of objects.

The medieval predilection for alliterative verse was consistent with a cultural propensity for repetitive forms in general, whether in the steps of a dance, the recitation of prayers, the pattern of a tracery, or the curves of a labyrinth. Labyrinths are particularly intriguing as sites that offered kinesthetic and visual pleasure in an engaging symbolic form. Located in or near many medieval churches, labyrinths may have been ritual sites of pilgrimages through which the devout would walk—or perhaps penitentially crawl—in pursuit of sanctification. In the case of labyrinths drawn on a wall, the journey through the maze would have been traced with a finger (Matthews 1922: 64).

Whether or not explicitly used as pilgrimage sites, the moral message of the labyrinth would probably have resembled that of the visionary voyages discussed in chapter 3, namely, that life is full of twists and impediments and careful, divinely guided walking is necessary to avoid ending up in Hell. As Claude Paradin put it in the early seventeenth century, "One can find one's way through the labyrinth to eternal life by holding in one's hands the thread of the holy commandments given by the grace of God" (89). The physical pleasure taken in threading one's way through labyrinthine patterns could hence be united with the moral satisfaction of undergoing corporeal and spiritual discipline.

The art form to least engage the sense of touch would seem to be that of painting. While the creation of a painting itself certainly requires manual labor and a painterly touch, the finished product—images on a flat surface—might appear to have purely visual relevance. There are a number of ways, however, in which even paintings participated in the culture of touch. One of these ways is through allegorical representations of the sense of touch. In his study of such representations from the Middle Ages to modernity, Carl Nordenfalk found a variety of images used to evoke the sense of touch. Normally the hand, either alone or engaged in an activity, served to represent touch. One thirteenth-century drawing shows a friar holding out a hand on which the word "tactus" ("touch") is inscribed. In the Lady and the Unicorn series of tapestries, the tapestry representing touch has the lady holding the unicorn's horn. A sixteenth-century engraving by Georg Pencz depicted touch as a weaving woman accompanied by her zoological counterpart, a spider in her web. A popular Renaissance motif showed a woman having her thumb bitten by a bird, illustrating the painful dimensions of touch. The thermal qualities of touch were brought out in Baroque illustrations of the senses by the use of a brazier or, in one case, of an old man warming his hands over a steaming bowl of soup.

While some of these images, such as the lady holding the unicorn's horn or having her thumb bitten by a bird, had sexual connotations, the iconography of the senses typically conveyed the sexual aspects of touch through the image of an embracing couple. The enduring notion of touch as a particularly female sense, brought out in a previous chapter, is made evident in a nineteenth-century cartoon on the theme of the senses by Charles-Joseph Travies (Nordenfalk 1990). While the other four senses are all represented by male figures engaged in a sensorially appropriate activity (for example, eating a licorice stick for taste), touch is represented by a naked female model. She does not need to do anything to illustrate her sense because her whole body is good for touching and being touched. The inscription tells us that she is "tout sentiment": "all feeling," suggesting there is nothing more to her than physical and emotional sensation.

THE FEEL OF ART

Another way in which the sense of touch was evoked in art was through representations of tactile contact and bodily movement. Though their depictions are often stylized, medieval and Renaissance paintings convey an immense amount of information about customary modes of touch, posture, and movement (see Quiviger 2010: 105–24). We see people holding hands, kissing, fighting, dancing, huddled round the hearth, soaking in a tub, kneeling in prayer, and bent over their work. They hold the objects characteristic of their times: spindles, flails, reins, swords, and thick prayer books, signaling a world of tactile sensations different from those of modernity.

Yet, however expressive of tactile experiences a picture might be, there was always the difficulty of conveying a physical sensation through a visual medium. Albrecht Dürer faced this dilemma in his own person when he tried to portray his sick body. To convey the site of his pain Dürer drew himself pointing to a yellow spot on his side. A written caption made his feelings clear: "There where the yellow spot is and the finger points, that is where it hurts." Language gave immediacy to an otherwise objective visual image (see Schott 2004).

Dürer, significantly, was a pioneer in the depiction of distant scenes, views apparently painted for the sole purpose of their visual interest: "Dürer's Alpine watercolors [are] the first landscapes in the history of Western art without utilitarian or allegorical significance" (Braunstein 1988: 513). When pain struck, however, the artist wanted to communicate how his body felt and not just how it looked: "That is where it hurts."

Pictures might convey tactile values not only through their subject matter but also through their representational style. The late-nineteenth-century art historian Bernard Berenson held that paintings have to appear three-dimensional and tangible to have an impact on their viewers. "[The painter's] first business . . . is to rouse the tactile sense, for I must have the illusion of being able to touch a figure . . . before I shall take it for granted as real, and let it affect me lastingly" (1967: 40). The masters of this sort of tactile representation in Berenson's view were the painters of the Italian Renaissance with their full-bodied figures and lively depictions of movement: Giotto's large-boned angels, Boticelli's Venus with tresses flying in the wind, Massaccio's Adam and Eve striding, heart-broken, away from Eden.

However, certain Renaissance artists, notably Michelangelo, went too far in their emphasis on tactility in Berenson's view.

> As he got older, and his genius, lacking its proper outlets, tended to stagnate
> and thicken, [Michelangelo] fell into exaggerations. . . . He seems to have

dreamt of presenting nothing but tactile values: hence his many drawings with only the torso adequately treated, the rest unheeded. I have already suggested that Giotto's types were so massive because such figures most easily convey values of touch. Michelangelo tended to similar exaggerations, to making shoulders, for instance, too broad and too bossy, simply because they make thus a more powerful appeal to the tactile imagination. (76–77)

While, as in Michelangelo's case, personal factors influenced the extent to which tactile values would be emphasized in a work, the general social impulse for this trend according to Berenson was to reveal "man's power to subdue and possess the world" (28). To illustrate the anthropocentric ideals of the Renaissance, real muscles had to be depicted interacting with a palpably physical world.

While medieval art fell far short of Renaissance art in the material realism of its depictions, it arguably had other modes of conveying tactile values. As mentioned above, a certain tactile emphasis can be found in the intimate subject matter and close-up views of medieval paintings, by means of which almost everything depicted appears to be close at hand. Medieval art has also been described as manifesting an "iconography of palpability" through its "hard outlines, flat planes of color, repetition and symmetry" (Olin 2000: 236). According to early twentieth-century art historian Alois Riegl, these latter qualities indicated an attempt to represent tactile (or "haptic") sensations in a visual form. Hard outlines, for example, conveyed the supposed tendency of touch to separate objects to ascertain their individual material reality. Riegl understood the tactile tendencies of medieval art to represent an earlier, more naive stage in the evolution of artistic styles (236–37).

Although contentious, Berenson's and Riegl's theories of tactile values in art are suggestive of how in different cultural periods the tactile imagination might find expression through particular modes of visual representation. To more fully appreciate the relationship between tactile values and visual art, however, it is essential to move beyond issues of representation to explore actual practices. By rejecting the modern assumption that art "is experienced by the eye only" (Barasch 1990: 208), it becomes possible to investigate how people actually did engage with art works through their senses.

In the hands-on culture of premodernity, many kinds of images—of sumptuous materials, of lifelike flesh, of a seemingly distant sky—would have prompted an inquiring touch. Touch would have served to verify that what looked so real was in fact just an optical illusion. It would also, however, have expressed a desire to feel and possess the objects so powerfully represented by the skills of the artist.

Not only the pictures but also the bright colors displayed in paintings had tactile appeal, as viewers were enticed to touch the vivid hues that so powerfully caught their eye. Bernard of Clairvaux even suggested that bright colors were employed in paintings for the purpose of luring people into touching them and then opening their purses: "Some beautiful picture of a saint is exhibited—and the brighter the colours the greater the holiness attributed to it; men run, eager to kiss; [then] they are invited to give" (cited by Morison 1884: 131).

The allure of bright colors in an era in which they were not always readily available and sometimes quite costly can be seen in the color obsessions manifested by some individuals with dancing mania in the sixteenth century: "No sooner did [such persons] obtain a sight of the favorite colour than . . . they rushed like infuriated animals towards the object, devoured it with their eager looks, kissed and caressed it in every possible way" (Hecker 1970: 22). It sounds very much like a more agitated instance of the situation described by Bernard of Clairvaux, with color inducing an irresistible desire to touch.

Although colors undoubtedly had a strong aesthetic appeal, the allure of the colorful lay also in premodern notions of the power of color. (Saint Bernard himself suggests that "the brighter the colors" of a painting "the greater the holiness attributed to it.") Colors, along with other sensory properties, could be thought of as cosmic forces. Green, due to its association with plant life, was held to contain vital energy. Twelfth-century abbess and visionary Hildegard of Bingen was a great believer in the power of green, which she and others thought to be most perfectly embodied in the emerald—a jewel that had "sucked up all the greenness like a lamb sucking up milk" (Flanagan 1998: 83). For this reason Hildegard recommended wearing an emerald next to the skin for the alleviation of many ailments. Blue, in turn, corresponded to the sapphire, which was attributed cooling and protective properties. Gold and golden colors were associated with the Sun and thought to communicate warmth and well-being. Perhaps most precious of all was the glowing red of the carbuncle. Associated with fiery light and with the salvational blood of Christ, the deep red of the carbuncle was described as a "joy-giving" color (Shackford 1913: 116).

The brightly colored, luminous stained-glass windows of churches would have seemed to their premodern parishioners to radiate color energies or "virtues" (see Gage 1993: 70–73). It might have been some notion of the life-giving virtues of the jewel-like colors employed in paintings that drew people to touch the bright images. As Hildegard pointed out, touching was a more effective means of receiving an influx of healing colors than simply looking (Flanagan 1998: 83).

Many colors, furthermore, had a close association with textiles: "Throughout history, fabrics have borrowed the names of colours and colours have used the names of fabrics. At one point . . . scarlet was the name of a cloth. As were beige . . . russet, tawny and turquoise. At other times, blanket, cashmere, chaulet, damask, flax . . . silk . . . were used as colour names. It is often hard to tell if you are looking at a cloth or a colour" (D. Salisbury 2009: 238). The overlapping of colors and cloths would have meant that a number of tints would have suggested a certain feel to their viewers. (In the seventeenth century natural philosophers discussed the possibility of different colors actually having different textures.) This tactile dimension of color would have been supplemented by the attribution of thermal properties to certain colors. The longest-lasting example of this was the attribution of warming and strengthening powers to the color red, due to which red colors might be added to medicaments, and red blankets and undergarments used to protect against the cold and against infectious diseases (Glynn and Glynn 2004: 26).

Colors were not considered to be all good, however. They could be associated with the Devil and his alluring, but deceitful enticements. To refrain from using or being drawn by gaudy colors was a sign of monastic simplicity and sobriety—as Saint Bernard emphasized in his work. The costliness of many pigments, furthermore, could make their use seem sinfully wasteful. One twelfth-century prior railed against episcopal palaces that had paintings of "Trojans dressed in purple and gold [while] a poor Christian has no right even to rags" (Pleij 2004: 67). Colors, it seemed, not only adorned the homes and clothing of the rich, they also took the clothing off the backs of the poor.

The literal as well as cosmological richness of colors, however, combined to give them immense popular appeal. Bright colors in clothing and in art did not go out of fashion until they began to be stigmatized as frivolous in the reform-minded sixteenth century, and less costly methods of production greatly diminished their prestige value. In the 1520s Baldassare Castiglione wrote in his guide to courtly behavior: "I am also always pleased when clothes tend to be sober and restrained rather than foppish; so it seems to me that the most agreeable colour is black, and, if not black, then at least something fairly dark" (2003: 101).

Whatever the appeal of their colors or lifelike representations, there is no doubt that painted images often seemed a very poor substitute for concrete objects, especially in the earlier Middle Ages. Discussing the long-standing practice of trying the dead for crimes they had committed while alive, sixteenth-century jurist Pierre Ayrault wrote that he could not understand the practice of having the corpse present in the courtroom and physically punished if condemned (Kadri 2005: 163). He suggested that a painting of the deceased be present and punished in place of the corpse. A brief overview of perhaps the most infamous trial of a corpse makes it clear that in making this suggestion Ayrault (although still maintaining the notion of vicarious punishment) was showing a poor comprehension of the importance of tangible objects in earlier periods.

In 896 Pope Stephen VI ordered that the corpse of his predecessor and rival Pope Formosus be put on trial. Formosus's corpse was disinterred, dressed in full papal regalia, with the apostolic ring on his finger and the miter on his head, and set up on a throne in an ecclesiastical council chamber. The corpse was then questioned on its former crimes, with Stephen mockingly urging it to reply to the charges. "The old man's body, like a monstrous doll, might nod and bend while the attendants supported it, or collapse in a ghastly bundle if they left it alone, but it made no sound" (Ives 1914: 262). Stephen VI then excommunicated the degraded Formosus and ordered that the three fingers of the right hand used for benediction be cut off. The body was divested of its robes of authority and thrown to the mob who, in turn, cast it into the Tiber river. How could the destruction of a mere painting of Formosus have had the impact of such a full-bodied degradation? Particularly considering that, as we saw in the second chapter, something of the spirit of the dead was considered to remain with their bodies.

While paintings might seem to offer a rather thin version of reality to those who liked thick sensations, even their meager tangibility provided something to hold on to. As proof of the superiority of painting to poetry, Leonardo da Vinci told the story of a king who preferred holding a portrait of his beloved to hearing a poem about her because the painting was something he could "see and touch, and not only hear" (cited in Cranston 2003: 226). That extra tactile dimension apparently made all the difference.

The pictures that people most wanted to see and touch were undoubtedly those mentioned by Saint Bernard: images of Christ and the saints. Religious art, indeed, provided most people with their predominant experience of artistic images. The personal possession of saintly pictures, which enabled one to touch an image at will without having to visit a church, became more common in the later Middle Ages as techniques of reproduction improved. The unlimited amount of contact made possible by the personal ownership of a picture could be intoxicating. The fourteenth-century mystic Margaret Ebner told of her desire for constant contact with an image she owned of the crucified Christ: "I possessed a little book in which there was a picture of the Lord on the cross. I shoved it secretly against my bosom, open to that place, and wherever I went I pressed it to my heart with great joy and measureless grace. When I wanted to sleep, I took the picture of the Crucified Lord in the little book and laid it under my face" (Ebner 1993: 96).

While the German nun's tactile devotion may have been particularly fervent, it was not unusual. Many, and probably most, people touched religious images. There was a widespread belief that touching an icon, similarly to touching a relic, could provide an infusion of divine virtue (Nyrop 1901: 129–30). In many

cases sacred images would be placed directly on the body for purposes of healing (Vauchez 1997: 452). Such images were manifestly not thought of simply as
representations, but rather as vehicles for the transmission of spiritual holiness
and physical wholeness. Painters of sacred images certainly would have known
that their works would be the subject of a devotional touch and this may well
have induced them to create paintings with touch appeal.

With the Reformation the role of images in religion came under attack. The
Old Testament prohibition on making "any likeness of anything that is in heaven
above, or that is in the earth beneath, or that is in the water under the earth" had
generally been interpreted by the Church as referring only to the idolatrous use
of images (Besançon 2000). This was a reasonable assumption as the commandment immediately following the prohibition on the creation of images read: "Thou
shalt not bow down thyself to them, not serve them." The Catholic Counter-
Reformation asserted the nonidolatrous nature of religious images "which we
kiss and before which we uncover the head and prostrate ourselves" by insisting
that such acts were not done because "any divinity or virtue is believed to be in
them" but because "we adore Christ and venerate the saints whose likeness they
bear" (Englander et al. 1999: 167).

Thinking the matter over, however, many reform-minded theologians arrived at
the conclusion that churchgoers, with all their kissing and parading of sacred icons
were dangerously close to crossing the line into idolatry. During the sixteenth and
seventeenth centuries, hence, some Protestant sects set about purifying churches
of such superstitious images. (Except among the strictest sects, secular art was
usually left alone.) The English Puritan William Dowsing, nicknamed "Smasher"
with good reason, left a record of his government-sponsored icon-breaking activities. An entry from a particularly busy day reads: "We brake down 1000 Pictures
superstitious; I brake down 200; 3 of God the Father, and 3 of Christ, and the
Holy Lamb, and 3 of the Holy Ghost like a Dove with Wings" (Dowsing 1885:
15). A reverential touch was replaced by a destructive touch, as the iconoclasts
strove to demonstrate that far from possessing any form of salvational power the
images they destroyed were powerless to save themselves. The pain and shock
such icon-smashing would have given more traditional believers, who would have
prayed before and kissed many of the images destroyed, can hardly be imagined.

While the importance and tactile value of religious art declined in Protestant
Europe as a result of the iconoclastic movement, touching still remained a popular
and meaningful way of interacting with art works. This was particularly true of the
art form that most seemed to invite a curious or appreciative touch: sculpture. A
seventeenth-century French courtier remarked on what was no doubt the case
through Europe at that time: that people "begin looking at sculptures by touching

them" (Chantelou 1985: 185). That is to say that the immediate sensory response to a sculpted work was to run one's hands over it.

In the case of sculpture the sense of touch revealed that the representations of humans and animals that looked so real were in fact made of hard stone—a sensory contradiction that never lost its power to fascinate (see Haskell and Penny 1981: 163, 235). At the same time this sense allowed people to vicariously handle what they would rarely, if ever, have been able to actually touch—emperors and goddesses and lions. Statues, with their lifelike forms, might also elicit a sensuous desire for tactile intimacy, as depicted, notably, in the influential myth of Pygmalion and Galatea. One prominent seventeenth-century collector in Rome, Hippolito Vitellesco, was reputed to embrace and kiss the statues in his collection (Evelyn 1955: 283). Some critics found such tactile interaction with sculpture too coarsely sensuous. Sixteenth-century art theorist Vicenzio Borghini denounced the practice of touching and kissing statues as vulgar (Johnson 2002: 66). Benedetto Varchi, by contrast, suggested that the particular value of touch in relation to sculpture was that it alone could appreciate the artifice involved in a sculpted work (Cranston 2003: 238–39). Referring to an ancient statue known as the Hermaphrodite, Lorenzo Ghiberti commented that "there was the greatest refinement, which the eye would not have discovered, had not the hand sought it out" (Johnson 2002: 64). Indeed, whatever the critics may have thought about it, handling sculptures wherever possible would have been a common practice.

With the rise of the visual arts in the eighteenth century, however, all such modes of tactile aesthetics began to fall out of favor. The practice of touching sculpture—the one art form deemed able to lay claim to some credible tactile value—still had its supporters. In the late eighteenth century Goethe poetically declared that by caressing flesh one comes to understand the tactile value of sculpture: to "see with a feeling eye, feel with a seeing hand" (1974: 45). The importance of touch for the aesthetic appreciation of sculpture was most notably upheld by the German philosopher Johann Gottfried Herder. Herder considered sculpture to be the highest form of art precisely because it was perceptible to the sense of touch, a sense he thought afforded a more profound appreciation of beauty than sight (Herder 2002; Norton 1990: ch. 6). From this perspective, preventing people from touching sculptures effectively denied them access to art at its highest level (see further Nichols 2006).

Such opinions however, did not have much effect on the growing trend among philosophers and art critics to deny touch any valid role in the encounter with art. Friedrich Schiller's claim in the late eighteenth century that the use of touch for aesthetic appreciation was a mark of savagery was indicative of this trend (Schiller 1982: 95). It would take time, however, for such high-minded notions of aesthetic appreciation to affect the ways in which ordinary individuals engaged with works of art.

CRAFTY LADIES

While touch would increasingly be dismissed as a valid mode for the appreciation of art in modernity, it nonetheless remained significant within the related field of craftwork. This was particularly the case with the often overlooked field known as "ladies' work"—the term used for the craftwork undertaken by women to adorn their homes and families. Ladies' work included such diverse practices as embroidering cushions, making shell mosaics, and fashioning jewelry out of hair. As interior decoration grew in importance from the seventeenth century on, so did the value and popularity of home crafts. One of the most renowned of the multitude of practitioners of ladies' work would be the eighteenth-century Englishwoman Mary Delany. Renown, however, was far from being considered an important, or even desirable, outcome of the practice of feminine craftwork.

As its name suggests, *ladies'* work was a sublimated version of *women's* work. It was the kind of work considered suitable (if sometimes frivolous) for women who had no need to perform everyday household chores. Though particularly the domain of leisured gentlewomen, ladies' work might be practiced by women of all classes or, for that matter, by nuns. Unlike artworks or masculine craftwork, ladies' work was not customarily made for purchase or for public view. As a branch of women's work it was considered essentially domestic, undertaken within the home for the home and of value nowhere else.

As with women's work in general, ladies' work was considered to be a work of the hand—handiwork. However visually engaging such work might be, it was associated with the tactile character of other domestic labors: sewing, cleaning, and caring for the family. This association was supported by the fact that feminine craftwork typically made use of materials with strong tactile associations, such as wool, hair, silk, feathers, shells, and beads. If an artistically inclined woman desired to produce or reproduce a picture, it was considered appropriate to work with a traditionally feminine material rather than with canvas, for example, to embroider the picture as a tapestry or to paint it on silk. In the case of those women who ventured into the masculine territory of the visual arts, their works (when considered at all) were usually brought back into the feminine sensory and social domain, by being described as tasteful or full of feeling.

Many of the crafts undertaken by women were extensions of skills developed in the practice of the quintessentially feminine art of needlework. These included lacemaking, beadwork, and papercraft—which involved delicate scissorwork. Whether or not a craft was directly related to needlework, practitioners would often employ two common features of needlework: assembling many smaller units to create a whole (as in embroidery or mosaic work)—and repetitive pattern. The former can be seen in the paper flowers created by Mary Delany in the eighteenth century, which were built up from hundreds of carefully cut pieces of colored paper pasted on a black background. An instance of Delany's use of the latter can found in an embroidered blanket that displays an elaborate pattern of white knotted thread couched on white fabric.

In the case of her paper flowers, which would come to number almost a thousand, an obvious question might seem to be why Delany did not simply paint the flowers, and then, if she wished, cut them out and mount them on a black background? The general visual result in most cases would have been much the same and the effort involved would have been considerably less. One likely reason Delany chose to work with scissors rather than with a paintbrush (in the use of which she was also adept) was because scissorwork was a particularly feminine practice cultivated by many women in her circle. Their reliance on highly skilled scissorwork made Delany's flowers a triumph of feminine craft, rather than merely a charming set of paintings (Delany 1974).

Another reason was that Delany aimed for more than mere visual representation in her flowers. The model for her flowers was the *hortus sicus,* or dried flower collection, popular among gentlewomen (Hayden 1980: 132). The layering of leaves, petals, stamens, and so on in her pressed paper flowers (which were composed with botanical accuracy) mimicked the physical qualities of real pressed flowers. The result was a richly layered effect rather than simply a flat visual image. The reliance on assemblage, repetition, and texture common in ladies' work (features that, from the perspective of modern aesthetics, made such work more decorative than artistic) had the result of creating works with a particularly tactile sensibility. Either actually or imaginatively, such craftwork invited the intimate, piece-by-piece exploration of an appreciative hand.

Women were generally expected to employ their skills at craft to add a feminine touch to a home, rather than to completely transform it. Yet many crafty ladies of means undertook large-scale projects of interior design, adorning whole rooms with their embroidery or paper collage, and decorating cavernous grottoes with their shellwork. When several industrious women—mothers, daughters, and friends—worked together on projects the results could be dramatic.

An example of a house transformed by accomplished craftswomen that is still largely preserved today is that of A la Ronde in Exmouth. A la Ronde was created by Jane Parminter and her cousin, Mary Parminter, in the late eighteenth- and early nineteenth centuries. The name of the house comes from its unusual sixteen-sided design, which the cousins were said to have based on the basilica of San Vitale at Ravenna. The house, however, looks less like a church than a cottage with white-washed walls and a thatched roof. Inside, a central octagonal hall rises up sixty feet and is encircled by an upper gallery (Hussey 1938; Tudor 1970). Situated between the hexadecagon of the exterior walls and the octagon of the interior hall, the rooms within the house are all of odd shapes, with furniture made to fit. Each room has a sliding panel leading into the next, making it possible to complete a circuit of A la Ronde by walking from room to room. Having rooms facing all directions ensured that the cousins would always have a warm, sunny spot in which to work. This novel configuration of interior space would have produced a heightened sense of self-positioning within the house.

The Parminters' creation of A la Ronde was influenced by the contemporary interest in pastoral life and in the picturesque. A la Ronde, however, was not simply a *cottage orné*, a gentrified simulacrum of a rustic residence for the recreation of the well-to-do. It was a large-scale example of feminine craftwork—an embroidered house, as it were. The upper walls of the house are covered in mosaics made out of shells, feathers, and porcelain fragments. Between the eight upper windows are sixteen representations of birds executed in feathers, twigs, and lichens. The narrow staircase leading up to the gallery was transformed by the cousins into a grotto, with its walls and vaulted ceiling encrusted with shells, rocks, and sparkling pieces of mirror. The rooms on the main floor of the house display examples of the Parminters' embroidery, pottery, and other craftwork, including a table inlaid with marble, shells, and cameos. The drawing room is decorated with an elaborate featherwork frieze and seaweed and sand landscapes, while the library is dominated by the cousins' extensive shell collection.

The use of shells, feathers, and other decorative materials on the walls creates texturally rich surfaces that invite tactile exploration and impinge on the interior space of the house. This ambience of textural diversity is enhanced by the numerous handicrafts displayed within the house. The use of similar materials for a variety of purposes produces a sensation of continuous transformation as collections become walls, walls become tables, and tables become pictures. In this context the surfaces in the house that remain flat and smooth become themselves texturally interesting by way of contrast.

Another significant feature of A la Ronde is its intimate relationship with the external environment. Situated on high ground, the house's gallery windows command an imposing view of the countryside in all directions. Through the use of natural materials such as feathers, twigs, lichens, rocks, shells, sand, and seaweed, however, the surrounding countryside is brought within the house. This makes it possible to not only look out onto the landscape from the house, but to enter into an intimate haptic relationship with it through its aesthetic reconstruction within the house. Diamond-paned windows, in turn, transform the view into a mosaic to match the mosaics inside. The fracturing of unified visual perspectives into a sensuous multiplicity is further enhanced by the fact that eight of A la Ronde's windows are placed on the angles of the house, creating two-sided vistas rather than flat pictures of the exterior.

In A la Ronde, therefore, we find craftswomen working at creating a total environment that engaged multiple senses. The Parminters did not just adorn a house with their handiwork, the house itself was their handiwork. They lived within their art. The importance of this total environment is suggested by the name of the house itself—A la Ronde, "in the round."

Ladies' work, such as that engaged in by Mary Delany and the Parminter cousins, can be seen as an artistic and sensory ghetto in which creative women were pressured by gender conventions to contain—and downgrade—their aesthetic and intellectual aspirations. Practitioners of feminine craftwork would find their work not only trivialized by men but also by women who saw in it a means of female subjugation (Hivet 2005). While many women undoubtedly felt disengaged or stifled by ladies' work, evidence indicates that many others found it stimulating and that they employed it as a means for developing and expressing their own creative interests. The endeavors of such women, even those of eminent craftswomen such as Mary Delany, would remain outside the established boundaries of art and for the most part unpreserved and undisplayed outside the home. Nonetheless, within a broader and more multisensory assessment of the history of aesthetics, traditional feminine craftwork occupies a key position, elaborating significant alternative practices and values to those of mainstream art.

TOUCH IN THE MUSEUM

In the late seventeenth century English traveler Celia Fiennes recorded a visit she made to the Ashmolean Museum of Oxford:

> There is a picture of a Gentleman that was a great benefactor to it being a cavalier, the frame of his picture is all wood carved very finely with all sorts of figures leaves birds beasts and flowers . . . there is a Cane which looks like a solid heavy thing but if you take it in your hands its as light as a feather, there is a dwarfe shoe and boote, there are several Loadstones and it is pretty to see how the steele clings or follows it, hold it on top att some distance the needles stands quite upright hold it on either side it moves towards it as it rises and falls. (Fiennes 1949: 33)

From this run-on description (which mimics the experience of rushing from one exhibit to another) we learn that touch had a role in the early museum.

Fiennes's interactive approach to the Ashmolean was of a piece with her behavior in related tourist sites. While in Oxford she also visited the Physic Garden (which in some ways constituted the botanical counterpart to the Ashmolean) with its collection of rare, curious, and beautiful plants. Among the exhibits she interacted with there were a mimosa—"take but a leafe between finger and thumb and squeeze it and it immediately curles up together as if pained"—and a humble plant—"do but strike it, it falls flatt on the ground stalke and all." Nor is she above sinking her teeth into certain of the exhibits—"the Wormwood sage [has] a narrow long leafe full of ribbs, in your mouth the flavour is strong of Wormwood to the taste" (22–27).

Fiennes's descriptions of her behavior at such sites offer no suggestion of the necessity of subduing one's senses within collection settings. The overall impression is of a lively exploration of whatever a particular site has to offer—and the more interactive that happens to be the better. The museum, along with other exhibition sites, is treated as a kind of gymnasium for the senses.

The acts of manual investigation taken for granted by Fiennes in the seventeenth century would scarcely be possible in most modern museums. In fact, it is now generally taken for granted that museums collections are not for touching (although certain groups and museums are challenging this rule [see Candlin 2010: chs. 5 and 6]). In the early museums of the seventeenth and eighteenth centuries, by contrast, touching within collection settings was commonplace, so commonplace as to customarily escape mention. Hence, in his account of his visits to English museums and collections, the German traveler Zacharias Conrad von Uffenbach made note of one place where his sense of touch was restricted rather than those where it was not. That place was the Chapel of St. Edward the Confessor in Westminster Abbey, where various historical and legendary artifacts were kept—coronation chairs and "the famous stone of the Patriarch Jacob" among others. Uffenbach wrote that he "should much have liked to scrape off a little" of this famous stone with his knife but "dared not, for one is liable to punishment for even sitting on one of these chairs" (1934: 92). A hint of modern museum policy is suggested here, except that the restrictions apparently did not go so far as to forbid all forms of touch, for Uffenbach records the heaviness of a great sword kept in the same chapel.

It cannot be assumed, moreover, that when visitors to early museums recorded seeing a collection that seeing was all they did. Then, as now, "to see" could be used in a general sense to mean to encounter or to perceive and could well include various sensory modalities. In a description of a visit to the Tower of London in 1710 Uffenbach noted that an attempted robbery had resulted in the crown jewels kept there being less accessible to visitors. The jewels were now displayed behind a "trellis work of strong iron . . . through which strangers can view the things." He adds, however, that it is still possible "to get one's hand through and pick up the articles to feel their weight, so that everything can still be seen tolerably"

(40). This was apparently the opinion of other visitors as well. William Hutton, who visited the Tower later in the century, describes putting his hands through the grate and picking up the crown jewels (1818: 124–25). For gallery-goers of the time, a satisfactory viewing involved handling.

Early museums retained many characteristics of the private collections on which they were based. The museum tour led by a curator matched the house tour that might be offered by a host. The curator, as gracious host, was expected to provide information about the collection and offer it up for handling. While in actual practice, many visitors to early museums felt that they were rushed through the exhibits, this model remained the ideal. The museum visitors, as polite guests, were expected to show their interest and goodwill by asking questions and by touching the proffered objects. In such cases etiquette mandated that deference be paid to the visitors or guests, particularly if they were of high rank, rather than to the objects on display. This was so much the case that the Ashmolean ordinances of 1686 allowed the Keeper to make presents of museum pieces to visitors "of extraordinary quality" (Ovenell 1986: 50). Thus, when Uffenbach visited the collection of historical records in Wakefield Tower in London he asked for and received a torn piece of a letter "of particular antiquity." (He noted the "fibrous and tough" quality of the paper [1934: 69].)

By allowing visitors to touch the objects within the museum, therefore, the curator enacted ancient notions of hospitality. Not all curators (or hosts) necessarily followed this model but it furnished the ideal and its poor performance was often the cause of complaint. Thus, when the underkeeper of the Ashmolean in 1760 tried to prevent a museum visitor from handling artifacts he was accused of incivility. "She desired me to take the Glass from off several of the Drawers, which I was somewhat unwilling to do, lest anything be lost by that means; which she perceiving she told me that I was not quite so civil as might be; that the last time she had seen the Museum . . . she had handled and examin'd the Curiosities in the Cabinet as long as she pleas'd" (cited in Ovenell 1986: 147).

Practical, as well as social, considerations contributed to the tactile accessibility of early museums. For one thing, glass cases were expensive and display space in the museum was usually at a premium. While certain particularly valuable or delicate artifacts would be placed under glass, many were hung on walls or stored in drawers. Exhibits in museums and collections that were placed out in the open—hanging on walls or arranged on tables—were particularly likely to be touched, but even exhibits in drawers and cases might be taken out and handled. Uffenbach describes "a calculus as big as a hen's egg" in the collection of St. John's College that was considered precious enough to merit "a carefully designed gold casket with a crystal lid," yet that was taken out of its case for the benefit of visitors (1928: 58.) The mere fact of an artifact being placed under glass hence did not necessarily signify untouchability. Furthermore, curators often received their salaries out of entrance fees. This constituted a considerable inducement to curators to make their museums attractive to visitors by allowing them to physically interact with the exhibits.

The reasons for touching museum pieces were wide ranging. Certain objects displayed in museums and collections were interactive by nature. Examples of this noted by Uffenbach were the sword kept in the Bodleian Library collection that had "a large knob of crystal, which can be unscrewed and in which is painted a golden hourglass," and a block of wood with a movable brass ring displayed in the collection of the Anatomy School in Oxford: "Not only can it be turned completely round, but it shows no sign of the place where it has been soldered" (13, 23).

More generally, touch supplemented sight as a means of investigating the traits of the objects on display. A visual impression of a sculpture, for example, could be complemented by a tactile impression of its contours. Smaller objects might be handled to enable them to be better seen—turned around or held up to the light. When visiting Hans Sloane's collection in London Uffenbach describes holding a shell up to the light so that he could see "the concham lying concealed within it" (1934: 186). According to Uffenbach the most remarkable item in the Bodleian collection in Oxford was a framed image of a lizard in white marble set in a black marble. He wrote that although this looked like a work of nature the eye might be deceived by skillful artifice. Touch, however, provided reliable evidence of the natural origin of the image: "A blind man even though he could not see could yet feel that this is a natural vein (*palpando experiri potest*)" (13).

For similar reasons, visitors to collections regularly lifted objects to ascertain their weight. When describing the collection in the Tower of London Uffenbach stressed the importance of being able to pick up the crown jewels and feel their weight. On her tour of the Ashmolean Fiennes tested the weight of a cane. In 1646 John Evelyn recorded lifting an antler in a Swiss collection to test its weight ("one branch of them was as much as I could well lift" [1955: 516]). When Samuel Pepys went to see two oversized children on display at Charing Cross in 1667 he "tried to weigh them in [his] arms" (1976: VIII, 326). The weight of an object (or person) might be taken as an indication of the material of its composition, of its value, or of the strength required to wield it. Attempting to ascertain the weight of something by lifting it, however, was not just a matter of data gathering, such as might otherwise and with better accuracy have been accomplished with scales, but of bodily knowledge. A hands-on approach to exhibits enabled visitors to acquire an embodied understanding of the nature of the display.

Not sight and touch alone, but hearing, smell, and even taste might also be used to investigate collection exhibits. Uffenbach, for example, records the following experience when visiting Sloane's collection: "Among other things [Sloane] pointed out to us the nests that are eaten as a delicacy. It is said that the material is formed in the sea like the succino and used by the birds to build their nests. But, judging from its taste, appearance and feeling, I took it for a gum or resin" (1934: 187).

Even if visitors to collections did not customarily taste the exhibits, their visit still might be informed by gustatory associations. Just as occurs today, museum visits might be coupled with meals. In early public museums, however, visitors sometimes brought food to eat within the collection space itself (i.e., M. Levy 1970: 8). In private collections, the owner, if so inclined, might provide a collation. Hans Sloane customarily ended his guided tour of his collection with coffee in the library (a fitting sequel to the viewing of the branch from a coffee tree exhibited in his museum) (187). In the library, as well as in the museum proper there were rare objects to be seen and touched. Indeed, the handling of these curiosities sometimes conflicted with the handling of the refreshments being served. When the composer Handel visited Sloane in 1740 he carelessly placed his buttered muffin on a precious manuscript, incurring the anger of his host (E. Miller 1974: 38–39). There were evidently limits to tactile license in the museum. For those who wished for more meal and less museum, there was Don Saltero's London coffeehouse, established by Sloane's former servant and embellished with a range of curious objects, many of them cast-offs from Sloane's museum.

Not only might meals be taken within a museum, the museum itself might be conceptualized as a meal. When the Prince and Princess of Wales visited Sloane's museum in 1748, exhibits were set up on and removed from tables like the courses of a meal. The first course was precious stones as found in nature. "The same tables were covered for a second course with all sorts of jewels, polish'd and set after the modern fashion, or with gems, carv'd or engraved." The third course consisted of gold and silver ornaments from around the world (Hudson, 1975: 19–20). While this carefully prepared feast of riches might indicate that Sloane's collection had outgrown its display space so that not everything could be exhibited at once (De Beer 1953: 133), it was also evidently a ritual strategy for offering the precious collection up for royal consumption. One can scarcely imagine that the Prince and Princess did not handle the objects laid so tantalizingly before them. Indeed, such royal handling would itself have added to the prestige and symbolic power of the collection.

Investigating rare and curious objects through a number of sensory modalities was supported by contemporary scientific practice. According to the seventeenth-century empirical philosopher Robert Hooke, the range of qualities to be examined in an object under study included "Sonorousness or Dulness. Smell or Taste. . . . Gravity, or Levity. Coarseness, or Fineness. Fastness, or Looseness. Stiffness, or Pliableness. Roughness, or Brittleness. Claminess, or Slipperiness" (cited in Arnold 2003: 76). Hooke, indeed, explicitly stated that "ocular inspection" must be accompanied by the "manual handling . . . of the very things themselves" (ibid.; see also Arnold 2006: 144; Candlin 2010: 67–68). Perhaps with some such scientific injunctions in mind, English diarist John Evelyn recorded a range of sensory interactions with artifacts in the cabinets of curiosities that were the antecedents to museums. He shook a petrified egg to hear the yolk rattle and a crystal with water inside to see the water move. He lifted an antler to test its weight and he smelled scented wood from the Indies (1955: 471, 516 and passim). Using multiple senses to investigate museum objects enhanced the impression of having comprehended their nature.

As mentioned above, an important advantage of touch lay in its presumed ability to access interior truths of which sight was unaware. Celia Fiennes wrote that the cane on display in the Ashmolean looked heavy, but when she picked it up she found that it was light. Touch functioned to correct the misconceptions of sight. Even in the eye-minded eighteenth century, when vision was widely lauded as fundamental to intellectual cognition, many still considered touch "to have the best and final access to the world that sense reveals" (Summers 1987: 326).

Visitors not only touched objects in museums to verify their true nature, they touched them because they wanted to experience them intimately. Sight requires distance to function properly, detaching the observer from the observed. Touch, by contrast, annihilates distance and physically unites the toucher and the touched. Handling museum artifacts gave visitors the satisfaction of an intimate encounter. In the case of human-made artifacts, it also provided the thrill of coming into vicarious contact with their original creators and users, and even—through, for example, hefting a sword or trying on a ring—a sense of what it would be like to *be* an artifact's original owner.

In 1786, for example, German traveler Sophie von La Roche wrote of her visit to the British Museum:

> With what sensations one handles a Carthaginian helmet excavated near Capua, household utensils from Herculaneum. . . . There are mirrors too, belonging to Roman matrons . . . with one of these mirrors in my hand I looked amongst the urns, thinking meanwhile, "Maybe chance has preserved amongst these remains some part of the dust from the fine eyes of a Greek or Roman lady, who so many centuries ago surveyed herself in this mirror. . . ." Nor could I restrain my desire to touch the ashes of an urn on which a female figure was being mourned. I felt it gently, with great feeling. . . . I pressed the grain of dust between my fingers tenderly, just as her best friend might once have grasped her hand. (1933: 107–8)

Here the sense of touch is essential to the visitor's experience of a museum collection, not because it provides her with an empirical knowledge of the artifacts' physical qualities, but because it enables her to establish an imaginative intimacy with storied ancient peoples. This potent sense of intimacy, which is evidently eagerly desired, is heightened by La Roche's perception of coming into direct contact with the bodily remains of the artifacts' former owners. Not only does she hold the objects that ancient peoples once held, she actually, through the funerary ashes she presses between her fingers, imagines herself to be holding the very hand of one of those long-dead persons. The sense of touch is perceived as annihilating both space and time. This oft-perceived ability of touch to bridge space and time gave it a special value in the museum setting, where visitors were separated by considerable spatial or temporal distances from the cultures of origin of many of the objects displayed.

For many visitors to early museums, however, touch did more than allow them an intimate experience of the artifacts inside, it allowed them to access the mysterious powers popularly associated with the rare and the curious. Cabinets of curiosities and museums were in many ways secular counterparts of shrines and churches. Many of the objects in museums were regarded as numinous by virtue of their marvelous and exalted status. Even in Protestant countries where the religious veneration of images and relics had been suppressed, the belief that extraordinary objects could be sources of power lived on in popular culture. Museum visitors hence often imagined that they might receive a supernatural boost by touching such objects of wonder as an Egyptian mummy or a "unicorn's horn" (both indispensable exhibits in early museums). So desirous, in fact were many to internalize the seemingly magical properties of many curiosities, that they not only touched them, they ate them. Unicorns' horns, mummified flesh, fossils, even prehistoric stone axes, might be ground up and ingested as potent medicine (Murray 1904: 40, 50, 73; see also Arnold 2003; Brown 1677).

The veneration that even minor museum artifacts could receive if invested with awe-inspiring associations was nicely satirized in an eighteenth-century poem by Edward Young. Young depicts Hans Sloane, whose collection formed the basis of the British Museum, impressing visitors with "a sacred pin, that touched the ruff that touched Queen Bess's chin" (cited in De Beer 1953: 125). The supposed sacrality of Queen Bess's pin must be understood within a cultural context in which the touch of a divinely ordained monarch, or of something that had been touched by a monarch, could have transformative effects. In fact, in the early eighteenth century the velvet lining of Henry VIII's suit of armor, kept in the collection of the Tower of London, was stuck full of pins that were given away to visitors as fertility charms (Uffenbach 1934: 41; see also Altick 1978: 88).

Even if no wonder-working effects were expected, coming into close contact with royalty exercised a powerful attraction for collection visitors. When Samuel Pepys toured Westminster Abbey in 1669, he was allowed to touch the corpse of

Queen Katherine, wife of Henry V, which was kept in a chest. "I had the upper part of her body in my hands. And I did kiss her mouth, reflecting upon it that I did kiss a Queen and that this was my birthday." (1976: IX, 457). It was obviously a meaningful moment for Pepys.

The museum collection as a whole was permeated with religious and mythological significance. Uniting all manner of objects from far and wide, it was often conceptualized as a microcosm, a little world in which the precious things gathered together were preserved from the chaos of the external world. The seventeenth-century Tradescant collection of curiosities, which would become part of the founding collection of the Ashmolean Museum, was called the Ark—the reference being to Noah's Ark that preserved the world in miniature during the biblical flood. The Tradescant collection was also described as "a world of wonders in one closet shut" (M. Allan 1964). Who would wish to enter such a world of wonders and not touch anything? Through asserting one's physical dominion over this little world, one symbolically became its ruler, and, by extension, master of all of those distant realms represented through their captive artifacts (see N. Thomas 1991).

The tactile interaction that museum visitors had with artifacts they also desired to have with art works. There was no perceived reason to stop touching just because one had turned from the perusal of an urn to that of a statue. Whether out of aesthetic sensibility, sensuous desire, or simple curiosity, seventeenth- and eighteenth-century gallery-goers routinely touched works of art (see Haskell and Penny 1981: 163, 235; Stewart 1999: 29–30; Hall 1999: 80–103).

Museum curators were not always pleased with the tactile practices of their visitors, just as hosts were not always happy to have guests handling their precious collectibles. However, the assumed importance of touch to the collection experience, along with contemporary norms of social etiquette, made its complete suppression difficult. (Unable to ask a visitor not to touch the valuable antiquities in his gallery without giving offense, the great seventeenth-century ecclesiastic and politician Cardinal Mazarin limited himself to reminding him that "these pieces break when they fall" [Chantelou 1985: 185].)

It is also true that, while not unconcerned about the preservation of their collections, early curators did not make conservation a high priority. For one thing, it was not usually considered necessary to maintain artifacts and art works in their original condition. Thus, for example, a head broken off from one ancient sculpture might be joined to the headless torso of another to form a new, historically inauthentic (but to the contemporary mind more aesthetically pleasing) whole. Paintings, similarly, might be cropped to fit frames or wall space, or altered to suit current tastes. For another thing, housed as they often were in damp conditions, museum collections were subject to processes of decay and dissolution. This was particularly true of biological specimens such as Egyptian mummies and stuffed dodos, but it also occurred with paintings and sculptures. The combination of these factors made early collections seem more fluid and organic in nature than the carefully preserved artifacts of the modern museum and this may have contributed to the presumption of their touchability.

The primary concern that early curators seem to have had with regard to touch was not with rough handling, but with visitors being light fingered. For this reason the Ashmolean kept its doors closed during tours in its early years and admitted only one group of visitors at a time. The eighteenth-century underkeeper cited above for being hesitant to allow a visitor to handle the collection (or at least the smaller pieces kept in drawers) was motivated by a concern over possible losses rather than potential damage. And, as he describes it, the loss of an antique gem did indeed occur:

> When we came to the Drawer of Antiques, she seem'd to be particularly enamour'd of them, and beg'd me to suffer her to have some of them in her hand, that she might inspect them more narrowly. She sat down at the Cabinet. Miss Arnold stood on one side of her, the Gentleman on the other at the Window in which the Chinese ivory Ball stands; now whilst I was engaged in handing the Curiosities to him, and in answering his Questions concerning them, (which were not a few) it was very easy for her to convey any of them into her Pocket, because you know my Back was then toward her. After she had left the Museum I went immediately to adjust the Drawers in which many Things had been displaced by her, but could not find the Gem. (Ovenell 1986: 147–48)

In this case the missing gem was later returned, but incidents such as this must have constituted a potent incentive to custodians to keep their collections hands-off. That they did not indicates that the use of touch in collection settings was strongly fortified by contemporary cultural ideologies and practices.

Given the established place of touch in early museums, its elimination in modern museums can by no means be regarded as a natural step in museological evolution. It is, rather, the result of a multiplicity of factors, some related specifically to the development of the museum (see Candlin 2010: ch. 3), others pertaining to broader cultural trends that will be discussed in the following chapters. The ousting of touch from the museum did not happen all at once. In the early nineteenth century Robert Southey noted that "seeing by the sense of touch" was commonplace in collection settings (1808: 124). Even in 1827 the regulations of the Ashmolean Museum still allowed visitors to handle artifacts with the custodian's consent (Ovenell 1986: 197). However, in 1844 the popular writer on art, Anna Jameson, could look back on the tactile practices she witnessed during her early gallery-going days with relief that they were over: "We can all remember the loiterers and loungers . . . [who] strutted about . . ., talking, flirting, peeping, and prying; lifting up the covers of chairs to examine the furniture; touching the ornaments—and even the pictures!" (1844: 34–35). In the late eighteenth century the elegant Sophie von La Roche had felt no sense of impropriety in fingering the exhibits in a museum. Anna Jameson's account indicates that by the mid-nineteenth century—at least in middle-class London— such behavior was seen to be a sign of vulgarity. Touch in the museum had become inappropriate and unnecessary.

If the educated elite in the nineteenth century increasingly accepted that museum exhibits were not for the handling, it would nonetheless take considerable time for the general public to learn to keep its hands off the art. In 1860 the director of the South Kensington Museum (today the Victoria and Albert Museum) noted of the "great multitudes" who visited the museum: "We have great difficulty in preventing them expressing the emotions they feel in looking at a picture, they will touch it, they say 'Look at the expression,' and the consequence is that they scrape off a little bit of the pigment. . . . We all know that though the public is generally becoming very well behaved, and is well behaved, still they very much want to touch things" (cited in Altick 1978: 501).

For the taboo on touch in the modern museum to be effective and accepted, visitors had to internalize a number of notions. First, that they must behave deferentially toward the exhibits on display. Second, that to touch museum pieces was disrespectful and damaging. Third, that touch had no cognitive or aesthetic uses and thus was of no value in the museum, where only cognitive and aesthetic benefits were to be sought.

The highly deferential model of behavior that became the standard in late nineteenth-century museums reflected not only a perceived need to impose order on heterogeneous museum visitors, but also a change in attitude toward museum holdings. In the 1800s the masterpieces and treasures of museums came increasingly to be regarded as inviolable (Hudson 1975: 52). Within the pseudo-sacred space of their museum-temples, artifacts were symbolically positioned outside of ordinary time and space, and thus removed from ordinary human interaction.

The increased reverence for museum pieces in the nineteenth century also led to intensified programs of conservation and to heightened concerns about the potential damage to collections caused by handling—particularly since ever-greater numbers of people were visiting museums. Even without being handled by visitors, many deteriorating artifacts required much effort on the part of specialists to remain in their seemingly timeless state. In this context, it seemed sacrilegious to allow the ideally eternal nature of museum pieces to be compromised by the presumptuous touch of a passing visitor's hand.

Museum patrons were assisted in their attempts to keep their hands to themselves by techniques of museum display that discouraged and reduced the perceived need to touch. Larger exhibits were protected by railings, smaller objects were ensconced within cases. Modern museums aimed to ensure visual accessibility by being well-lit and displaying their artifacts behind clear glass. At the same time, placing artifacts out of reach reduced the risk of theft and allowed visitors to see the collection at their leisure, rather than be marshaled through by a vigilant curator.

The popular link between looking and touching, however, was a difficult one to sever. One tactic employed to counter this tendency was to convince people that, instead of "seeing by the sense of touch," they could "touch with the sense of sight." Thus in the late nineteenth century Charles Dickens Jr. reported of the Picture Gallery of the Bodleian Library in Oxford that "on one of the walls is the following humorous admonition: 'Touch what you like with the eyes, but do not see with the fingers'" (1880: 153). Through admonitions such as this, along with the practices described above, the sensing body was gradually taught to direct itself exclusively through the faculty of vision in the modern museum.

CHAPTER SEVEN

The Modern Touch

PETRARCH'S VISION

On April 26, 1336, Petrarch climbed Mont Ventoux in Provence to see the view. It might not seem that noteworthy an event to a modern mind but it was one of those moments that marked the beginning of the end for the medieval way of understanding the world. Petrarch, who has often been called "the first modern man," knew he was doing something novel. He wrote afterwards that he was the first person since antiquity to climb a mountain purely for the sake of the panorama that awaited at the summit. "My only motive was the wish to see what so great an elevation had to offer," he declared with a sense of his great originality (1898: 308).

The climb had been prompted by an account in Livy's *History of Rome* in which Philip of Macedon is said to have seen two seas from the summit of Mount Haemus in Thessaly. It surprised Petrarch that commentators on this event were content to consider the possibility of such a view without endeavoring to see for themselves. This incited him to do what others had failed to do, but at a point closer to home. Hence by gazing out from the summit of Mont Ventoux, Petrarch demonstrated his own visual mastery of the world. Perhaps for Petrarch, who was among the first to think of the medieval period as an age of darkness, his visionary expedition was a step toward the age of pure radiance he looked forward to in a more enlightened future (Mommsen 2002: 234).

Although Petrarch credited himself with keen vision, he was at first dazed by "the unaccustomed quality of the air and the effect of the great sweep of view spread out before me" at the summit. Almost like a blind man learning to see, Petrarch slowly distinguished the vast landscape below him, struck by the ability of sight to present clearly to his eyes places that it would take days of exertion to reach physically: "I could see with the utmost clearness, off to the right, the mountains of the region about Lyons, and to the left the bay of Marseilles and the waters that lash the shores of Aigues Mortes, altho' all these places were so distant that it would require a journey of several days to reach them. Under our very eyes flowed the Rhone" (1898: 59, 313, 316).

Petrarch was still medieval-minded enough to turn his thoughts from the view before his eyes to a consideration of the spiritual significance of his climb. With a copy of Saint Augustine's *Confessions* to guide his thoughts, he sternly reproached the vanity of his ascent, proclaiming, "How earnestly should we strive, not to stand on mountain-tops, but to trample beneath us those appetites which spring from earthly impulses" (1898: 319; see further Quillen 1998: ch. 3). Self-discipline was of more value than worldly dominance. Nonetheless, he had had his moment of visual epiphany and the world had opened up before his eyes.

On the way up Mont Ventoux Petrarch and his younger brother met a shepherd who had also once climbed the mountain: "We found an old shepherd in one of the mountain dales, who tried, at great length, to dissuade us from the ascent, saying that some fifty years before he had, in the same ardour of youth, reached the summit, but had gotten for his pains nothing except fatigue and regret, and clothes and body torn by the rocks and briars" (1898: 310). The shepherd said nothing, notably, about the glorious view from the top. Indeed he might have made the ascent blindfolded for all the visual impact it seems to have made on him. What he recalls are the intimate muscular and tactile experiences of the climb. This emphasis on the tactile could be found in the name of the mountain itself, which signified "windy" (308). The contrast, perhaps by design on Petrarch's part, is thus striking between the sweeping view attained by the visionary poet and the aches and scratches that impressed themselves on the body and memory of the humble shepherd. When Petrarch ascended Mont Ventoux he seemed to have at least temporarily left the old tactile mentality, signified by the shepherd, behind. For a moment he was the first modern man with the first modern sensorium.

THE DECLINE OF SACRED TOUCH

The sense of touch first fell from grace in the Garden of Eden when Adam and Eve took hold of the forbidden fruit after being expressly warned by God that it was hands-off. The second fall of the sense of touch—which was less of a fall than a gradual displacement from social centrality—began in the later Middle Ages. It was at this time that practices of visual contemplation increased in importance, preparing the way for the more eye-minded culture of modernity (see Denery 2005).

The growing desire of the public to see the consecrated host—the body of Christ—is an important indication of this cultural shift toward prioritizing visual experience. The practice of the elevation of the host during Mass instituted at this time responded to and fostered this desire. In some churches where the rood screen might block the view of the host, "elevation squints" or peep holes were made so that communicants would not be denied their moment of visual fulfillment. In larger towns dedicated host-watchers would go from church to church seeking to catch as many glimpses as possible of the elevation of the host in one day. This was not mere religious sightseeing: viewing the consecrated host was widely believed to confer considerable benefits, including protection against fire, hunger, and disease.

The new feast of Corpus Christi, instituted in the thirteenth century, fed the popular desire to see "the body of Christ" by displaying the host during processions and within churches. Such practices emphasized the importance of visualizing the Divine rather than entering into direct contact with it. This sensory and ritual shift would make some churchmen distinctly uneasy. The Eucharist was "instituted as food, not as an item of display," Nicolas of Cusa scolded in the fifteenth century (Kieckhefer 1987: 98). However, in contrast to the numerous times in which believers would see the Eucharist, the times when they actually consumed it might well be few and far between (Muir 2005: 171, Biernoff 2002: 140–44).

Not only the host, but also relics, became the subject of increased visual attention during this period. Relics were taken out of ground-level tombs and placed in ornate elevated shrines. Shrines were still touched by pilgrims but they also had an important new visual role as objects of a reverential gaze (Binski 1996: 78). The significance of such elevations of hosts and relics did not lie solely in their enhanced visuality. The elevated position and the corresponding raising of the eyes were in themselves significant, suggesting the high authority of the Church and the upward movement of the soul toward God. The particular importance they gave to seeing, however, was reflected in another development in religious practice: the shift from touching saintly relics to viewing saintly images.

From the thirteenth century on, images of saints began to proliferate and to provide a focus for private devotions. Correspondingly, "an increasing number of miracles began to happen without direct contact with relics, mediated instead by an image of the saint in question or by a vision or prayer" (Park 1998: 74). While sacred images were quite likely to be touched as well as viewed by devotees, direct contact with a relic was no longer seen as absolutely necessary (Vauchez 1997: 444–53). This change in attitude indicates a transition from a more concrete to a more diffuse understanding of the nature of spirituality. The idea of saints' bodies containing a holy essence that must be touched for an effective transfer of sacred power to occur was gradually being supplanted by a notion of saintly virtue being accessible anywhere, through intangible as well as tangible means.

The Church had its own reasons for promoting a less tactile form of Christianity. One of these was to ensure that God and his saints not be treated with too much familiarity by believers. The elevations of hosts and relics and the substitution of sacred images for sacred bodies not only gave a new prominence to sight, but also created a sense of distance between the worshipped and the worshipper. Not infrequently, as we have seen, attempts were made in the Middle Ages to control the power of the sacred through direct physical domination. By replacing tactile proximity with visual distance the Church sought to put an end to such rough handling. For similar reasons the old practice of humiliating relics was outlawed in the thirteenth century. The Church was seeking to move away from "the close reciprocal relationships between men and saints which had belonged to an earlier sort of Christianity, one in which both men and saints could honour or humiliate, reward or punish each other" (Geary 1983: 138). And for this purpose it was increasingly important to keep believers at arm's length.

The terrible plagues and famines of the Middle Ages also played a role in reducing the religious importance of touch. These catastrophes left many disaffected with traditional religious forms that seemed unable to provide the necessary aid in times of desperate need. This disaffection helped open the door to reformulations of Christian practice and belief that were often less concrete and tangible in nature.

Experience of quick and deadly contagion during the Black Death furthermore made people fearful of close contact with their fellows and contributed to a shrinking sacred touch. The bodies of plague victims had been "anti-relics," radiating disease instead of holy vitality and serving as objects of tactile avoidance rather than tactile desire. This fear of contagion may be one of the reasons why in the later Middle Ages it became the custom in many places for church-goers to kiss a tablet with a devotional image during the service instead of kissing each other.

One also finds growing doubt in the late Middle Ages over the authenticity of the relics pilgrims traveled from far and wide to touch. If a supposed relic turned out to have come from the body of an ordinary mortal and not that of a saint, a pilgrim could hardly hope to gain any special benefits from touching it. While an inauthentic relic was basically useless, however, a visual image of a saint was not required to be true-to-life to serve as an efficacious mediator between the human and the Divine. This gave images a definite advantage over remains.

Suspicions that certain so-called relics might be inauthentic circulated throughout the Middle Ages (most notably voiced by the Benedictine Guibert of Nogent). Such suspicions, however, became increasingly widespread from the fourteenth

century on as a new attitude of worldly skepticism—perhaps one of the consequences of the Black Death—began to take hold of society. Thus in *The Canterbury
Tales,* the Pardoner is said to carry spurious relics, including the shoulder bone
of a sheep belonging to a "holy Jew," which he offers to let pilgrims kiss for a
price. In *The Decameron* Friar Cipolla returns from a trip to Jerusalem with such
manifestly absurd relics as a feather from the Angel Gabriel along with "a small
phial containing some of the sound from the bells of Solomon's temple" (Marshall
2006: 132).

In the following centuries such skepticism would only increase. When the
sixteenth-century Franciscan François du Moulin visited the shrine of Mary Magdalene and was shown her skull with the supposed imprint of Jesus's fingers he
noted that, while monks called the relic "*Noli me tangere,*" "Do not touch me" (in
reference to Jesus's injunction to Mary Magdalene), he called it "*Noli me credere*"—
"Do not believe me" (Boyle 1998: 122). Taking Chaucer's spoof of false relics
one step further, the sixteenth-century playwright John Heywood had his own
Pardoner say:

> And another holy relic here may ye see:
> The great toe of the Holy Trinity;
> And whosoever once doth it in his mouth take,
> He shall never be diseased with the toothache . . .
>
> Here is another relic eke, a precious one,
> Of All-Hallows the blessed jaw bone,
> Which relic without any fail
> Against poison chiefly doth prevail;
> For whomsoever it toucheth without doubt,
> All manner venom shall issue out. (1905: 7)

Heywood satirizes the notion that the intangible Divine can reside in such unim-
pressive objects as bones. Even the most intimate and devout touch, the reader
is led to conclude, is completely useless with such obviously inauthentic and
impotent relics.

With the Protestant Reformation not only the authenticity of many relics,
but the efficacy of *any* relics was put into question. Touching relics was simply
not the way to get "in touch" with God in this new form of Christianity. As we
saw in the previous chapter, sacred images were also considered suspect by the
more puritanical Reformers. However, the sense of sight could at least be put
to an appropriate religious use in the study of Scripture. Not only the touching
of relics, but the sense of touch in general, seemed to have no genuine religious
purpose for the Protestants. Martin Luther dismissed the value of traditional
gestures of piety by saying that "it is of no great importance whether one stands,

kneels, or falls to the ground because these are bodily practices, neither prohibited nor commanded as necessary" (cited by Kolofsky 2005: 27). These words came from a man who, while a Catholic monk, had climbed Pilate's stairs in Rome on his knees, kissing each step on the way in the hope of releasing his grandfather's soul from purgatory (Bainton 1977: 32).

Along with the downplaying of traditional external signs of piety, the Protestants' emphasis on interiorized forms of spirituality signaled a transition from corporate practices of worship to individual modes of devotion. Thus it was not only the old tactile bonds linking believers to the Divine that were loosened by the new religious approach, but also those that linked believers with each other. The traditional Christian greeting of the kiss of peace, notably, was declared by some Reformers to be an inappropriate and meaningless ritual. Peace, it was said, could only come from God and could not be made by humans among themselves by physical acts, such as kissing. Besides, kissing smacked of immorality. "Among us kisses are not considered proper," pronounced Luther (Kolofsky 2005: 26). The days in which kisses and hand-holdings served to join people together in binding relationships of vassalage and friendship were evidently coming to an end.

While Catholic thinkers did not go so far as the Protestant Reformers in dismissing the religious value of touch, they were not immune to the new theological trends. The reform-minded Catholic theologian Erasmus wrote, "Should anyone produce a tunic worn by Christ, we would hurry to the ends of the earth to kiss it. But you might assemble his entire wardrobe, and it would contain nothing that Christ did not express more explicitly and truly in the evangelic books" (28). This statement, which may seem sensible enough from a modern point of view, has no trace of the old notion that direct contact with a sacred object can establish a vital connection with the Divine in a way that merely reading "dead" letters cannot. Far from it, one is rather said to be better off reading than touching: the former rewards you with clear significance the latter only offers imprecise sensations. It is an indication of the increasing privileging of linguistic texts and utterances over tactile signs—and perhaps also of a growing rift between self and body, thought and action. To revere no longer automatically meant to fall on one's knees.

As religion became more intangible, however, it also lost something of its perceived reality. When the new science began demanding empirical proofs for metaphysical claims, religion often seemed to come up empty-handed. The materialist eighteenth-century philosopher Denis Diderot made his own point about this by reporting (or inventing) the deathbed speech of the prominent blind mathematician Nicholas Saunderson. When encouraged by an attending minister to turn his thoughts to God, Saunderson reputedly said, "If you want me to believe in God, you have to make me touch him" (Diderot 1749: 72–73). This, however, was something that the modern world was no longer able to do.

NEW SENSORY WORLDS

Many developments contributed to the changing relevance of the tactile sense, and indeed of all the senses in the late Middle Ages and Renaissance. The old feudal relationships and contracts, so often sealed with a kiss and a handclasp, were becoming obsolete as more complex and impersonal social networks evolved in the growing urban centers. The dissolving of traditional social ties allowed a greater sense of individuality to develop. The rise in importance of the individual should not be overestimated, for most people during this period still derived much of their identity from social networks (see Martin 2006). The Renaissance individual was by no means a modern individual. However, the social transformation that would result in the notion of the person as an autonomous agent was under way.

As we saw in chapter 1, the safeguarding of the specific interests that proliferated in this new social context required precise written documents rather than generalized customary gestures. This, together with the increase in literacy among the educated classes, promoted noncontact modes of interacting and acquiring knowledge. Eventually these modes would penetrate even into the intimacy of the family. In Renaissance France, and perhaps elsewhere as well, new "taboos against expressions of affection and strong emotions by males led to the creation of a literary genre: letters and wills in which fathers expressed their love for their sons and sons for their fathers." Such letters might be exchanged "even when father and son lived under the same roof" (Ranum 1989: 259).

A technological development that would come to have a profound effect on Western sensory life was the invention of printing with movable type in the fifteenth century. The consequent mass production of books would make vision an evermore important sensory avenue for acquiring knowledge about the world. As regards religion, literate Europeans would come to rely less on such nonverbal means of accessing the Divine as touching relics and smelling odors of sanctity, and more on reading the Word of God.

In the emergence of the individual, as in other areas, Petrarch, with his interest in self-analysis and self-depiction, was a forerunner of what was to come (He was, indeed, groundbreaking in his inclusion of a brief, physical description of himself in his autobiographical account [1898: 60].) This shift from the social body to the personal body was marked in art by the development of a domestic portraiture in which ordinary middle-class individuals and their families might leave a visual record of their appearance and their lives. Like mirrors, which would soon come into fashion (having become much clearer due to technical improvements), such portraits encouraged individuals to see themselves from the outside as visual objects, rather than to kinesthetically and tactually feel their integration with the world from the inside. The growing use of eyeglasses during the Renaissance enabled more people to clearly perceive such visualizations of the self, as well as giving an added value to the sense of sight in general.

As the notion of the person changed from being based on corporate membership to being grounded in individual identity, the public rites and spaces that had bound people together grew less important while the construction of private personae and spaces became more important. One religious expression of this was an increased stress on the importance of individual as opposed to communal confession. Eventually, in the seventeenth century, the Catholic Church would largely replace rites of communal confession and absolution with the practice of each penitent privately confessing sins to a single priest and receiving an individual absolution. This development had its counterpart in Protestant churches in their emphasis on personal piety (LeBrun 1989:75–86).

The new concern with interior sensibilities made the rough and tumble physical interaction that had previously characterized much of social life more problematic. One's neighbor might not wish to be poked in the ribs, to participate in a spontaneous wrestling match, or to share a piece of bread—and a consideration of such feelings had become a requirement of good manners. Changes in standards of polite behavior occurred first in the upper classes in urban centers and only penetrated rural areas and lower-class culture much later. These changes contributed to a widening gap between the upper and lower classes from the late Middle Ages on. One area in which this growing class separation can be traced is in the displacement of servants within upper-class homes. In the Middle Ages personal servants often slept in their masters' bedrooms. From there they moved into rooms close to their masters' bedrooms and finally to servants' quarters in a separate part of the house, often the attic.

Not all the social and sensory changes that occurred during the Renaissance and after were generated solely by internal stimuli. The discovery of new lands overseas and the consequent influx of new peoples, products, foods, and ideas opened up the minds of Europeans to alternative ways of living in and making sense of the world. Even if the tales of other lands were often largely fictitious, they served as a stimulus to the imagination. It is partly for this reason, and partly because of the ongoing social upheaval, that stories about fantasy worlds, from Thomas More's *Utopia* to Margaret Cavendish's *New Blazing World,* were popular during this period. (Cavendish's work is particularly interesting for its reversal of sensory and gender values and its jab at the optical obsessions of natural philosophers [Classen 1998: 103–4].) The general notion was that people might invent new worlds and new customs for themselves and not simply be content with what had been handed down by their forefathers.

It is in the eighteenth century that we clearly see the emergence of modern sensory values. As Norbert Elias brought out in *The Civilizing Process,* rules of etiquette are an excellent source of information on how individual behavior is shaped on the most intimate level to conform to contemporary social and sensory standards. Eighteenth-century etiquette shows that the use of touch was increasingly restricted. The 1774 edition of Lasalle's popular guide to good manners, *Les règles de la benevolence et de la civilité*, included the following advice: "Children like to touch clothes and other things that please them with their hands. This urge must be corrected, and they must be taught to touch all they see only with their eyes" (cited in Elias 1994: 166). Significantly, these lines are absent from the first edition of Lasalle's work published in 1728. Between those two editions, evidently, changes had occurred that made it necessary to denounce touch as an inappropriate means for finding out about and deriving pleasure from the surrounding environment. As we saw in the previous chapter in the case of the museum, the aesthetic and cognitive roles of touch were transferred to the visual faculty in the new age.

Table manners provide another instance of this sensory shift. While in premodernity dining was a time for communal intimacy, with people eating off shared plates and drinking from a single cup, by the eighteenth century, even when eating in company, dining had become an individual affair. "Each person had his or her own plate, glass, knife, spoon, fork, napkin, and bread. Whatever was taken from common serving dishes, sauceboats, or saltcellars had to be served with utensils and placed on one's own plate before being transferred to the mouth. Thus, every diner was surrounded by an invisible cage" (Flandrin 1989: 266). Every diner was also by this time sitting on an individual chair, a practice that had become common in the seventeenth century, rather than squeezed in between other bodies on a bench. If in the Middle Ages shared touch at the table had created an impression of a common social body, here we see the reverse happening, an isolated touch emphasizing that each diner is a separate individual.

Another indication of a waning importance of touch was the growing use of gloves as a customary article of apparel. Beginning in the late Middle Ages, gloves became highly popular among the middle and upper classes, serving as a mark of elegance, cleanliness, delicacy, and social status. What might seem like a relatively insignificant item of clothing, hardly worthy of historical attention, served to mark the social transition from a hands-on to a hands-off way of life. By the time gloves came off in the twentieth century, the transition was complete: the skin had been liberated but modern mores had placed much of the world out of hand's reach.

It was not only what one did with one's body but also how one talked about one's body that required strict regulation according to the polite manners of modernity. A letter writer to the eighteenth-century journal *The Spectator* complained of the "young Creature" with whom he had the "misfortune" to be in love that she was constantly committing faults against "Delicacy": "After our Return from a Walk the other Day, she threw her self into an Elbow Chair, and professed before a large Company, that she was all over in a *Sweat*. She told me this Afternoon that her Stomach *Aked* and was complaining yesterday at Dinner of something that stuck in her *teeth*" (R. Porter 2005: 119, emphasis in original). Perhaps this letter was an editorial fiction meant to instruct *The Spectator's* readers in decorum. Whether written by a disapproving lover or by a moralizing editor, however, the message was clear. Just as one must take care not to physically transgress the corporeal boundaries of others, one must avoid inappropriate verbal presentations of one's body.

One phenomenon in particular made a potent contribution to the development of the new hands-off culture. This was the deadly plague outbreaks that ravaged many European cities during the second half of the seventeenth century. If the Black Death in the Middle Ages had made many people somewhat wary of touch, the epidemics of the seventeenth century seemed to spawn a mass "tactophobia." Daniel Defoe's fictional *Journal of the Plague Year*, based on accounts of the Great Plague of London in 1665, contains many powerful passages concerning people's changing attitudes to touch during the outbreak. In one section Defoe describes how the plague affected methods of marketing: "When any one bought a joint of meat in the Market, they would not take it off the butcher's hand, but take it off the hooks themselves. On the other hand, the butcher would not touch the money, but have it put into a pot full of vinegar which he kept for that purpose. The buyers always carried small money to make up any sum, that they take no small change" (1830: 114). In another passage Defoe tells of the horror of a family who suddenly realized they had a plague victim for a visitor:

> It is easy to believe, though not to describe the consternation they were all in; the women and the man's daughters, which were but little girls, were frighted almost to death, and got up, one running out at one door, and one at another . . . [and] locked themselves into their chambers, and screamed out the window for help, as if they had been frighted out of their wits. The master, more composed than they, though both frighted and provoked, was going to lay hands on the [plague carrier], and throw him down stairs, being in a passion; but then considering a little the condition of the man, and the danger of touching him, horror seized his mind, and he stood still like one astonished. (223)

These and numerous other references in the *Journal* indicate that the notion of touch as contaminating had made a deep impression on the popular psyche.

Accounts of the tactile climate of the time in Italy are provided by seventeenth-century Milanese chronicler Giuseppe Ripamonti. According to Ripamonti, any conspicuous touching in public places was viewed with suspicion during the plague that struck Milan in the 1630s. In one case an old man was severely beaten by locals who feared he was spreading plague poison when he wiped a pew with his handkerchief. In another case three Frenchmen were taken to prison for touching the marble in a church (Manzoni 1834: 377–78). The negative associations of touch brought about by the terrifying experience of the plague must have done much to hasten the ousting of this sense from social centrality in the seventeenth and eighteenth centuries.

During the same period, significantly, new visual worlds were opening up and catching the popular imagination. Scientific advances in the field of optics led to the development of microscopes, which made minute inner worlds available to the eye, and telescopes, which brought the outer worlds of space into view. Within medicine, the practice of anatomical dissection exposed the mysterious interior of the body.

The ocular discoveries and obsessions of the seventeenth and eighteenth centuries had a strong influence on the development of a new culture of sight. Already during the Renaissance, the artistic interest in naturalism and linear perspective had emphasized the realism of visual images and turned canvasses into seeming windows on the world. During the Enlightenment attention was focused on the organization of space. To give an example of the changing spatial aesthetic, in the Middle Ages the ideal garden was a walled enclosure redolent with the scents of flowers and resonant with the singing of birds and the splashing of water. In the eighteenth century the ideal garden became a park, a seemingly infinite expanse of space that celebrated picturesque views rather than intimate experiences of inhaling herbal aromas or sitting on turf benches. Unbounded by walls, the eye was free to roam, seeking the distant horizon: "Sight wanders up and down without Confinement, and is fed with an infinite variety of images" (cited in Classen 1993: 26).

This shift in spatial aesthetics paralleled the changing understanding of the nature of the universe. As previously noted, the Middle Ages and the Renaissance imagined the universe to be concentric, an enclosed space of enclosed spaces animated and ordered by a network of multisensory powers. The Enlightenment swept away these old sensory cobwebs, broke down the enclosing walls of the cosmos, and opened up the universe to infinite space.

While the heavens opened up during the Enlightenment, however, Hell started to close in. From being a spatial realm, an infernal landscape populated by devils and sinners, Hell was beginning to be perceived as an interior state. The modern individual required a personal Hell. Already in Milton's "Paradise Lost" there is a suggestion of this transition when Satan proclaims "Which way I flie is Hell; my self am Hell" (4: 75). This Hell of the self was less one of external tortures than of inner pangs of remorse: the hair shirt internalized. While plenty of preachers still cowed their followers with images of a very tangible Hell, the notion of a physical site of corporeal punishments was beginning to seem crude to enlightened theologians. The way was being prepared for the twentieth-century notion of Hell as a painful state of consciousness (Wheeler 1990: 179).

THE PERSISTENCE OF TOUCH

As charges of treason and tyranny were being brought against Charles I of England in 1649 the king rapped the prosecutor on the shoulder with his cane and called on him to stop. The cane broke, its gold tip falling to the floor. The prosecutor, heedless of the king's command, carried on. No one bent a knee to offer the golden head of the cane back to the sovereign and Charles was obliged to stoop and pick it up himself.

This seemingly trivial incident was taken to foretell the king's own imminent beheading. However, it also seems to signify another loss, that of the power of the royal touch. The king—whose hand had grasped the scepter symbolizing his rule by divine right—had been stripped of tactile importance. By even submitting a monarch to trial the Parliamentarians showed their disregard for the monarchy as a divinely ordained institution. The power to rule could not reside within the body of any one individual, they claimed, it was an impersonal public office. As for the supposed healing powers of the royal touch, the Republican Henry Marten wryly suggested that sufferers from scrofula might touch the Great Seal of Parliament instead (K. Thomas 2005: 357). The execution of the king brought the point home: his body was no different from the body of any other "enemy of the people." As Milton's work of political propaganda *Eikonoklastes*—"Iconbreaker"—made clear, the king was but one more spurious icon to be smashed.

In retrospect the failed touch of Charles I appears emblematic of a whole cultural turn away from the notion of tactile authority. A little over a decade after Charles's execution, however, a change of fortune restored the monarchy in England and the son of the executed monarch became King Charles II. John Cooke, the Republican who had ignored the tactile summons of the former king, was hanged, drawn and quartered in the traditional fashion for traitors, together with a number of others accused of the crime of regicide. Even the corpses of Republican leaders who were already dead were exhumed and hung for having spilt the precious blood of a divinely ordained monarch.

The new king did his part to restore faith in personal, hands-on authority by ritually touching thousands of people a year. (One sufferer from a "fungus nose," went so far as to rub his nose in the royal hand, which, it was said, "disturbed the king but cured him" [Molloy 1885: 72].) Not only the scrofulous or ill wished to touch the king, but, it seemed, almost the whole populace. "The eagerness of men, women, and children to see his majesty, and kisse his hands was so great," Evelyn wrote, "that he had scarce leisure to eat for some days" (64). This enthusiastic king-touching was accompanied by a general indulgence in tactile pleasures, as freedom from puritanical mores created a carnavalesque atmosphere of sensual exuberance. The power of touch, it seemed, was as great as ever.

There can be no straightforward narrative of a decline in the cultural impor-tance of touch accompanied by a corresponding rise in the cultural importance of sight. The sensory patterns of history are too complex. Older tactile practices long coexisted with the new emphasis on more disembodied modes of social interaction and religious practice. Indeed, the centuries in which religion was increasingly becoming a visual, or audiovisual practice, were also the centuries in which mystics were ardently clasping Christ to their breasts in visionary ecstasies. Some of the reasons for this heightening of mystical tactility in the later Middle Ages have been discussed earlier. It may also be the case that the rise in impor-tance of individualism created a sense of alienation from both God and society and that consequently there was a greater perceived need to be enveloped in a cosmic embrace. Were these elaborations of mystical touch the last gasp, or rather, grasp of a dying tactile culture? Or were they evidence of a generally heightened sensibility that would give rise to a new social emphasis on interior sentiments?

So people still wanted to touch, and would continue avidly touching. The desire for and interest in tactile experience not only existed at a popular level among the uncultured masses. Early modern scholarship also grappled with the nature of physical sensation. One instance of this was the attempt by seventeenth-century natural philosophers to find physiological reasons for the seeming power of certain persons—whether kings, saints, or folk healers—to heal by touch. In his study of the Irish tactile healer Valentine Greatrakes, Robert Boyle attempted to answer such questions as whether Greatrakes could cure persons of any religion, how many touches were necessary for a cure, and whether his glove could cure as well as his hand. Boyle even had a dab at therapeutic "stroking" himself. Greatrakes was convinced his extraordinary ability came directly from God to confound atheists and provide a Protestant counterpart to the tactile miracles claimed by the Catholics. While not ready to leave God entirely out of the picture, Boyle and others determined that Greatrakes's touch worked by some form of "sanative contagion"—the obverse of the pathogenic contagion of the plague-sufferer's touch. (Greatrakes was also said to emit a "herbous Aromatick Scent," another traditional sign of healing virtue and corrective for the presumed infectious odors of disease.) The Royal Society's secretary, Henry Oldenburg, dutifully summed up these and related researches into "the effects of touch and friction" in the Society's Philosophical Transactions (Schaffer 1998: 83–120).

Another, more novel, form of tactile healing would be introduced in the eighteenth century by German physician Franz Anton Mesmer, who postulated the existence of a universal magnetic fluid that could be felt but not seen. In his treatments of patients Mesmer attempted to channel this magnetism through his hands for healing purposes. A commission appointed to investigate his work concluded, however, that what Memser manipulated was not any physical fluid, but rather his patients' imaginations.

As the above examples suggest, along with the persistence of old notions of tactile transmission, new interests in the science of sensation had developed. A number of prominent thinkers, notably John Locke in England and Étienne Bonnot de Condillac in France, gave a major boost to the empirical study of sensation by making the senses the starting point for human knowledge. In the discussion of how we learn through our senses, the phenomenon of blindness was of particular interest, for the blind evidently acquired a great deal of their knowledge through one sense—touch. One question that exercised Enlightenment minds and became known as "Molyneux's Question" after the philosopher who raised it, concerned whether a man born blind and suddenly endowed with vision would be able to distinguish a sphere and a cube by sight after having previously known them solely through touch. Could the different senses communicate with each other? To what extent did sensation correspond to external reality and to what extent was it subjective? (see Riskin 2002: ch. 2).

The intellectual ferment over these issues led Denis Diderot to examine the matter for himself by interviewing and gathering material about the blind. He published his conclusions in his "Letter on the Blind for the Use of Those Who See" (which, because of its religious skepticism, landed him in prison). Diderot was greatly impressed by the hands-on knowledge and practical approach to life exhibited by the blind. When he asked one blind man whether he would like to see, the man replied that he would rather have very long arms, "for it seems to me that my hands could better inform me about what's happening on the Moon than your eyes or your telescopes" (1749: 18). As a result of his sensory studies, Diderot claimed that "of all the senses the eye [is] the most superficial. . . . [and] touch the most profound and the most philosophical" (1751: 23). With this controversial statement Diderot was probably trying to emphasize the value of empirical investigation; however, it certainly turned the customary hierarchy of sensory values on its head.

One major consequence of the eighteenth-century interest in the capacities of the blind was the founding of schools for the blind that made use of tactile, as well as oral, modes of education, and the eventual creation in the nineteenth century of a tactile form of writing (Braille) and tactile manual languages. Although it went against the grain of Western sensory ideology (and although the fact would be virtually ignored by linguists), it would be proven possible for the sense of touch to serve as a medium of thought and language.

The philosophy of sensation spawned an interest in the physiology of sensation. The workings of the nervous system, in particular, received an enormous amount of attention from the late seventeenth century on. Traditionalists held that nervous impulses were conveyed by "animal spirits" (vital fluids) traveling through hollow nerves. Isaac Newton, however, argued influentially that sensations were rather carried by vibrations along solid nerves to the sensorium—the cerebral terminus of nerve endings that coordinated all the incoming messages.

Just as medieval thinkers had tried to harmonize their understanding of the workings of nature with their understanding of the workings of God, so did many of the modern philosophers. Newton attempted to bring the deity into his theory of the nervous system by making God the "boundless uniform Sensorium," a being who instantly senses everything without any need of sense organs and within which all the little sensoria of humans are contained (Leshem 2003: ch. 6). In another analogy, Newton characterized God as the Great Clockmaker, who created the machinery of the cosmos and then set it in motion. (Did God need to "wind up" his creation every now and then, philosophers wondered, or did he put it in a state of perpetual motion and then just watch it from afar?) The notion of God as Clockmaker, suggested already prior to Newton, would have a long afterlife in the intelligent design argument for God's existence.

One tactile phenomenon related to the investigations into the nervous system that was of particular interest to eighteenth-century physicians was the experience of pain. Within the more secular culture of the Enlightenment it was possible to separate suffering from religious considerations and investigate pain solely as a physiological reaction. Physicians eagerly compiled pain typologies: gravative pains, pulsating pains, itching pains, burning pains, and so on (Rey 1998: 94–95). Even nonphysicians became interested in the matter, with one patient who had a leg amputated questioning his physician as to "why the pain that he felt the moment his skin was cut was completely different from the awful feeling that he experienced when his flesh was sectioned . . . and why this last feeling differed again from that which took place when his marrow was sectioned" (98).

The scientific investigations on the interesting subjects of nerves and pain would be seized on by the literary community of the eighteenth century and given a thrilling new cultural life. The literary interest in suffering manifested itself most infamously in the writings of the Marquis de Sade, who devoted almost as much space to the physiology and philosophy of pain as he did to the relationship between pleasure and cruelty. More than just perverse pleasure-seekers, Sade's protagonists were experimental philosophers who, flush with current medical theories, conducted their experiments on what seemed the most sensitive of organisms: the human body. The materialist Sade held that both physiological sensations and moral sentiments were no more than differing excitations of the nervous system, and that, as excitations of the nervous system went, physical pain was the liveliest and therefore most interesting. With the human soul out of the picture, the only remaining source for meaning appeared to be the body. Although endlessly pressed for responses, however, the Sadean body, being just a nervous system, could never provide any ultimate answers (Vila 1998; Classen 2005a: 112; Morris 2005).

Unlike Sade, most writers of the period were more interested in exploring the emotional effects of nervous sensibility than its physiological reactions (although the two were seen as intertwined). It was accepted that refined individuals would have acutely sensitive nerves that would react not only to physical stimuli but also to emotional influences. The heroes and heroines of eighteenth-century novels are full of talk about nerves, fibers, and heartstrings that have been weakened or broken by shock or sorrow and that need to be braced (see Barker-Benfield 1992; Van Sant 1993). By contrast, Frances Burney's villain in *The Wanderer* had a "constitutional hardness of nerve that cannot feel." In the state of heightened sensibility promoted by the novelists even a slight touch could have profound effects. Essayist Mary Hays wrote of "the thousand tremulous touches that convulse the tender and impassioned heart" (cited in Barker-Benfield 1992: 17, 20). Coarse physical sensations were therefore to be eschewed by the man, or woman, of feeling in favor of exquisitely delicate perceptions. "The greatest happiness that love can give," Stendhal would write in 1822, "is the first hand-pressure of the woman one loves" (1927: 105).

Despite the fascination with physical and sentimental suffering in the eighteenth century, this was a period that increasingly appreciated bodily comfort. Modern Westerners, in fact, generally did not strive after keen pleasures. Instead they desired comfortable housing with comfortable furniture and comfortable ambient temperature. A good deal of the increased comfort of life in modernity can be attributed to advances in technology, such as the more efficient chimneys and windows discussed in chapter 1. However, the institution and diffusion of many basic modern comforts were as much the result of cultural developments as they were of technical inventions. For instance, the inhabitants of England endured the rain for many centuries before they finally took to using umbrellas in the late 1700s. Previously, a cloak or a hat had seemed to provide sufficient protection against the rain. The first daring users of umbrellas were often ridiculed: to hold a little canopy over one's head to ward off a few drops of rain seemed to indicate an excessive delicacy (Crowley 2005: 85–86). For umbrellas to become popular, there first had to occur a cultural refinement of the sense of touch, indeed, precisely that fostered by the cult of sensibility.

In premodernity the importance of clothing, furniture, and housing lay largely in their role as markers of social status. Displaying an elegant set of tableware was therefore more desirable than having an armchair by the fire. A chair, in fact, was traditionally a symbol of authority, not a site for relaxation. Even "noblemen sat on benches, stools and chests, shivering in their furs, their eyes smarting as the fire in the great hall swirled smoke up to the roof" (Gloag 1934: 5). The word "comfort" at that time referred more to spiritual consolation than to physical ease (Morris 2005: 82).

In the eighteenth century the home became not just a place in which to take shelter or a place with which to impress others, but a place in which to live *comfortably*. Hence in Daniel Defoe's novel of 1719, Robinson Crusoe, stranded on his desert isle, sets right to work making himself comfortable, building a home and furniture, sewing clothing, and even constructing his own umbrella (Crowley 2005: 85; see further Barker-Benfield 1992: xx–xxiv). At the other end of the scale of home comforts from Crusoe's meager furnishings were the alluring images of soft delights presented—and criticized—by James Thomson in "The Castle of Indolence":

> Soft quilts on quilts, on carpets carpets spread,
> And couches stretch around in seemly band:
> And endless pillows rise to prop the head,
> So that each spacious room was one full-swelling bed. (1876: 227)

One finds in all this a definite move away from the medieval emphasis on hard bones to a modern emphasis on soft flesh.

The new concern with comfort aroused fears that, once the poor (who were still far from being comfortable) got wind of it, they would no longer be content with their austere lifestyle. The justification, if one were needed for a trend whose time had come, was that the increase in domestic comforts would prove a stimulus to manufacturing that would eventually place the new products within every one's reach and improve standards of living across classes. Indeed one might expect the working classes to work harder than ever to attain the ideal of a comfortable home. Another point in favor of the new culture of comfort was that greater comfort often went hand in hand with greater efficiency. A fireplace that radiated heat more effectively also made more efficient use of fuel. Smoother roads not only made for a more comfortable ride but also for more efficient transportation. Labor-saving devices made life easier and freed up time for other activities (Crowley 2005).

By the late eighteenth century, the comforts of life had come to be seen as necessities. Their gratification would be said by Thomas Malthus to constitute "the principal happiness of the larger half of mankind" and an indispensable require-

ment for "the more refined enjoyments of the other half" (67). When, across the
sea, Thomas Jefferson famously declared the pursuit of happiness to be a human
right, it was arguably the acquisition of just those material comforts that he had
in mind. After all, Jefferson himself, with his enthusiasm for the latest conveniences—smokeless fireplaces and swivel chairs—"epitomized the new obsession with comfort" (89).

In the Middle Ages the pursuit of happiness, which would only have been
considered a worthwhile quest if it concerned spiritual joy, might well have
been thought to involve a considerable amount of physical discomfort and pain.
The most joyful saints were often great sufferers. In modernity happiness and
comfort seemed to go together. Pain still had moral and social uses. Locke, for
instance, advised regularly inflicting pain on children ("with good will and kindness") to strengthen their resolve (1779: 168–69). Within conventional religious
circles saintly suffering still carried ideological weight. However, suffering was
now often considered an unnecessary interference in human welfare that should
be avoided or alleviated whenever possible. Except among the military-minded,
who preserved a strong notion of the value of corporeal discipline, deliberately
inflicting pain on oneself in the fashion of the Middle Ages began to seem perverse. Why sleep on the cold, hard ground when a comfortable bed could be had?

Furthermore, with the assistance of opium, eighteenth-century physicians
could suppress both physical and mental suffering more effectively than ever before. Indeed any one who bought a bottle of Sydenham's Laudanum or any of the
other opium-based medicines on the market, could dose themselves out of their
troubles—a custom that would culminate in Thomas De Quincey's nineteenth-
century paean to opium, *Confessions of an Opium Eater* (Porter and Porter 1989:
150–51). It would take a long time for the dangers of opium addiction to be
fully recognized and, by then, other analgesics to soothe the pangs of the afflicted
would be discovered.

Ironically, the pampering and protection the sense of touch received in the
new culture of comfort may have contributed to a certain deadening of tactile
sensation. The most comfortable furnishings, the most agreeable ambient temperature, the smoothest rides, are, after all, ones that adapt themselves to one's
body and thus can hardly be felt. This neutralizing of touch may have worked to
promote visual culture. People who are not distracted by the cold biting at their
hands, by rain trickling down their backs, by hunger gnawing at their bellies, by
smoke burning their eyes or, on top of all that, by hair shirts pricking their skin,
can pay more attention to what they see around them. The decrease in tactile
stimuli in modernity may well have created a desire for a corresponding increase
in visual excitement, for the infinite variety of images said to be required by the
newly liberated sense of sight.

THE FINISHING TOUCH

On October 7, 1793, in the city of Reims, the *sainte ampoule,* the vial that contained the wondrously aromatic balm used to anoint French kings and said to have been brought by a dove from heaven to Saint Remi in the fifth century, was publicly smashed by an official of the new Republican assembly. The tiny bottle, kept in a red velvet bag in Saint Remi's shrine, had previously been brought out only for coronation ceremonies, when the archbishop of Reims touched the new king's head, chest, back, shoulders, elbows, and hands with a minute amount of chrism drawn out from the vessel with a golden needle. The ceremonial touch of this heavenly balm was believed not only to confer kingship on the anointed monarch, but also the miraculous power to heal scrofula. Now with one revolutionary gesture the *sainte ampoule* shattered into fragments on the empty pedestal of a toppled statue of Louis XV—a fitting site for this dramatic repudiation of the divine right of monarchs. The official responsible, Philippe Rühl, proclaimed afterwards that the broken vial had emitted an "offensive exhalation," like that of an old medicine bottle. What could be less wondrous? What could be less worthy of a reverential touch?

After the monarchy was (temporarily) restored under constitutional safeguards in the nineteenth century there was an attempt to revive the old customs. Broken fragments of the shattered *sainte ampoule* were miraculously located and a holy vial was recreated for the coronation of Charles X in 1825. So there would be no question of the validity of his kingship, Charles was anxious that everything be done according to the age-old rites. However, the time for such things had passed. It did not happen all at once, with the beheading of any one king or the destruction of any one relic, but the impact of cumulative blows meant that a whole worldview had been broken. Volney wrote during the preparations for the great event that he was surprised to see "a constitutional government proposing a sham medieval specatacle in nineteenth-century Europe" (Le Goff 1998: 243). It was good theater but hard to take seriously. When Charles prostrated himself during the ceremony, many in the audience felt uncomfortable: "What is royal about the posture of a monarch who lies flat on his stomach?" (245). Prostration was evidently not an acceptable posture in modernity.

The coronation took place on May 29. On May 31 King Charles proceeded with a grand cortege to the Hospital of Saint Marcoul to demonstrate the healing powers invested in him by the touch of the holy chrism during his coronation. The rite of the royal touch had been discontinued in both France and England in the eighteenth century and there were few left who had a personal recollection of the practice. In contrast to the thousands of patients who had lined up to be healed by earlier monarchs only some 120 scrofulous patients had been rounded up for Charles X's tactile benediction. In this last enactment of the royal touch, Charles made a cross with his finger on the forehead of each, saying "May God heal thee! The King touches thee! The king then allowed the nuns who had charge of the hospital to kiss his hand, whereupon they reportedly wept for joy (Imbert de Saint-Amand 2006: 76).

While the pious nuns may have been moved by the ceremony, others remained skeptical. If even Mesmer, with his seemingly scientific basis for a curative touch, had been discredited, what modern mind was likely to believe in the healing power of a royal touch? "There is no longer any hand virtuous enough to cure scrofula," Chateaubriand commented dourly (Le Goff 1998: 245). (Nor, he added, was there any *sainte ampoule* miraculous enough to prevent an anointed king from losing his head.) An English commentator wrote more brusquely that, whereas not long ago few would have doubted the miraculous nature of the holy ampulla, "any one would now be accounted an idiot that should believe it" ("Holy Oil" 1831: 234).

When Philippe Rühl smashed the *sainte ampoule* in 1793 it was still considered an object of great authority. Such smashing would hardly have been necessary in the nineteenth century when the above comments were written. Rather than a medium of divine power, the vial, like the tactile practices that surrounded it, had come to be considered a museum piece.

CHAPTER EIGHT

Sensations of a New Age

THE DRILL

Ironically, or perhaps necessarily, the very period when the fully fledged modern individual was finally appearing on the scene was also the period when modern institutions—schools, prisons, armies, workhouses—that promoted the social conformity of individuals were reshaping society. These limited the possibilities for the new emphasis on individuality to result in idiosyncratic behavior or a personal touch. The individual, disconnected from the corporate sensibilities of the past, was trained by the new institutions to conform to a standardized model: to wear a uniform (a term that first came into use in the eighteenth century) and to be uniform. The body, liberated from the harsh disciplinary techniques of the Middle Ages, was subjected to the exacting regimen of the drill.

Modern military drill was a product of the late sixteenth century when it was implemented in the Dutch army by Maurice of Nassau, Prince of Orange. Its effectiveness as a military tactic, along with its embodiment of modern efficiency, led to the drill being adopted across Europe in the seventeenth century. The drill consisted of training soldiers in basic maneuvers until they were able to perform them at command and in unison. No longer could each soldier develop his own corporeal techniques. No longer was bodily movement a matter of fluid action. To enable a methodical, synchronized performance each military maneuver was broken down into its component movements and postures. Drill manuals identified forty-eight postures to be performed with muskets and thirty-six postures to be used with pikes. The dancing movements said to characterize predrill warriors were banished. In the drill all body parts not involved in a particular maneuver were required to keep rigidly still. Officers were told to rehearse their men in the prescribed postures "over and over againe" until they could perform the motions like clockwork (Lawrence 2009: 133–34).

It is no coincidence that the spread of the military drill occurred at the start of the age of machinery. The drill was based on a precise analysis of corporeal action. This same form of analysis—breaking down a required action into a series of constituent elements and eliminating all inessential movements—was necessary to the construction of machines. The result, in both cases, was movement that was precise, regular, and inflexible. The movements of the drill "stood in exact opposition [to] the sturdy peasant behaviour with its loose, flexible, but occasionally wild movements" (Kleinschmidt 1995: 164).

The drill was not the only technique used to remake the bodies of soldiers. Almost every bodily action had to be relearned in the army. According to one eighteenth-century general, the new recruit had to be taught "how to put on his shoes, dress himself . . . be diligent, bold, adroit and agile, and to rid himself utterly of his base peasant habits and vices, like pulling faces, or scratching himself when he talks" (cited by Duffy 1987: 97). Before they could even begin to march in military fashion, many recruits had to learn to tell their left foot from their right. It was an immense task and there could be no letting up on the pressure to conform. Even after hours of exhausting drill practice, soldiers needed to ensure that all their belongings were in perfect order before they could rest. (In the eighteenth century this might include sleeping with curlers in order to manifest the correct military hairstyle.) The slightest deviation from the routine would be met with harsh reprisals, beatings, and kicks, or "the ordeal of walking the gauntlet under a hail of blows with sticks" (98). The body itself needed to be broken down to be remade.

Given that in the seventeenth and eighteenth centuries European states began to maintain large standing armies, this military reconstruction of the body became an increasingly common experience. In those countries that later enforced compulsory service, it would be a virtually universal male experience. Even those people who did not personally experience the drill would likely have seen it being practiced and have felt its influence.

The military emphasis on the conformity of individuals to a set pattern of norms expresses a major concern of the early machine makers: the need for uniform components. The individuality of each piece in premodern craftwork was detrimental to the construction of machines, which relied on precise standardization. Until the mid-nineteenth century, however, "nearly every part of a machine had to be made and finished . . . by mere manual labour, that is, [by] the dexterity of the hand of the workman" (cited by Musson and Robinson 1969: 474–75). The problem of inaccuracy produced by manual workmanship could not be solved until the process of machine making was itself mechanized by the invention of machine-making tools in the nineteenth century. In the meantime the drill expressed the quest for standardization in a social form.

The mechanical nature of the drill was recognized even in the eighteenth century, when commentators remarked on the machinelike movements of the soldiers: "A regiment of Prussian infantry is like a machine directed by the officers" (Duffy 1987: 99). Although drill practices would be reformed to render their motions more fluid, the ultimate goal remained to reconstruct the bodies of individual soldiers so that, when called upon, they would act in a coordinated fashion with precision and unquestioning obedience.

The drill not only made people act like machines, it also prepared them to work with machines in the developing factory system. In the factory it was necessary for the rhythms of the body to be attuned to the rhythms of the machinery. Everyone was required to work in concert with the mechanical pace, performing the same meticulous actions over and over again. For good reason many of the best factory workers would be said to be former soldiers, trained in the drill (Chadwick 1861: 136).

The drill's emphasis on regularity, efficiency, and diligence stimulated and paralleled a wider social obsession with these traits. Nowhere was this better manifested than in mid-eighteenth-century Prussia, where the king himself—a renowned military leader who had mastered the drill before the age of five—set the example for his subjects. In the strict daily regimen adhered to by Frederick the Great, the monarch was "up at daybreak, at his desk until late afternoon . . . riding, reading, or writing in the evening, and then retiring regularly at ten o'clock." "Every day I become more economical with time," he wrote with satisfaction, "I begrudge its loss and hold myself accountable for its use" (cited in Van Horn Melton 1988: 111). What kind of a royal life was that, one might wonder? What peasant would choose to live in that fashion if he were king? However, diligence had been decreed to be the new happiness. "For my subjects to be happy," Frederick declared in 1775, "they must grow accustomed to diligence and hard work" (132).

Frederick the Great's creed of industriousness was not unique to Prussia. It had become commonplace throughout Europe that industriousness was the key to prosperity, respectability, and a competitive economy. There could be no industrial revolution without industrious workers. Of course, national differences existed regarding conceptions of industriousness and the development of industrialization. For example, while the state promoted the expansion of industry in Germany and France, in England it remained in private hands (Henderson, 2006: 10). However, just as the practice of the drill spread across Europe's armies, so did the perception of the necessity of a disciplined workforce to deal with the demands of modern industry.

According to Frederick the Great, the first step to take toward the creation of such a workforce was to put the children to work (Kleinschmidt 1995: 164). "While children of eight or nine years can do little in the way of strenuous work, they can at least spin during the evenings when they have nothing better to do. In this way they could earn their keep and grow into disciplined laborers, instead of growing accustomed from youth onwards to a life of idleness" (cited by Van Horn Melton 1988: 132).

Children would, in fact, come to form a large percentage of factory workers. Although children had worked before the Industrial Revolution, many essential tasks had been beyond their skills and strength. However, just as the implementation of the drill in the military minimized the importance of the exceptionally strong and skillful warrior, the use of machinery in factories minimized the need for muscle power and technical competence. The actions required by factory work were usually neither very physically demanding nor complex. Just as very young children could master the drill, so could they master the movements required by factory work. They could, moreover, be paid much less than adults.

Though it might not be physically demanding, factory work nonetheless took its toll on the body, as Engels would describe in *The Condition of the Working Class in England* (1844). Operatives, frequently children, worked fourteen-hour days in conditions that were often highly detrimental to their health and that put them at risk of being injured by the machines they tended. As in the army, strict discipline was enforced within the workshop and infractions of regulations were harshly punished.

This mechanization of industry met with considerable opposition from those members of the working classes who felt that their traditional employments were being taken from their hands by the new machines. In the early nineteenth century handloom weavers known as Luddites set fire to textile mills throughout England. During the agricultural uprisings of the 1830s impoverished farm workers smashed the threshing machines that had rendered the traditional practice of flailing obsolete. Such acts of sabotage led to machine-breaking becoming a crime punishable by death in England. However, while workers protested their loss of income and social status in the new industrial order, they apparently had little objection to the new forms of corporeal discipline. Many of the fledgling workers' groups were themselves enthusiastic practitioners of military drill (Blackburn 2000: 446).

The language and methods of the drill would eventually penetrate even religious institutions. The organization that went furthest in this regard was the Salvation Army, founded in 1865. The Salvation Army ordered itself along military lines, referred to its members as soldiers, held its meetings in "barracks," marched in procession along city streets, and called kneeling in prayer "knee-drill."

Influenced by the Salvation Army, evangelical members of the Church of England started their own "Church Army." In a typical group: "Sundays began with a drill at seven, then an open-air meeting at ten, which was followed by a church service at eleven. There was an afternoon Bible class and in the evening a band and army banner would lead a procession to the mission hall" (Hylson-Smith 1988: 180). These military methods seemed to many to be the most effective and engaging way to inculcate a sense of Christian discipline in the dissolute masses.

THE SCHOOL, THE PRISON, AND THE MUSEUM

With the institution of compulsory education in the nineteenth century (the eighteenth century in Prussia), the drill extended its reach. One trait the school had in common with the army and the factory (to which it was sometimes attached) was a strict adherence to a standardized set of bodily practices. Indeed, for many of its proponents, the greatest advantage of schooling the working classes was not the mental attainments that would result from it—for these might lead students to desire further education rather than a future in manual labor—but rather the inculcation of values of "duty, self-restraint, order, punctuality, and obedience." Public schooling was intended to provide a moral and physical training more than a cultivation of the intellect (Van Horn Melton 1988: 119).

The lower orders had a widespread reputation for laziness. It was stated time and again that laborers only worked as hard as was necessary to make a bare living. In his social satire *Fable of the Bees*, Bernard de Mandeville declared that "Every Body knows that there is a vast number of Journey-Men Weavers, Tailors, Clothworkers, and twenty other Handicrafts; who, if by four Days Labour in a Week can maintain themselves, will hardly be persuaded to work the fifth; and that there are Thousands of labouring Men of all sorts, who will, tho' they can hardly subsist, put themselves to fifty Inconveniences, disoblige their Masters, pinch their Bellies, and run in Debt, to make Holidays" (cited by S. Jordan 2003: 37). Such on-and-off habits of work would not do in the factory, which required continuous, repetitive effort, day after day. "This penchant for idleness," complained one German administrator, "is certainly a cause for the failure of many manufacturing establishments" (Van Horn Melton 1988: 127). Writing in support of the factory system, Andrew Ure pronounced, "When the handicraftsman exchanges hard work with fluctuating employment and pay, for continuous labour of a lighter kind with steady wages [in a factory], he must necessarily renounce his old prerogative of stopping when he pleases, because he would thereby throw the whole establishment into disorder" (1967: 279).

Another impediment to the making of a good industrial worker according to contemporary views was an engrained willfulness. The worker, like the peasant of old, was regarded as a wild animal requiring breaking in. "No animal, whether on four legs or two, however he may enjoy life, can be of any use in the workshop of man until he has been sufficiently divested of that portion of his natural inheritance commonly called 'a will of his own'" (cited in Chadwick 1861: 148).

Schools aimed to correct these two social problems of modernity—indolence and idiosyncracity—by transforming idle, willful children into disciplined, obedient pupils. Within the school, time was rigidly ordered by bells, and space by lines of bodies and benches. There was to be no stepping out of line, no failure to perform the correct action at the correct time, no attempt to deviate from established routine in even minor ways. As in the army and in the factory, any infraction of the regulations met with a stern reprimand if not with physical punishment. As in the army and the factory, maximum attention, compliance, and efficiency were demanded.

To forward the creation of a disciplined student body many schools introduced the drill or related exercises as an addition to the routine. In a mid-nineteenth-century report on the subject, English social reformer Edwin Chadwick concluded that the practice of drill in schools not only constituted useful training for future soldiers, but also contributed "to the eficiency and productive value of pupils as labourers . . . in afterlife" (144).

In Chadwick's report the drill was described as a kind of breaking in of boys, similar to that of horses, which would render them useful to society. "Now as . . . a couple of little straps have proved sufficient . . . to divest . . . horses, mules, and donkeys of that portion of their self-will which had made them useless, instead of useful, to man, so must a system of military drill in our public and private schools incline the rising generation of boys 'to do their duty in that station of life unto which it shall please God to call them'" (149). Significantly, the drill here is stated to be good for all classes, for in modernity everyone alike must become a cog in the social machinery—the king must be as industrious as the laborer. However, the underlying assumption was that the laboring classes should not aspire to move beyond the lowly station of life to which they had been called by God.

Schools were by no means so universal or so uniform in the nineteenth century as to be able to entirely succeed in the creation of a standardized, drilled, modern body. Idiosyncratic traits and postures still flourished among people of all classes. Thus we hear in the autobiography of the Victorian writer Augustus Hare of a literary man who let his dog sit on his head, an Oxford student who held his hands in front of him like a kangaroo, and a cleric who turned over the pages of his book of service with his nose (1896: 265, 441, 468). Such eccentricities of manner (which bring to mind the corporeal vagaries criticized so many centuries earlier by the author of *The Cloud of Unknowing*) were deemed less harmful when exhibited by the ruling classes than by the laboring classes, however. Uncouth behavior among the latter always carried a suggestion of rebelliousness.

The perception of the working classes as prone by nature to disorder and violence made them appear particularly in need of social constraints. Continuing a typology inherited from Aristotle and carried over into the modern discourse on race (see M. Smith 2006), working-class bodies were seen as harder and coarser than middle- and upper-class bodies. (In his examination of such sensory markers of class, George Orwell would recount that "the very texture" of servants' skins seemed "mysteriously different" [1937: 159].) Coarse bodies, bodies prone to violence, bodies called to serve, naturally seemed to require more thorough disciplinary tactics. While military drill formed a minor part of the physical training in elite schools therefore, it tended to dominate the provision made for physical education in the state schools (Atkinson 1978: 94).

When, usually to cut costs, the practice of drill was discontinued in a school, anarchy was said to result. The superintendent of one English school where drill was discontinued wrote, "The immediate effect of the discontinuance of the drill was to make the school quite another place. I am sure that within six months we lost about two hundred pounds, in the extra wear and tear of clothing, torn and damaged in mischievous acts and wild plays, in the breakage of utensils from mischief, and the damage done to the different buildings. . . . A spirit of insubordination prevailed amongst the boys during the whole of the time of the cessation of the drill . . . and I was under the disagreeable necessity of reverting to corporal punishment" (cited by Chadwick 1861: 52) It was a frightening omen of the kind of social mayhem that could erupt from an insufficiently disciplined population. What was remarked of soldiers in the eighteenth century, "if they are not employed doing something useful, they will get up to something bad" (cited by Duffy 1987: 100), was held to be true of the public in general. The fear of such mayhem, after the recent bloody scenes of the French Revolution and the various workers' uprisings, was strong in the nineteenth century.

The suggestion that the drill provided a preferable alternative to corporal punishment is significant for it reflects a wider social tendency to see routine physical discipline as generally preferable to extraordinary physical punishment as a means for achieving social control. As Michel Foucault (1979) detailed in *Discipline and Punish,* this general transition is best seen in the nineteenth-century preference for penal servitude over corporal punishment as the modern way of dealing with criminal deviance. Along with the abandonment of dramatic criminal penalties such as burning or drawing and quartering, the use of torture to obtain confessions was also largely phased out during the modern period (Langbein 2004).

The notion of penal servitude—along with occasional hangings conducted out of public sight within the prison yard—grated less on the refined sensibilities of the modern man and woman than that of bloody beatings and gruesome public executions. Anthony Trollope wrote in the introduction to his 1859 novel, *The Bertrams:* "This is undoubtedly the age of humanity. . . . A man who beats his wife is shocking to us, and a colonel who cannot manage his soldiers without having them beaten is nearly equally so. We are not very fond of hanging; and some of us go so far as to recoil under any circumstances from taking the blood of life. . . . If disgrace be absolutely necessary, let it be inflicted; but not the bodily pain" (1859: 5). Aside from their presumed inhumanity, bloody punishments were, in any case, perceived as too emotionally stirring, too likely to arouse the very passions responsible for deviance. Sentences must rather manifest the unemotional and irrefutable power of reason. And for a society that wished to emphasize the social value and redemptive power of work, a sentence of hard labor made more sense than one of mutilation or flogging. Prisons became "houses of correction" and not just places of confinement in which the accused awaited trial and punishment.

To maintain discipline and instruct inmates in new corporeal habits the nineteenth-century prison employed its own forms of the drill. One of the most notorious and widespread in England was the shot drill. As one contemporary observer described it: "The exercise consists is passing the shot [cannon balls], composing the pyramids at one end of the line, down the entire length of the ranks, one after another, until they have all been handed along the file of men, and piled into similar pyramids at the other end of the line; and when that is done, the operation is reversed and the cannon balls passed back again" (Mayhew and Binny 1862: 308–9). The practical uselessness of this drill indicates that its sole function was to reform the bodies of the inmates and to ensure they carried out their sentence of hard labor. Similar useless prison exercises included turning a crank connected to nothing but a counterweight and walking a treadmill that moved nothing but a large fan. "The prisoners style the occupation 'grinding the wind,' and that is really the only denomination applicable to it—the sole object of the labour of some 150 men employed for eight hours a day, being simply to put in motion a big fan, or regulator as it is called, which, impinging on the air as it revolves, serves to add to the severity of the work by increasing the resistance" (303). While ostensibly working on nothing (i.e., "grinding the wind"), the prisoners, in fact, worked on themselves.

Not all the hard labor of the prisoners was unproductive. One common task imposed on prisoners was that of picking oakum. This involved painstakingly separating out strands of tarry old pieces of rope until they were "fine as silk" and could be reused (Priestly 1985: 121). Another common prison chore was doing the laundry, which had the particular appeal for the prison authorities of symbolizing the cleansing of moral filth. In the case of female prisoners, while they might also be required to walk the treadmill, the preference was to assign them tasks that formed part of traditional women's work, such as laundry, sewing, and baking (A. Smith 1962).

The repetitive, tedious, and physically wearing nature of the work undertaken in the prison closely resembled that of the factory, as a comparison of narratives by Victorian prisoners and factory workers clearly shows (i.e., Priestly 1985; Simmons 2007). Superficially the work routine in both cases evoked the endless rounds of genuflections and prayers of the medieval ascetics, or, at the other end of the scale of virtue, the painful and repetitious penalties of the inhabitants of Dante's *Inferno*. Rather than serving as a sign of spiritual heroism or damnation, however, it now suggested the tireless, unfeeling operations of a machine.

Foucault justly emphasized the importance of visual surveillance in the modern prison, and his observations in this regard have been taken up and extended by a multitude of scholars (1979: 149–50). Yet visual surveillance was not the central function of the prison. It was there to ensure corporeal discipline: the prisoners had to be watched to see that they behaved. Inmates were generally in prison for what were deemed to be aberrant uses of their sense of touch—breaking and entering, theft, assault, prostitution—and it was the sense of touch in particular that the prison addressed. New, regulated, tactile mechanisms had to be learned to replace the old deviant impulses, and this required a vigorous reprogramming involving sensory deprivation, hard labor, and painful chastisement. Even in the darkness, prisoners were required to labor, tidying their cells before sunrise when the simplest task became "like working on a Chinese puzzle" (Priestly 1985: 84), groping their way like newborns to an orderly world by touch alone. This tactile training was not only intended to shape external actions but also to serve as a guide and an occasion for the remaking of interior dispositions. While spending hours picking apart oakum till it was fine as silk, prisoners were also supposed to be picking apart their hardened consciences until they too were fine as silk and ready to be refashioned according to the dictates of contemporary morality (Classen 2005a: 262).

One of the striking characteristics of the modern prison was the segregation of prisoners. Whereas in the prisons of the eighteenth century and earlier, prisoners had often been herded together, in the modern prison they were kept in individual cells. Victorian prisons, furthermore, commonly enforced a rule of silence, forbidding prisoners to speak to each other. A visitor describing a room of prisoners picking oakum wrote, "The building was full of men, and as silent as if it merely contained so many automata, for the only sound heard was like . . . the ticking of clockwork—something resembling that heard in a Dutch clockmaker's shop, where hundreds of time-pieces are going together" (Mayhew and Binny

1862: 311). Even in the labor of the treadmill each prisoner walked in a separate compartment. In some prisons this rule of separation was extended to church services, where prisoners sat in separate cubicles. When working together on a bench inmates were likewise required to remain out of touch with each other: "'You're getting too close together on that back seat,' . . . a warder shouts to some men . . . who instantly separate, till they are spaced out like tumblers on a shelf" (312). At the same time as the monotonous uniformity of the prison routine ensured conformity to a set standard, these practices of segregation emphasized the solitary condition and individual responsibility of each prisoner, indeed, of each person in contemporary society.

There was resistance. Prisoners secretly communicated by knocking on walls, talking through pipes, and scratching messages on tin plates. The need for friendly contact led many prisoners to make pets out of the animal life of the prison: rats, mice, even spiders. One prisoner recorded tolerating the bites of mosquitoes for the sake of their enlivening presence in the cell (Priestley 1985: 47). The memoirs of prisoners themselves indicate that outward conformity was no assurance of inward compliance. While intensive, the disciplinary regimen of the prison did not always achieve its intended results, and a rebellious spirit was often nurtured within a prisoner's apparently docile body.

One last modern institution concerned with social discipline to be considered here is the museum. We saw in a preceding chapter how museum tactics changed in the nineteenth century and artifacts were placed out of hands' reach. One key factor in this transition had to do with the public nature of the modern museum. When collections were private, owners could limit access to those they deemed worthy of the privilege. When they became public, controlling the quality of the visitors became more difficult. Thus, during his visit to the Ashmolean in 1710, Uffenbach reported finding the museum full of country folk in town for market day. This was evidently not the class of visitors he expected to find there and their undisciplined behavior met with his disapproval: "The people imperiously handle everything . . . even the women are allowed up here for sixpence; they run here and there, grabbing at everything and taking no rebuff from the [caretakers]" (Uffenbach 1928: 24, 31).

Uffenbach was not opposed to museum pieces being touched, as he also handled exhibits during his visit to the Ashmolean. He was opposed to the uncultured touch of the masses (and especially, it seems, of women). The rowdy behavior of certain members of the working classes was not only considered to disrupt the order of the museum and endanger its artifacts, it was also understood to constitute an affront to the social order. Many of the museum objects subject to such apparent contempt were traditional trappings of power and authority. As museums were more frequented by the general public in the nineteenth century there was consequently not only an increased risk of damage, but also an increased sense that the vulgar touch of the common visitor profaned the exhibits and, implicitly, the social elite who acquired collections and supported museums.

One way of dealing with this problem of social discipline was to restrict public access to museums; various practices, such as requiring written application for admission or keeping entrance fees high, contributed to this end (see Hudson 1975: 9–17). Nevertheless, the hope of many museologists was that the museum would have a civilizing and educational effect on the general public. For this to happen, however, visitors could no longer be permitted to run around and grab everything—they must learn to control their bodies as they enlightened their minds. The formation of the modern state required that visitors to a public museum be both awed by the splendor of this emblematic state institution and impressed with a sense of its inviolability.

The perceived importance of fostering respect toward the cultural and political authority museum pieces were understood to represent was a major factor in the exclusion of touch from the museum in the mid-nineteenth century. After all, a characteristic act of revolution is the toppling of statues, as had been dramatically illustrated during the French Revolution. Louis-Sébastien Mercier described visiting a post-Revolutionary museum of toppled monuments in Paris: "I walked on tombs, I strode on mausoleums. Every rank and costume lay beneath my feet. I spared the face and bosoms of queens. Lowered from their pedestals, the grandest personages were brought down to my level; I could touch their brows, their mouths" (cited by McClelland 1994: 166–67; see also Mercier 1929: 225–29).

Perhaps because of scenes such as this, the fear that museums might be a target of public riots seemed ever-present in the minds of nineteenth-century administrators in England (see E. Miller 1974: ch. 7; Bennet 1995: ch. 2; Auerbach 1999: 38–39). No wonder one mid-nineteenth-century official wrote with satisfaction and relief of the working men visiting the National Gallery of London that one could see them "sitting, wondering and marvelling over those fine works, and having no other feeling but that of pleasure or astonishment, they have no notion of destroying them" (cited by Teather 1984: 4).

The museum, then, with its strict rules regarding bodily comportment and its guards, was not only a site of aesthetic enjoyment and intellectual stimulation, it was also itself a house of correction. However, it was not just the working classes who were subject to such correction, for everyone in industrial society would come to be expected to have a regulated body. The museum, hence, spread its regulatory net over as many citizens as possible. Although at the beginning of the nineteenth century, exceptions to the hands-off rule of the modern museum might be made for persons of quality, by the end of the century, everyone was required to conform to the rules. Indeed, the artifacts themselves, imprisoned in their cases, corrected by cleaning and restoration, silenced and isolated, were both bearers and recipients of the disciplinary regime of modernity.

THE FEEL OF THE CITY

Morning in a modern city was a very different experience from morning in a medieval city. In his poem "The Art of Walking the Streets of London," John Gay described a typical morning scene in eighteenth-century London:

> Now industry awakes her busy sons,
> Full charg'd with news the breathless hawker runs:
> Shops open, coaches roll, carts shake the ground
> And all the streets with passing cries resound. (1730: 201; see further
> Corfield, 1990)

There is no mention of church bells here or of roosters crowing. Instead we have the cries of the newspaper vendor, the bustle of shops opening, and the rumble of coaches rolling through the streets. It is not the Church or the agricultural round that calls the sleeping citizens to their duties, but industry. This would be one of the defining characteristics of the modern city. In many rural areas of Europe, the routines and rituals of life arguably still had much in common with those of the Middle Ages. However, whereas the rural experience had been central in premodernity, the immense growth of cities from the sixteenth century on meant the urban experience would dominate in modernity.

While medieval life had partaken of a communal nature, the modern city seemed rather to be a conglomeration of strangers. This was due in part to the decline in importance of the corporate activities of the Church. It was also a result of improvements in housing which meant that activities previously undertaken outdoors could now be accomplished indoors, out of contact with neighbors.

Furthermore, the new sense of personal privacy in modernity made people more reluctant to share their lives and bodies with others. Village life, where everyone knew everyone else, seemed too intrusive to many urbanites who craved the anonymity of the crowd. Conversely, if a city-dweller longed for the touch of others, the anonymity of the people one passed in the street put them out of tactile bounds. One might bump into people in the crowd but not deliberately enter into contact with them. The sensory motto of modernity was look but don't touch.

A frequently noted characteristic of the modern city was the accelerated pace of life: "All are in a hurry, running up and down, with cloudy Looks and busy Faces," one eighteenth-century traveler to Bristol noted (cited by Morgan, 1993: 9). In his novel *The Expedition of Humphry Clinker,* Tobias Smollet described the bustle of a modern city street: "Everywhere rambling, riding, rolling, rushing, jostling, mixing, bouncing, cracking, and crashing, in one vile ferment" (2008: 101; see also Sennett 1994: 18). The activity of the street mimicked the hustle of industrial production, with its emphasis on the quick and constant production of goods. It was in the eighteenth century, indeed, that vagrancy and loitering became public offenses. Everyone needed to be on the move in the modern city.

In the nineteenth century the sense of acceleration was increased by the entrance of trains into the city. Racing along at thirty miles an hour, train passengers felt as though they were being swept away in a whirlwind. As one early train traveler wrote, "Riding in an open and shaking carriage so elevated was at first somewhat startling. Dragged along backwards by the snorting engine with such rapidity, under thundering bridges, over lofty viaducts, and through long dark tunnels filled with smoke and steam! By and by, however, we became accustomed even to this" (cited by Hibbert 1975: 82). In premodernity touching the stone walls of the church had conveyed a sense of stability and of the immutable cosmic order. In modernity rushing along in a steam-powered train exemplified contemporary ideals of speed and progress.

At this time the European imagination began to shake off antiquity's hold and wrap itself in dreams of a completely new and vastly superior future. Many of the early thinkers who had helped to shape modernity, from Petrarch with his vision of a luminous age of learning to the Prince of Orange with his institution of the military drill, had looked to the ancient world for models. While antiquity would still provide a touchstone in the nineteenth century—Greece for learning, Rome for public order—there was little doubt now of the preeminence of the new.

The social and physical changes wrought by railways can hardly be overestimated—one of Thackeray's characters exclaims that "we who lived before railways . . . are like Father Noah and his family out of the Ark" (84). Whole areas of cities were demolished to make room for railway stations, engine sheds, and station hotels. The London station of Euston, for example, was built over a dairy-producing district of cow sheds. However this did not mean that local residents would no longer be provided with milk, for the train, with its milk run, could bring in fresh milk from the countryside. Indeed, by transporting goods quickly over long distances, the train allowed for and encouraged the increased separation of rural and urban activities.

The industrial feel of the modern city was, in fact, heightened by the ongoing removal of natural and rural spaces from the urban center. As cities grew, their orchards, gardens, and fields were built over with houses and workplaces. To accommodate more people on smaller areas of land, buildings grew upwards. When space within the city was unavailable urban development extended into the countryside. City dwellers, consequently, had less and less experience of country life. The only way large sectors of the population could encounter nature in the modern city was in the form of the park, an orderly space for urban recreation that reminded people that they must not go wild even in their time off.

The experience of being detached from the natural world was intensified by contact with modern machinery (Giedion 1955). One of the first and most important crafts to be mechanized, textile making, was, indeed, closely identified with the sense of touch. While in traditional iconography the spinner served as an emblem of the sense of touch, however, the same hardly seemed possible with the worker in a textile mill. The worker's touch appeared automatic, almost unfeeling, simply part of the production process. The machine, in fact, seemed to direct the hand, rather than the reverse. The very fact that the machines that powered industrialization were made of metal rather than organic materials contributed to a sense of their unresponsive, alien tactility, a sense that perhaps accorded with the feel of the modern city itself.

The use of a train for travel, the use of machines at work, all of the modern innovations that created a gap between the body and the natural world contributed to a sense of being out of touch with the Earth. Romantic souls longed to get back in touch with nature. Samuel Coleridge, among them, feared that the modern disconnection of the self from the natural world—which he linked to a repression of the sense of touch—might lead to insanity (Modiano 1978). More prosaic minds, however, thought that rather the reverse was happening: life was becoming more orderly and rational.

Yet the nineteenth-century city was far from being a place of inorganic sterility. While green spaces were in short supply, the city had a high density of both humans and animals. The increase in urban populations meant a corresponding increase in waste products. Refuse lay piled up in the streets and overflowing cesspools leaked into the surrounding ground and water supply. The hardest hit were the crowded working-class districts that often had little in the way of sanitary facilities. Nineteenth-century medical officers and sanitary reformers described scenes of overwhelming squalor in working-class tenements: "In pursuance of my duties, from time to time, I have visited many places where filth was lying scattered about the rooms, vaults, cellars, areas, and yards, so thick, and so deep, that it was hardly possible to move for it. I have also seen in such places human beings living and sleeping in rooms with filth from overflowing cesspools exuding through and running down the walls and over the floors" (Jephson 1978, 19).

Many members of the middle and upper classes had a hard time separating the poor from the filth in which they often lived. Cleaning up the urban environment, therefore, was strongly associated with cleaning up the working classes—or even cleaning them out from certain neighborhoods (see Stallybrass and White 1986: ch. 3). Not coincidentally, one of the most prominent promoters of sanitary reform in England, Edwin Chadwick, was also a proponent of military drill in state schools. The urban body, as well as the individual body, it seemed, needed discipline. An organizer of the "Columbian Guards"—youth squads dedicated to cleaning up Chicago for the World's Fair—combined the two practices by suggesting that the boys employ military tactics on dirt: "I suggested to the boys that we work out a drill with sewer spades, which, with their long narrow blades and shortened handles were not so unlike bayoneted guns . . . [and explained] that it was nobler to drill in imitation of removing disease-breeding filth than to drill in simulation of warfare" (Addams 1990: 254).

Not until regular garbage collection was instituted and underground sewers built, however, did the filth start to disappear from the city. This mechanization of waste occasioned vigorous protests and even riots by workers—cesspool cleaners, street sweepers, rag pickers—who depended on refuse for their livelihoods. However not only the filth in the streets and the stench in the air (which rose to a peak during "The Great Stink" of 1858), but also the cholera epidemic of the mid-nineteenth century had made the sanitary reform of the city and its citizens seem imperative (Classen 2005b). Victor Hugo would write of the new sewage system in Paris: "Today, the sewer is clean, cold, straight, correct. . . . The mire there comports itself with decency" (1887: 5: 96).

Another way in which the modern city was made to exemplify modern principles of order and efficiency was through the straightening and widening of its streets. It is no coincidence that Paris, the European city that went the furthest in straightening out its convoluted city core, was also a city that had been repeatedly shaken by popular revolts and riots. The way rioters could set up barricades in narrow medieval streets, the way they could hurl rocks down on soldiers from the rooftops, the way they disappeared from view in the shadows or around twisting corners, made it evident that broad, straight, and well-lit streets would greatly forward social control. A broad street would be difficult to barricade and a straight, well-lit street would provide no hiding places. Furthermore, a clear sight line also meant a clear line of fire.

The man who undertook the work of transforming Paris's center was the civic planner Baron Haussmann (who also oversaw the construction of the Parisian sewer system). In his memoirs Haussmann recalled his dislike of the twisting, narrow, odorous streets of the medieval city center. When given his chance, therefore, Haussmann, in his own words, "disembowelled" the old city and eliminated the stench of antiquated medievalism and working-class subversion that festered there. Up came the old streets of bumpy cobblestones. Flat paving stones not only smoothed the way for vehicular traffic but also facilitated the marching of troops. Down came the old houses with overhanging stories projecting so far over the street below that "persons at opposite windows could converse in whispers" (McCabe 1869: 104). Instead, expensive new houses stood aloof and set back from the street. One would have to possess a loud voice indeed to get in touch with someone living across the way in one of the new, widened city streets. It was a dramatic move toward the modern city of unknown neighbors.

The wide, straight boulevards Haussmann created in the gutted urban center of Paris offered majestic vistas terminating in monumental structures such as the Arc de Triomphe. They were places to see and to be seen, for fashion parades and military parades. There need be, it was thought, no more fear of rumblings from the city's belly. Not everyone approved of this transformation, however. According to Marx, Haussmann razed Paris "to make place for the Paris of the sightseer" (1988: 78). However, it satisfied the desire of the time not only for increased public order but also for more light and views within the city. The closeness of the medieval city no longer pleased. The Vicomte de Launay declared in 1838, "How one chokes in these dark, narrow and dank corridors that we like to call the streets of Paris. One would think that one was in a subterranean city, that's how heavy is the atmosphere, how profound is the darkness! . . . And thousands of men live, act and press against each other in these liquid shadows, like reptiles in a swamp!" (cited by Rice 2000: 9). Within the broad spaces of modern boulevards, by contrast, the sense of touch shrank while the range of sight vastly increased.

The emphasis on visibility in the modern city was indicative of the new status given to visual experience. It was not only because they had learned to control their tactile impulses, or because they had come to see themselves as aloof from their surroundings, that nineteenth-century gallery-goers accepted the sensory restrictions of the museum. It was also because touch was no longer understood to provide any important information about the world. The important thing was to *see*.

Nineteenth-century evolutionary theory would declare that attending to sights over tactile or olfactory sensations was a defining trait of the human species, which at some point in its long transition from animality had learned to take its hands and nose away from the ground and stand up and look around. Aping the evolutionists, social theorists claimed that the most evolved peoples—namely Europeans—manifested a similar interest in sight as the most evolved and rational sense. So-called primitive races—namely indigenous peoples—by contrast, were assumed to remain mired in an irrational tactile world. Any people still living in this fashion in the modern age were, in Launay's phrase, like unevolved "reptiles in a swamp." Later, Freud would psychologize this evolutionary theory of the senses by asserting that in their passage to maturity individuals progressed from a desire to mouth and feel the environment to a focus on audiovisual perception. A hands-off approach to life, hence, would come to signify not only an appropriately disciplined body, but also a civilized and mature self.

The increased visibility that modernity demanded was forwarded by improvements in lighting. By the mid-1800s inexpensive gas lighting was providing homes and streets with a never-before-seen level of illumination. Improvements in the manufacture of glass had already made for brighter interiors and allowed most of the work of the city to be undertaken behind closed doors rather than outside. Gas lighting would make it possible to extend working hours: regardless of the time of day work could go on. At the same time the visual activity of reading flourished with the improved availability of light in the after-work hours. Superior lighting not only enabled a greater practice of visual activities, it also made all activities more visible. The role of surveillance in maintaining order in public places after dark was therefore enhanced. Moreover, the increase in lighting—along with the spread of mirrors and the growing practice of having oneself photographed—heightened the consciousness of the visible body as compared to the felt body.

Both gaslight and the railway, often compared in the nineteenth century, were seen as taking away individual autonomy and obliging all to be dependent on and interconnected through a dominating industrial system: "A gas work, like a railway, must be viewed as one entire and indivisible machine; the mains in one case being analogous to the rails in the other" (cited by Schivelbusch 1995: 29). To the networks of gas mains and rails could be added the modern water and sewer systems, to which all likewise would be connected. People might finally be regarded as individuals in modernity, but they could not stray far from the public utilities that allowed them to exercise a modern lifestyle. Even without walls, the modern city contained and constrained its inhabitants.

THE ELECTRIC CREED

Near the end of the century a new source of power, one that would further increase dependence on and interconnection through industrial networks, began to transform the cityscape. This was electricity. One of the perceived advantages of electricity was that, as a clean form of energy, it promised to reduce the amount of smoke and soot in the atmosphere. These had added their own textures to modern urban life, shrouding the city and leaving its citizens, in Dickens's words, "with smarting eyes and irritated lungs . . . blinking, wheezing, and choking" (1885: 1).

Not only the utilitarian value of electric power was appreciated, therefore, but also its hygienic value. "As gas superceded candles and oil, so, in turn, will it come to be superceded by a more sanitary electric illuminant" wrote one sanitary reformer with satisfaction in 1884 (Allan 1884: 67). Another great advantage of electrical energy was that it was much less likely to cause fires than traditional sources of light and power. With electric light many institutions, including museums, which had been fearful of using gaslight due to the risk of fire, could finally keep their doors open after dark.

Compared to the ease with which one could observe one's surroundings in a street lit with electric lights, negotiating a gas-lit street seemed almost to be a matter of feeling one's way in the dark: "In the middle of the night, we emerge into the brightest daylight. Shop and street signs can be recognised clearly from across the street. We can even see the features of people's faces well from quite a distance. . . . As soon as we look away from the broad thoroughfare into one of the side streets, where a miserable dim gaslight is flickering, the eye-strain begins. Here darkness reigns supreme, or rather, a weak, reddish glow, that is hardly enough to prevent collisions in the entrances of houses" (cited by Schivelbusch 1995: 118).

Beyond the actual transformations electricity occasioned within cities, industries, and homes, was the influence it exercised on the public imagination. Already in the mid-1800s excitement about the new form of energy had penetrated the popular consciousness. This can be seen in the following lines on electricity (sandwiched in between articles on "The Profit of Raising Pork" and "A New Description of Bricks") from a farming journal of 1852.

> It has now become very well known that the electric fluid pervades all nature, and that its properties are in many respects analagous to those of light and heat. It is probably identical also with the attraction of gravitation, and some have even supposed that it is one and the same thing with the vital principle. . . . The electric fluid pervades all matter, all bodies and all space. . . . Some human beings are fuller of it than others, and possess the property of giving off sparks of electricity when in a particular state of health. (*Plough* 1852: 170)

This understanding of electricity as a vital fluid flowing through everything and every one gave it the appeal in the nineteenth century that magnetism had enjoyed in the eighteenth. (It was not until the late 1800s that electricity and magnetism would be confirmed to be different aspects of one force.)

Early enthusiasts even courted the novel experience of the electric shock: "In the old days of semi-scientific exhibitions, what a delighted and terrified circle, rapturously apprehensive, was that which used to gather, taking hands, round the 'battery' from which an electric shock was to be received" (Oliphant 1896: 135). More than just being a source of thrills—or of deadly shock—the sparking vital fluid was widely reputed to have restorative properties. Why shouldn't the human body be empowered by the force that was energizing industry, that seemed indeed to vivify the whole universe?

Nervousness, caused by the hectic pace of modern life, had been widely declared to be the malady of the age. The prominent physician George Beard asserted that "unusual exertion," had turned the contemporary nervous system into "a badly conducting circuit," or an "electric battery" without "a reserve force" (1881: 11–12). A jolt of electricity, therefore, seemed to many to be just the thing to recharge the battery of the run-down modern body and enable it to get back to work (which in the case of women meant "women's work"). Following this reasoning, physicians and entrepreneurs devised different methods of administering electrotherapy to their patients. Popular devices marketed to the public included electric belts and corsets and "Dr. Cram's Fluid Lightning," said to contain liquid electricity (Peña 2005; Nye 1992: 153).

The enthusiasm engendered by electricity and its seemingly limitless potential inspired Victorian novelist Marie Corelli to invent an electrical version of Christianity (Siebers 2006). According to Corelli's "Electric Creed," God was "pure Electric Radiance" residing within a heavenly "Electric Ring." Cast out of this Electric Ring, the planet Earth was in danger of losing contact with its heavenly energy source until God kindly reconnected it by means of an electrical cable in the form of Jesus Christ: "In brief, the Earth and God's World were like America and Europe before the Atlantic Cable was laid. Now the messages of goodwill flash under the waves, heedless of the storms. So also God's Cable is laid between us and His Heaven in the person of Christ" (Corelli 1886: 110). According to Corelli, Jesus's electrically charged body explained his ability to heal the sick with a touch and also why Mary Magdalene was forbidden to touch him after his resurrection—his voltage had grown dangerously high.

"It has been asked whether the Electric Theory of Christianity includes the doctrine of Hell," Corelli wrote (114). However, those readers who had envisioned "the electric germ of the Soul—delicate, fiery and imperishable" undergoing hair-raising shocks at the hands of demon electricians were doomed to disappointment. Corelli was thoroughly modern in her notion of Hell; it consisted only of the pangs of a tormented conscience. "There is no greater torture than to be compelled to remember, in suffering, joys and glorious opportunities gone for ever" (123–24).

Corelli's vision of all humanity plugged into one great electrical circuit, which captivated many thousands of readers in the last years of the nineteenth century, almost seems to presage the Internet. It was however, perhaps the last attempt to place God at the center of a tangible cosmos.

As well as sparking religious fervor, electrical energy also inspired the artistic imagination. The artistic movement that would most celebrate the electrical revolution was Futurism, founded in the early twentieth century by F. T. Marinetti. Marinetti anticipated that the new form of energy would bring about a world in which vibration and speed were the dominant sensations. According to the Futurist leader, this electrification of the world would lead to visual aesthetics and eye-minded rationalism being superseded by a kinesthetic fusion of force, thought, and feeling (Classen 1998: 156–57).

One novel trait of electrical power that would prove to be a defining characteristic of touch in the twentieth century was that it could be switched on and off instantaneously. Once the infrastructure was in place, virtually no effort or time was needed to put all its immense energy to work. A French journalist reported of the use of electricity at the Parisian Exposition of 1900 (which featured electrically powered walkways, escalators, rides, and, of course, thousands of lights): "A single touch of the finger on a switch and the magic fluid pours forth: everything is immediately illuminated, everything moves" (Goodall 2002: 212). It would take many decades to fully materialize, but it was the start of push-button culture.

TOUCH AT HOME

The nineteenth-century middle-class home was distinctive in its ostentation of all those technological conveniences developed by modern industry: plate-glass windows, running water, smokeless fireplaces, gas lighting. It was also distinctive in its specialization of domestic space. In contrast to the multipurpose rooms of the past, each room in the modern house had its own unique purpose: the bedroom was not for dining and the dining room was not for sleeping. This creation of specialized spaces was proclaimed to be in accordance with "the well-understood principle that every important function of life required a separate room" (Flanders 2003: 1). House-dwellers by no means always adhered to the rules about what should be done where, but the principle was, nonetheless, well understood. Within the house, therefore, the body was divided into its component functions and each allotted a separate space. The home thus provided the physical setting for a domestic version of the drill, whereby the occupants learned to regulate their bodies by moving from room to room to perform the different activities and postures deemed suitable for each.

Yet the middle-class home was no mere machine for living in, for it offered an extraordinarily rich assemblage of material goods. Take the plate-glass window in the Victorian parlor: "Windows were usually covered with at least two layers of fabric: a lightweight, transparent muslin or lace next to the glass was overlaid with heavier and showier fabric drawn up in complex folds, often lined or tied back with decorative braid, cord, fringe, or tassels, and surmounted by a valance" (Logan, 2001: 43). Here a device created for the purpose of increasing light within the house becomes the site of an extraordinary visual and tactual elaboration as the plain, flat glass is swathed in folds, braids, fringes, and tassels.

Even the architectural details of the homes of the well-to-do were suggestive of a tactile plenitude. In the dining room of the Sambourne house in Kensington (preserved as a museum), "there is an elaborate series of carved moldings along the ceiling, an embossed frieze designed to look like Spanish leather, a frieze rail and bracketed shelf for the display of china, and a dado; the ceiling is covered in stamped gilt paper [and] the wall in William Morris' Pomegranate pattern" (20). One cannot say that the Victorians had no interest in exploring the voluptuous potential of touch, as least insofar as it concerned home decor.

The Victorian home encompassed a greater collection of objects—and objects made for objects (doilies, antimacassars, spectacle cases, umbrella stands, pincushions, and so on)—than any previous home in history. Although explicit fingering might be discouraged as vulgar, there was nonetheless much to handle, much to take in and out, to put on and off, to position and reposition. Walter Benjamin attributed the preference of the bourgeoisie for "velvet and plush covers, which preserve the impression of every touch," to a concern to leave a personal trace on an increasingly impersonal world (2006: 77). Perhaps this concern for the tangible traces of existence is most noticeable in the nineteenth-century practice of creating ornaments, such as bracelets or artificial flowers, out of the hair of (often deceased) family members (Pointon 1999). The bourgeois accumulation of goods, however, was also a celebration of the new material culture and the satisfaction of a yearning for products—sumptuous textiles, furnishings, ornaments, pictures, books—that had been beyond the means of most people in the preindustrial age. The predilection for cases and covers not only multiplied the number of desirable objects to be bought or made, it also exemplified the same basic principle that ordered the space of the modern house: everything must have its place.

In the medieval home there had hardly been anything to touch but other bodies. In the Victorian home, there was often everything to touch *but* other bodies. An insistence on physical separation, except for prescribed, ritualized moments—the hand offered to a friend, the morning kiss on the wife's cheek, the storytime on father's knee, the spanking of the naughty child, the bedtime kiss from mother—was reinforced by the use of individual chairs for sitting on and single beds for sleeping in. To be forced to sleep alone as a child in the eighteenth century might have been regarded as a punishment. In the nineteenth century, while numerous children might necessitate communal sleeping arrangements, the ideal was one person per bed. Any piece of furniture that allowed contact between two bodies—the sofa, the "loveseat," the matrimonial bed—was suggestive of an extraordinary physical intimacy. When Charles Darwin was considering marriage, what decided him in its favor was the image of "a nice soft wife on a sofa with [a] good fire," a combination of softness, warmth, and intimacy that seemed irresistible (Flanders 2003: 214).

There *were* moments of playful exuberance when the customary social barriers preventing interpersonal touch broke down—moments that might well strike us today as surprisingly indecorous or downright childish. Such could occur when ever-popular parlor games—descendants of boisterous medieval frolics—were played at home by adults. These games, including Hot Cockles and Blind Man's Buff, often involved a considerable amount of hand-holding, lap-sitting, groping, or hitting. (The author of a guide to parlor games, indeed, felt obliged to remind readers that, for a well-bred player, a light touch sufficed [Waterman 1853: 16].) A mild spoof of one such parlor game, "Cutlets," appeared in *Punch* in the late nineteenth century:

> [Gowings] suggested we should play "Cutlets," a game we never heard of. He sat on a chair, and asked Carrie to sit on his lap, an invitation which dear Carrie rightly declined.
>
> After some species of wrangling I sat on Gowings' knees and Carrie sat on the edge of mine. Lupin sat on the edge of Carrie's lap, then Cummings in Lupin's and Mrs. Cummings on her husband's. We looked very ridiculous and laughed a great deal. (Grossmith and Grossmith 1962: 103)

Undoubtedly, the playful disruption of ordinary tactile decorum permitted by many of such games added to their popularity. Even strait-laced Victorians occasionally needed to unwind.

Rather than by direct physical contact, however, the communal life of the nineteenth-century home was imagined to be fostered by the more delicate medium of warmth. The Victorians extolled the virtues of the fireside circle, whose kindly heat countered the cold indifference of the outside world. John Ruskin's father wrote: "Oh! how dull and dreary is the best society I fall into compared with the circle of my own Fire Side with my Love sitting opposite irradiating all around her, and my most extraordinary boy" (cited in Flanders 2003: xxiv). No one is explicitly touching in this scene, yet all are connected by the warmth of the family circle. As indicated by this quote (which implies that Ruskin's wife is a fireside in herself), domestic warmth was particularly associated with the lady of the house. A shift had taken place from the thermal values of premodernity; now heat was more likely to be associated with feminine sensuality, while coldness was linked with masculine reason. The housewife had become the human hearth of the home.

Such housing arrangements were, however, very different in the homes of the poor. In fact, the dwellings of the poor were often taken by the middle classes to exemplify everything a modern home should not be. Instead of having separate rooms with separate functions, whole families were "compelled to herd together in a single apartment" (Moore 1988: 286). Instead of ample furnishings, "not a stick of furniture" could be seen. Instead of separate beds, a family might crowd together on one mattress, sometimes in close proximity to strangers sleeping nearby. It was evident that such accommodations, which required people to herd together rather than be separated out, afforded plenty of opportunity for indiscriminate touching.

The possession of only one or two rooms for living in also prevented the separating of domestic and bodily functions deemed to be so important in the nineteenth century. Working-class wives were frequently advised to have the house and children in order, a cheerful fire blazing, and a hot meal ready for when their husband arrived home. Yet with all household activities occurring within one space, the creation of a pleasant fireside atmosphere was often impossible. One earnest social worker wrote: "Think of the life of many a working man coming home from his day's hard labour, tired and depressed, to one of these houses. It may be that his wife has a washing, and the atmosphere is full of the steam of the washing-tub and of the clothes hung up to dry, and . . . the children [are] noisy and restless. . . . What can a man in these circumstances do?" (286). Instead of femininity being associated with a cheerful fire and social order, here it exudes steam, disorder, and noise—the chaotic fluidity of the stereotypical female body. Driven—or flooded—from his home (there is no suggestion that he give a help-ing hand), the working man "is met by the chill air of the foggy frosty night and an atmosphere laden with the smoke and fumes of manufactories" (ibid.). Only the local tavern, with its more enticing liquid offerings, provides a refuge.

If the ideal of the nineteenth-century housewife associated her with the warmth of the home, there was nonetheless one room in which she was reputedly rather cold: the bedroom. Indeed, one can hardly be surprised if a lifetime of studied avoidance of sexual matters, coupled with an often-startling introduction to the subject on her wedding night and followed by painful experiences of childbirth, left many a woman unenthusiastic about sexual activity. However, nineteenth-century men, if not faced with the same physical consequences, were not neces-sarily much better prepared for their marital duties. John Symonds, ambivalent about his sexuality and recalling a disastrous wedding night, denounced the "bar-barism" of taking a refined modern man and woman and "fling[ing] them naked in bed together, modest, alike ignorant, mutually embarassed by the awkward situation, trusting that they will blunder on the truth by instinct" (cited by Michie 2006: 259). However, as Peter Gay has amply documented, a good number of nineteenth-century women and men attested, in language that spoke of tender caresses and sweet communions, to their enjoyment of marital relations (1984). The popular notion of Victorian frigidity, if not entirely a myth, would seem to be a misrepresentation of the reality.

The question of the extent to which women, as well as men, should have their bodies regulated by the mechanisms of industrial society was a vexing one. Girls might either be excluded from the drill at school, or given a cane to use instead of the rifle shouldered by the boys. In a number of girls' schools therapeutic exercises imported from Scandinavia replaced the performance of the drill. Feminine versions of the drill were also available to be performed as entertainments. These included fan drills, dairymaid drills with milking stools, and a broom drill that involved marching with brooms and mops (*Fancy Drills* 1897). The main point of such "fancy drills" was probably not to inculcate a military approach to women's work but to show off female bodies performing an amusing and unthreatening variation on actual military drill.

Women, it was thought, could not become too mechanical, for they still needed to perform the organic function of childbearing and, as we have seen, to irradiate a tender domestic warmth. (In the case of female factory workers, who were often given minimum time off from the assembly line to give birth, such "niceties" were little regarded.) However, the feminine tenderness that was extolled by some was also seen by others as highly detrimental to the rearing of children. This was the case with the influential nineteenth-century German physician Daniel Schreber. In books that were translated into many languages, Dr. Schreber advised mothers to treat their children with rigid discipline, ignoring their cries, punishing them frequently, and strapping them into bed at night to prevent any self-touching. Rather than enveloping her children in maternal warmth, a conscientious mother was supposed to administer regular cold baths. This scientific method of child care, backed by the authority of the medical establishment, seemed to make a mockery of all the soft plush and cozy firesides of the nineteenth-century home (Synnott 2005).

The practice of systematically alienating the sense of touch in childhood had many adherents among physicians in the late nineteenth century (although some found Schreber's methods excessive). The widely read pediatrician Emmett Holt, for example, warned against sleeping with or rocking babies, and denounced the kissing of children as a means of communicating disease. Such hands-off methods of child rearing would later find a strong proponent in John B. Watson, the founder of Behaviorism. "Mothers just don't know," Watson scolded, "when they kiss their children and pick them up and rock them, caress them and jiggle them upon their knee, that they are slowly building up a human being totally unable to cope with the world it must later live in" (cited by Synnott 2005: 42). Touch created emotional dependency and this was an unacceptable trait in a world that demanded self-control and emotional detachment.

According to such theories of child care, a well-drilled child would no longer even desire a mother's touch. This result can be clearly seen in the case of Ernst von Salomon. In 1913 at the age of eleven Salomon entered a German military academy. There he experienced a reordering of his body and his psyche through intensive disciplinary practices—the drill enforced to the limits of endurance.

The new cadet found the process of being transformed into a component of the military machine excruciatingly painful, but also immensely satisfying. "I began to notice my body stiffening, my posture gaining in confidence," he noted. "It had become quite impossible to move with anything but dignity. On the rare occasions when a senseless desire for freedom surfaced it invariably shattered against a new determination and will." After the harsh and relentless discipline of the academy, young Ernst found home life unbearably soft and engulfing: "I found any kind of solicitous care quite intolerable, and the broad stream of my mother's empathy only made me wish to breathe the harsher air of the corps again" (cited by Theweleit 2005: 184). If his mother had followed the child care regime propounded by Dr. Schreber and his disciples, far from feeling overwhelmed by maternal warmth when he returned home from the academy, Ernst might have felt right at home.

THE STUFF OF DREAMS

Many of the goods on display within the mid-nineteenth-century home came from an important new commercial and cultural venue: the department store. The great stores of the nineteenth century—Le Bon Marché in Paris, Harrod's in London, Marshall Field's in Chicago, among others—were a dominant feature of the urban environment of modernity. As their owners boasted, these immense shopping complexes contained "a city within a store," a private, enclosed city with its own sensory and social ambience.

Department stores were distinguished by the vast array of goods contained within their cavernous premises, including textiles, furniture, hardware, books, toys and even food. The growth of urban populations and the expansion of public transportation ensured a sufficient clientele for these large-scale shops. Trade and industrial production provided the goods with which to stock the shelves.

The profusion of merchandise within the store helped to create an atmosphere of abundance and sensuous luxury. In *Au bonheur des dames* Emile Zola described a fictional department store that overwhelmed shoppers with "piles of ribbons," "clouds of lace," and "palpatations of muslin": "There were silks of a cloudy fineness, surahs lighter than the down falling from the trees, satined pekins soft and supple as a Chinese virgin's skin" (1886: 222, 224). The ultimate touch of luxury is provided by velvet-covered handrails that caress the hands of shoppers as they make their way from floor to floor.

Walking through the store's seemingly endless number of departments, Zola's customer feels the "slow exhaustion of her strength amidst the inexhaustible treasures displayed on every side" (230). This was quite a change from older-style shops that kept much of their goods out of sight and touch behind counters and in store rooms. Somewhat overstating the case, one pioneer in the new marketing methods recalled, "On entering a [traditional] dry goods store . . . one found long stretches of bare counters with clerks standing at attention behind them. . . . The customers were expected to make their wants known. . . . There was no such thing as 'counter display'" (F. W. Woolworth 1954: 9).

Just as significant as the abundance of goods on display in the department store were the new techniques of marketing employed. The relatively novel practice of fixed pricing eliminated the age-old practice of bargaining, reducing tensions between client and sales clerk, and facilitating a quick turnover of goods. The sales clerks themselves were trained to conform to a norm of neatness, respectability, and courteous demeanor—a departure from the situation in many smaller stores in which the staff might well be rude or overbearing. It was now possible to enter a store and just look—without having to ask for anything, without a particular purchase in mind, and without being subject to a continuous sales patter. This silencing of clerks made it easier to walk around a store and examine the goods in peace, but it also contributed to a demise of shopping as a dynamic social interaction between buyers and sellers.

To attract more customers to the store and keep them within the store once there, department stores offered a range of services, such as a restaurant, a post office, a beauty salon, and perhaps a concert hall as well. Le Bon Marché in Paris had a reading room and an art gallery, as well as a buffet, on its second floor. The British Selfridge's housed a library, an exchange bureau, a travel and theater booking office, a post office, and a bank, as well as restaurants (see Flanders 2006: ch. 3). In a number of key cities, such as Paris, London, and New York, department stores became symbols of the cities in which they were situated. These stores were—and continue to be—important tourist sites, not only because they were deemed to embody something of the mystique of celebrated cities but also because they enabled tourists to bring part of that mystique back home in the form of a tangible purchase, however humble that purchase might be.

As a city within a store the department store offered its visitors an environment that both mimicked that of the city outside and differed from it in key respects. The aisles of the store were like city streets through which visitors were free to wander. Unlike city streets—or open marketplaces—however, the store offered patrons a perpetually ideal climate no matter what the weather outside. Zola wrote of shoppers entering his fictional store: "A feeling of comfort invaded them, they seemed to be entering into spring-time after emerging from the winter of the street. Whilst outside, the frozen wind, laden with rain and hail, was still blowing, [inside] the fine season . . . was already budding forth" (1886: 214). Other potential annoyances of the city outside were also avoided within the store: there was no traffic, no dirt, no malodor, and no disagreeable spectacles of poverty. In return, customers tacitly agreed to conform to the behavioral norms of the store.

The enforcement of norms of polite behavior was facilitated by the fact that the store was an enclosed, private space as opposed to the open, public space of the city. Long ago city officials had discovered that if open markets were placed in enclosed market halls the traditional rowdiness of the marketplace became much more governable. Architectural design also played a role in encouraging self-control. As in the modern museum, the palatial setting of the department store both provided an imposing setting for the display of goods and contributed to inspiring attitudes of reverence and respect on the part of patrons. However, while a disciplined body was required within the department store as in the museum, in the former it had to be allowed to unbend sufficiently to indulge itself in the purchase of those modern luxuries and homey comforts now deemed to be eminently desirable.

Unlike in the modern museum, therefore, in the department store visitors were allowed to touch. Allowing customers to come into direct contact with goods without the mediation of a sales assistant was the most compelling feature of the department store: "All merchandise was arranged on the counters so the purchaser could see and handle everything. This radical departure from the customary method of displaying goods was the greatest innovation of all. . . . The people were not accustomed to being invited to handle and see for themselves" (F. W. Woolworth 1954: 9–10). While increasing the risk of theft and damage, allowing customers to handle the merchandise promoted sales. It did so by increasing customer confidence in the desirability and quality of a product, and more subtly by creating a bond of attachment between customer and product. An article one has held in one's hands is harder to leave unpurchased than an article one had simply seen.

Here then was a palatial edifice full of beautiful things to look at and touch, staffed with courteous, quiet "servants" (undoubtedly quite unlike many of the servants the middle classes dealt with in their homes). When electric lighting was installed in the late nineteenth century the store was further transformed into "a dazzling hall of light" (Lancaster 1995: 51). It was a dramatic change from the often muddy, rainy, dingy, and malodorous conditions of traditional marketplaces and shopping streets.

Department store owners wanted people to think of shopping as an enjoyable recreational activity. In London, ads for Selfridge's grandiosely announced that the new department store had turned shopping from a chore into a pastime. While previously "shopping was merely part of the day's work . . . Today, shopping—at Selfridge's . . . is an important part of the day's pleasure" (Rappaport 2004: 57). Store owners also wanted to attract visitors who had no immediate intention of shopping. Along with making extensive use of advertising, therefore, department stores had striking window displays to catch the attention of passersby and entice them inside. Once inside, visitors were encouraged to buy through the placement of tempting, portable goods near the entrances. Allowing unwanted purchases to be returned facilitated impulse buying as customers could purchase articles with little forethought knowing that they might return them later if they changed their minds. The department store made it a simple matter for a customer to pick something up, buy it, and walk out of the store with it.

The majority of the customers thronging the new department stores were women. For good reason Zola titled his novel on the department store *Au bonheur des dames,* "The Ladies' Delight." The conventional explanation for this predominance of female shoppers was that stores catered to women's inherent sensuality. Shopping excursions could also be accepted, or excused, as extensions of a woman's homemaking duties. Whatever its sensuous attraction or practical value for women, however, the department store offered housewives the immense attraction of an interesting, diverse, and respectable alternative to staying at home.

The nineteenth-century city was primarily a male space that did not provide unaccompanied middle-class women (who were not expected to work, conduct business, or eat alone in restaurants) with many places to go. Even walking in the street was considered a suspicious activity for women, associated as it was with prostitution. By contrast, unescorted women could walk freely through the "city within a store," browse at leisure through its offerings, and make use of its multiple services without fear of being snubbed or harassed. All in all, middle-class women enjoyed a degree of freedom in the department store that they rarely experienced elsewhere. Aware of this, the founder of one department store described his shop as an "Adamless Eden" (Lancaster 1995: 171).

However, Eden was not without its snake and the department store was not thought to be without its own dangers for the female shopper. The simple situation of a woman walking about on her own in a semi-public space seemed to some to promote a corrupting moral laxity. The primary danger, however, was imagined to be that the sight and touch of so many highly desirable and readily accessible luxuries would make a woman lose her self-control and buy beyond her needs or means. Many store owners, indeed, tried to encourage this situation by creating a layout that obliged customers to walk around a great deal to complete their shopping and in the process see—and desire—much that was not on their shopping list. When the founder of Le Bon Marché decided to reorganize his store in 1872 he wrote, "What's necessary . . . is that [women] walk around for hours, that they get lost. . . . It would really be too much if, as they wander around in this organized disorder, lost, driven crazy, they don't set foot in some departments where they had no intention of going, and if they don't succumb at the sight of things which grab them on the way" (cited by Bowlby 1985: 74). Though women might be safe from predatory men within the department store, the store goods themselves were potentially predators, reaching out to grab unsuspecting women who had lost their way. Playing on this theme, one novel of the period, *Les grands bazars,* likened a woman shopping in a department store to a man visiting a prostitute. Both have become depraved by desire. "The husband . . . leaves [his wife in a store] for long hours as prey to the seductions of lace . . . her eyes on fire, her face reddened, her hand shivering, placed on that of a gloves salesman, while he [the husband] goes off during this time with shady women" (cited by M. Miller 1981: 192).

So seductive, it was feared, would women find the atmosphere of the store, and so alluring and accessible its merchandise, that many would simply take goods without paying for them. It was indeed the case that increasing numbers of middle-class women were caught shoplifting in the nineteenth century. The phenomenon even became the subject of a popular music hall song:

> A beauty of the West End went,
> Around a shop she lingers,
> And there upon some handkerchiefs
> She clapped her pretty fingers,
> Into the shop she gently popped;
> The world is quite deceiving,
> When ladies have a notion got
> To ramble out a-thieving. (cited in Lancaster 1995: 184)

One nineteenth-century French psychiatrist who made a study of the subject wrote, "These immense galleries . . . enclose and expose . . . the richest cloths, the most luxurious dress articles, the most seductive superfluities. Women of all sorts . . . fascinated by so many rash provocations, dazzled by the abundance of trinkets and lace, find themselves overtaken by a sudden, unpremeditated, almost savage impulse." The account of one female shoplifter confirmed this analysis: "Once plunged into the sensuous atmosphere of the [store] I felt myself overcome little by little by a disorder that can only be compared to that of drunkenness. . . . I saw things as through a cloud, everything stimulated my desire and assumed, for me, an extraordinary attraction. I felt myself swept along towards them and grabbed hold of things without any outside and superior consideration intervening to hold me back" (cited by Miller 1981: 202). Allegedly sensuous and irrational by nature, torn from the civilizing influences of her home, a woman, it was said, could not resist the sensory enticements of the department store. Her hands picked up goods against her will. Perhaps the city in a store was not actually any safer for women than the city outside. Or perhaps the notion of *any* predominantly female space outside of the home aroused concerns of female insubordination. Imagine the dismay of the bourgeois husband, arriving home expecting to find "a nice soft wife on a sofa with a fire," and discovering instead that she was out feverishly perusing the merchandise at a department store—or ardently discussing women's suffrage with friends in a department store tea room (Lancaster 1995: 190–92).

The women, and customers in general, who shopped at department stores were largely middle class. Though department store goods were often mass-market products, they were nonetheless frequently out of the financial reach of the working classes. In the late nineteenth century, however, a new kind of department store sprang up to cater to the working and lower-middle classes. These stores offered a wide range of products, like the *grands magasins,* but at less expensive prices. One classic example of such variety stores (as they came to be known) was Woolworth's, which originated in the United States and then expanded into other countries. Variety stores allowed lower-income families to participate in the sensory splendor of consumer society at prices they could afford. One of the distinctive characteristics of the variety store, indeed, would be the intensity of the sensory experiences it offered. It was as though the deprivations of the working classes required strong palliatives—the brightest colors, the sweetest flavors, the headiest perfumes, the chunkiest costume jewelry, the catchiest tunes thumped out on the store piano. Nor were the middle and upper classes adverse to occasionally entering a variety store in search of a bargain or of bolder sensory experiences than those available in the more refined great stores. With the variety store, the modern consumer experience became available to all.

A common complaint of the cultural elite in the late nineteenth and early twentieth centuries was that modern science and industry had created a dry and drab world. A number of artists and writers responded by attempting to recreate in their work the sensuous, holistic qualities they associated with a preindustrial worldview. Arguably, however, it was not Baudelaire with his poems of sensory correspondences, nor Moreau with his rich representations of textures, nor Husymans with his fantasies of gustatory symphonies, nor William Morris with his handcrafted textiles, who went the furthest in this direction (see Classen 1998: ch. 5). It was the department store.

With its silk hangings and oriental rugs, its floral displays, its perfumes, its musicians, its thronging masses, the department store resembled a medieval street decked out for a holiday. (The founder of Selfridge's boasted that his store had "the atmosphere of the old-time fair at its best" [Rappaport 2004: 161].) More than that, however, the store's ideal climate and festive decor, its pyramids of merchandise and hand-on accessibility, made it into a contemporary, commercial realization of the premodern fantasy of an eternally sunny land of plenty. Indeed, the sensory world of the department store was at its height a synesthetic world in which all the sensory effects shimmered and merged into one captivating whole.

Perhaps the shopping process was, underneath it all, only a variation on the drill swathed in silk. Perhaps the store itself was only a glamorous machine for positioning the end results of the assembly line. Yet, of all the founding institutions of modernity, it would be the department store that offered the nineteenth-century public the fullest hands-on experience. No wonder then that many in the new age would increasingly look not to rural life or to communal life or to religious life to satisfy their tactile hunger, but to consumer culture.

BIBLIOGRAPHY

Adair, James M. 1812. *An Essay on Diet and Regimen.* 2nd ed. London: James Ridgway.

Addams, Jane. 1990. *Twenty Years at Hull-House with Autobiographical Notes.* Edited by James Hurt. Urbana: University of Illinois Press.

Aelfric. 1961. *Aelfric's Colloquy.* Edited by G.A. Garmonsway. London: Methuen & Co.

Ahlgren, Gillian T. W. 1998. *Teresa of Avila and the Politics of Sanctity.* Ithaca, NY: Cornell University Press.

Allan, John. 1884. *Practical Guide on "Healthy Houses" and Sanitary Reform.* London: Simkin and Marshall.

Allen, Mea. 1964. *The Tradescants: Their Plants, Gardens and Museum, 1570–1662.* London: Michael Joseph.

Allen, Peter Lewis. 2000. *The Wages of Sin: Sex and Disease, Past and Present.* Chicago: University of Chicago Press.

Allen, Prudence. 1985. *The Concept of Woman: The Aristotelian Revolution 750 BC–AD 1250.* Montreal: Eden Press.

Allen, Prudence and Filippe Salvatore. 1992. "Lucrezia Marinelli and Woman's Identity in the Late Italian Renaissance." *Renaissance and Reformation* 28, no. 4: 5–39.

Altick, Richard D. 1978. *The Shows of London.* Cambridge, MA: Harvard University Press.

Angela of Foligno. 1999. *Angela of Foligno's Memorial.* Edited by Cristina Mazzoni; translated by John Cirignano. Cambridge: D.S. Brewer.

The Anonimalle Chronicle. 1927. Edited by V.H. Galbraith. Manchester: University of Manchester Press.

Ardo. 1979. *The Emperor's Monk: Contemporary Life of Benedict of Aniane.* Translated by Allen Cabaniss. Ilfracomb, England: A.H. Stockwell.

Ariès, Philippe. 1974. *Western Attitudes Toward Death, From the Middle Ages to the Present.* Translated by Patricia M. Ranum. Baltimore: Johns Hopkins University Press.

Armstrong, Edward A. 1973. *Saint Francis: Nature Mystic.* Berkeley: University of California Press.

Arnold, Ken. 2003. "Skulls, Mummies and Unicorns' Horns: Medicinal Chemistry in Early English Museums." In *Enlightening the British: Knowledge, Discovery and the Museum in the Eighteenth Century.* Edited by R. G. W. Anderson, M. L. Caygill, A. G. MacGregor and L. Syson. London: The British Museum Press.

—————. 2006. *Cabinets for the Curious: Looking Back at Early English Museums.* Aldershot, England: Ashgate.

Asbridge, Thomas. 2004. *The First Crusade: A New History.* Oxford: Oxford University Press.

Ashton, John, 1882. *Social Life in the Reign of Queen Anne,* Vol. 1. London: Spottiswood and Co.

Asua, Miguel de. 1999. "Medicine and Philosophy in Peter of Spain's Commentary on *De animalibus.*" In Steel, Goldentops, and Beuliens, *Aristotle's Animals in the Middle Ages and Renaissance.*

Asua, Miguel de and Roger French. 2005. *A New World of Animals: Early Modern Europeans on the Creatures of Iberian America.* Aldershot, England: Ashgate Publishing Limited.

Atkinson, Paul. 1978. "Fitness, Feminism and Schooling." In *The Nineteenth-Century Woman: Her Cultural and Physical World.* Edited by Sara Delamont and Lorna Duffin. New York: Harper & Row.

Aucassin & Nicolette. 1887. Translated by Andrew Lang. London: David Nutt.

Auerbach, Jeffrey A. 1999. *The Great Exhibition of 1851: A Nation on Display.* New Haven, CT: Yale University Press.

Augustine. 2006a. "On Free Will." In *Augustine: Earlier Writings.* Edited by J. H. S. Burleigh. Louisville, KY: Westminster John Knox Press.

Augustine. 2006b. "Two Books on the Catholic Way of Life and the Manichean Way of Life: Book Two." In *The Works of Saint Augustine: A Translation for the 21st Century,* Pt. I, Vol. I. Translated by Edmund Hill and John E. Rotelle. New York: Augustinian Heritage Society.

Bacci, Pietro Giacomo. 1902. *The Life of Saint Philip Neri, Apostle of Rome and Founder of the Congregation of the Oratory.* London: Kegan Paul, Trench, Trübner and Co.

Baer, Richard A. 1970. *Philo's Use of the Categories Male and Female.* Leiden: E. J. Brill.

Bainton, Roland H. 1977. *Here I Stand: A Life of Martin Luther.* Peabody, MA: Hendrickson Publishers.

Barasch, Moshe. 1990. *Theories of Art: From Winckelmann to Baudelaire.* New York: Routledge.

—————. 2001. *Blindness: The History of a Mental Image in Western Thought.* London: Routledge.

Barker-Benfield, G. J. 1992. *The Culture of Sensibility: Sex and Society in Eighteenth-Century Britain.* Chicago: University of Chicago Press.

Barthélemy, Dominique and Philippe Contamine. 1988. "The Use of Private Space." In *A History of Private Life,* Vol. II: *Revelations of the Medieval World.*

Barton, Carlin A. 2001. *Roman Honor: The Fire in the Bones.* Berkeley: University of California Press.

Battestin, Martin C., and Ruth R. Battestin. 1993. *Henry Fielding: A Life.* London: Routledge.

Bayless, Martha. 1996. *Parody in the Middle Ages: The Latin Tradition.* Ann Arbor: University of Michigan Press.

Beard, George M. 1881. *American Nervousness: Its Causes and Consequences.* New York: G.P. Putnam's Sons.

Bede. 1990. *Ecclesiastical History of the English People.* Translated by Leo Sherley-Price. London: Penguin Books.

Bedford, Ron. 2002. "Historicizing Irony: The Case of Milton and the Restoration." In *The Touch of the Real: Essays in Early Modern Culture in Honour of Stephen Greenblatt.* Edited by Philippa Kelly. Crawley: University of Western Australia Press.

Bellamy, J. G. 1970. *The Law of Treason in the Later Middle Ages.* Cambridge: Cambridge University Press.

Benjamin, Walter. 2006. *The Writer of Modern Life: Essays on Charles Baudelaire.* Edited by Michael W. Jennings. Cambridge, MA: Harvard University Press.

Bennett, Tony. 1995. *The Birth of the Museum: History, Theory, Politics.* London: Routledge.

Bentham, Jeremy. 1779. *An Introduction to the Principles of Morals and Legislation.* Oxford: Clarendon Press.

Benthien, Claudia. 2000. *Skin: On the Cultural Border Between Self and the World.* T. Dunlap, trans. New York: Columbia University Press.

Berenson, Bernard. 1967. *The Italian Painters of the Renaissance.* London: Phaidon Press.

Bergman, Charles. 2007. "A Spectacle of Beasts: Hunting Rituals and Animal Rights in Early Modern England." In Boehrer, *A Cultural History of Animals in the Renaissance.*

Besançon, Alain. 2000. *The Forbidden Image: An Intellectual History of Iconoclasm.* Translated by Jane Marie Todd. Chicago: University of Chicago Press.

Bestiary: Being an English Version of the Bodleian Library, Oxford, MS Bodley 764. 1993. Translated by Richard Barber. Woodbridge, England: Boydell Press.

Biernoff, Suzannah. 2002. *Sight and Embodiment in the Middle Ages.* New York: Palgrave Macmillan.

Bingley, William. 1805. *Animal Biography,* Vol. 2. London: Richard Phillips.

Binski, Paul. 1996. *Medieval Death: Ritual and Representation.* London: British Museum Press.

Birgitta of Sweden. 1990. *Life and Selected Revelations.* Edited by Marguerite Tjader Harris. Translated by Albert Ryle Kezel. Mahwah, NJ: Paulist Press.

Bishop, Louise M. 2007. *Words, Stones and Herbs: The Healing Word in Medieval and Early Modern England.* Syracuse, NY: Syracuse University Press.

Blackburn, Robin. 2000. *The Overthrow of Colonial Slavery, 1776–1848.* London: Verso.

Bloch, Marc. 1961. *Feudal Society.* Translated by L. A. Manyon. Chicago: University of Chicago Press.

———. 1973. *The Royal Touch: Sacred Monarchy and Scrofula in England and France.* London: Routledge & Kegan Paul.

———. 1989. *Feudal Society: The Growth of Ties of Dependence.* Translated by L. A. Manyon. London: Routledge.

Boccaccio, Giovanni. 1977. *The Decameron.* Edited and translated by Mark Musa and Peter E. Bondanella. New York: W. W. Norton and Co.

Boehrer, Bruce, ed. 2007. *A Cultural History of Animals in the Renaissance.* Oxford: Berg.

Bondeson, Jan. 1999. *The Feejee Mermaid and Other Essays in Natural and Unnatural History.* Ithaca, NY: Cornell University Press.

Born, Bertran. 1990. "Be'm plai lo gais tems de pascor." In *Lyrics of the Middle Ages: An Anthology.* Edited and translated by James J. Wilhelm. New York: Garland.

Boswell, James. 1873. *The Life of Samuel Johnson.* Edinburgh: William P. Nimmo.

Bougeant, Guillaume-Hyacinthe. 1739. *Amusement philosophique sur le langage des bêtes.* The Hague: Antoine Van Dole.

Bowlby, Rachel. 1985. *Just Looking: Consumer Culture in Driesler, Gissing and Zola.* London: Methuen and Co.

Boyle, Marjorie O'Rourke. 1998. *Senses of Touch: Human Dignity and Deformity from Michelangelo to Calvin*. Leiden: Brill.

Braunstein, Philippe. 1988. "Toward Intimacy: The Fourteenth and Fifteen Centuries." In *A History of Private Life*. Vol. II: *Revelations of the Medieval World*.

Bray, Alan. 1995. *Homosexuality in Renaissance England*. New York: Colombia University Press.

Bremmer, Jan and Herman Roodenburg, eds. 1991. *A Cultural History of Gesture*. Ithaca, NY: Cornell University Press.

Brentano, Robert. 1968. *Two Churches: England and Italy in the 13th Century*. Princeton, NJ: Princeton University Press.

Briffault, Robert. 1919. *The Making of Humanity*. London: G. Allen & Unwin.

Brody, Saul Nathaniel. 1974. *The Disease of the Soul: Leprosy in Medieval Literature*. Ithaca, NY: Cornell University Press.

Brown, Edward. 1677. *An Account of Several Travels through a Great Part of Germany*. London: Benjamin Tooke.

Bueil, Jean de. 1887. *Le Jouvencel par Jean de Bueil: suivi du commentaire de Guillaume Tringant*. Vol I. Edited by Leon Lecestre and Camille Favre. Paris: Librarie Renouard.

Burke, Peter. 2009. *Popular Culture in Early Modern Europe*. Farnham, England: Ashgate Publishing.

Burns, E. Jane. 1993. *Bodytalk: When Women Speak in Old French Literature*. Philadelphia: University of Pennsylvania Press.

Burrow, J. A. 2002. *Gestures and Looks in Medieval Narrative*. Cambridge: Cambridge University Press.

Butler, Alban. 1956. *Lives of the Saints*. Vol 1. New York: P. J. Kennedy.

Bynum, Caroline Walker. 1987. *Holy Feast and Holy Fast: The Religious Significance of Food to Medieval Women*. Berkeley: University of California Press.

——————. 1995. *The Resurrection of the Body in Western Christianity, 200–1336*. New York: Columbia University Press.

Bynum, W. F., and Roy Porter, ed. 1993. *Medicine and the Five Senses*. Cambridge: Cambridge University Press.

Byrne, Joseph P. 2006. *Daily Life During the Black Death*. Westport, CT: Greenwood Press.

Caciola, Nancy. 2003. *Discerning Spirits: Divine and Demonic Possession in the Middle Ages*. Ithaca, NY: Cornell University Press.

Cadden, Joan. 1995. *Meanings of Sex Difference in the Middle Ages: Medicine, Science and Culture*. Cambridge: Cambridge University Press.

Caius, Johannes. 1576. *Of Englische Dogges, the Diversities, the Names, the Natures, and the Properties*. Translated by Abraham Fleming. London: Rychard Johnes.

Camille, Michael. 1999. "Bestiary or Biology? Aristotle's Animals in Oxford, Merton College, MS 271." In Steel, Goldentops, and Beuliens, *Aristotle's Animals in the Middle Ages and Renaissance*.

Camporesi, Piero. 1989. *Bread of Dreams: Food and Fantasy in Early Modern Europe*. Translated by David Gentilcore. Cambridge: Polity Press.

——————. 1991. *The Fear of Hell: Images of Damnation and Salvation in Early Modern Europe*. Translated by Lucinda Byatt. University Park, PA: Penn State University Press.

Candlin, Fiona. 2004. "Don't Touch! Hands Off! Art, Blindness and the Conservation of Expertise." *Body & Society* 10: 1.

——————. 2010. *Art, Museums and Touch*. Manchester: Manchester University Press.

Carew, Thomas. 1899. *The Poems of Thomas Carew.* London: George Routledge & Sons.

Carruthers, Mary. 2008. *The Book of Memory: A Study of Memory in Medieval Culture.* Cambridge: Cambridge University Press.

Castiglione, Baldassare. 2003. *The Book of the Courtier.* Mineola, NY: Dover Publications.

Cavendish, Margaret. 1969. *Sociable Letters.* Menston, England: Scolar Press.

———. 1972. *Poems and Fancies.* Menston, England: Scolar Press.

———. n.d. *The Life of William Cavendish, Duke of Newcastle.* Edited by C. H. Firth. London: George Routledge and Sons.

Caxton, William. 1813. "Prologue." In Raoul Lefèvre, *The History of Jason.* London: Kegan Paul, Trench, Trübner & Co.

Chadwick, Edwin. 1861. *Communications from Edwin Chadwick, Esq., C.B., Respecting Half-Time and Military and Naval Drill.* London: n.p.

Chantelou, Paul Fréart de. 1985. *Diary of Cavaliere Bernini's Visit to France.* Edited by Anthony Blunt and George C. Bauer. Translated by M. Corbett. Princeton, N.J.: Princeton University Press.

Chartier, Roger. 1989. "The Practical Impact of Writing." In *A History of Private Life.* Vol. III: *Passions Of the Renaissance.*

———. 2007. *Inscription & Erasure: Literature and Written Culture from the Eleventh to the Eighteenth Century.* Philadelphia: University of Pennsylvania Press.

Clark, Gillian. 1998. "The Fathers and the Animals: The Rule of Reason?" In Linzey and Yamamoto, *Animals on the Agenda: Questions about Animals for Theology and Ethics.*

Classen, Constance. 1993. *Worlds of Sense: Exploring the Senses in History and Across Cultures.* London: Routledge.

———. 1998. *The Color of Angels: Cosmology, Gender and the Aesthetic Imagination.* London: Routledge.

———. 2001. "The Senses." In *Encyclopedia of European Social History.* Edited by Peter Stearns. New York: Charles Scribner's Sons.

———, ed. 2005a. *The Book of Touch.* Oxford: Berg.

———. 2005b. "The Deodorized City: Battling Urban Stench in the Nineteenth Century." In *Sense of the City: An Alternate Approach to Urbanism.* Edited by Mirko Zardini. Montreal: Canadian Centre for Architecture.

The Cloud of Unknowing. 1981. Edited by James Walsh. Mahwah, N.J., Paulist Press.

Cohen, Esther. 1993. *The Crossroads of Justice: Law and Culture in Late Medieval France.* Leiden: E.J. Brill.

———. 2003. "The Expression of Pain in the Later Middle Ages: Deliverance, Acceptance and Infamy." In *Bodily Extremities: Preoccupations with the Human Body in Early Modern European Culture.* Edited by Florike Egmond and Robert Zwijnenberg. Aldershot, England: Ashgate Publishing.

———. 2010. *The Modulated Scream: Pain in Late Medieval Culture.* Chicago: University of Chicago Press.

Cohn, Samuel Kline Jr., ed. and trans. 2004. *Popular Protest in Late Medieval Europe: Italy, France, and Flanders.* Manchester: Manchester University Press.

Connor, Steven. 2004. *The Book of Skin.* Ithaca, NY: Cornell University Press.

Constable, Giles. 1996. *The Reformation of the Twelfth Century.* Cambridge: Cambridge University Press.

Cook, Dutton. 2007. *A Book of the Play: Studies and Illustrations of Histrionic Story, Life and Character.* Teddington, England: Echo Library.

Corbin, Alain. 1986. *The Foul and the Fragrant: Odor and the French Social Imagination.* Translated by M. Kochan, R. Porter, and C. Prendergast. Cambridge, MA: Harvard University Press.

———. 1995. *Time, Desire and Horror: Towards a History of the Senses.* Translated by Jean Birrell. Cambridge: Polity Press.

———. 1998. *Village Bells: Sound and Meaning in the 19th-century French Countryside.* Translated by Martin Thom. New York: Columbia University Press.

———. 2005. "Charting the Cultural History of the Senses." In Howes, *Empire of the Senses: The Sensual Culture Reader.*

Corelli, Marie. 1886. *A Romance of Two Worlds.* London: Richard Bentley and Son.

Corfield, Penelope J. 1990. "Walking the City Streets: The Urban Odyssey in Eighteenth-Century England." *Journal of Urban History,* 16, no. 2: 132–74.

Coulton, George Gordon. 1989. *The Medieval Village.* Mineola, NY: Dover Publications.

Cowan, Alexander, and Jill Steward, eds. 2007. *The City and the Senses: Urban Culture since 1500.* Aldershot, England: Ashgate.

Cranston, Jodi. 2003. "The Touch of the Blind Man: The Phenomenology of Vividness in Italian Renaissance Art." In Harvey, *Sensible Flesh: On Touch in Early Modern Culture.*

Crouch, David. 2005. *Tournament.* London: Hambledon and Continuum.

Crowley, John E. 2005. "Homely Pleasures: The Pursuit of Comfort in the Eighteenth Century." In Classen, *The Book of Touch.*

Dalarun, Jacques. 1992. "The Clerical Gaze." Translated by Arthur Goldhammer. In Georges Duby and Michelle Perrot, ed., *A History of Women in the West: Silences of the Middle Ages.* Cambridge, MA: Harvard University Press.

Darwin, Charles. 1958. *The Autobiography of Charles Darwin and Selected Letters.* New York: Dover Publications.

Das, Santanu. 2005. *Touch and Intimacy in First World War Literature.* Cambridge: Cambridge University Press.

Davis, Susan E., and Margo DeMello. 2003. *Stories Rabbits Tell: A Natural and Cultural History of a Misunderstood Creature.* New York: Lantern Books.

De Beer, G. R. 1953. *Sir Hans Sloane and the British Museum.* London: Oxford University Press.

Defoe, Daniel. 1830. *A Journal of the Plague Year.* Edited by Edward Wedlake Brayley. London: Thomas Tegg and Son.

Delany, Mary. 1974. *The Autobiography and Correspondence of Mary Granville, Mrs. Delany.* Edited by Lady Llanover. New York: AMS Press.

Denery, Dallas George. 2005. *Seeing and Being Seen in the Later Medieval World: Optics, Theology and Religious Life.* Cambridge: Cambridge University Press.

Desaguliers, John Theophilus. 1728. *The Newtonian System of the World.* London: J. Roberts.

Deyle, Steven. 2005. *Carry Me Back: The Domestic Slave Trade in American Life.* Oxford: Oxford University Press.

Dickens, Charles. 1885. *Our Mutual Friend,* vol. 1. Philadelphia: J.B. Lippincott & Co.

Dickens, Charles, Jr. 1880. *Dickens's Dictionary of the Thames* London: Charles Dickens.

Dickenson, Victoria. 2007. "Meticulous Depiction: Animals in Art." In Boehrer, *A Cultural History of Animals in the Renaissance.*

Diderot, Denis. 1749. *Lettre sur les aveugles a l'usage de ceux qui voyent.* London: n.p.

———. 1751. *Lettre sur les sourds et muets, A l'Usage de ceux qui entendent & qui parlent.* n.p.

"A Discussion with an Infidel." 1874–75. In *New Catholic World*. New York: The Catholic Publication House.

Dowsing, William. 1885. *The Journal of William Dowsing*. Edited by C. H. Evelyn White. Ipswich, UK: Pawsey and Hayes.

Drogin, Marc. 1989. *Biblioclasm: The Mythical Origins, Magic Powers, and Perishability of the Written Word*. Savage, MD: Rowman & Littlefield Publishers.

Duby, Georges. 1988. "Public Power, Private Power." In *A History of Private Life*, Vol. II: *Revelations of the Medieval World*.

Dudden, Frederick Homes. 1905. *Gregory the Great: His Place in History and Thought*, Vol. I. London: Longmans, Green, and Co.

Duffy, Christopher. 1987. *The Military Experience in the Age of Reason*. London: Routledge & Kegan Paul.

Ebner, Margaret. 1993. *Margaret Ebner, Major Works*. Edited by Leonard Patrick Hindsley. New York: Paulist Press.

Edwards, Elizabeth. 2001. *Raw Histories: Photographs, Anthropology and Museums*. Oxford: Berg.

Ekirch, A. Roger. 2005. *At Day's Close: Night in Times Past*. New York: W. W. Norton.

Elias, Norbert. 1994, *The Civilizing Process: The History of Manners and State Formation and Civilization*. Translated by E. Jephcott. Oxford: Blackwell.

Elliot, Paul. 1990. "Vivisection and the Emergence of Experimental Physiology in Nineteenth-Century France." In Nicolaas A. Rupke, ed., *Vivisection in Historical Perspective*. London: Routledge.

Englander, David, Diana Norman, Rosemary O'Day, and W. R. Owens, ed. 1999. *Culture and Belief in Europe, 1450–1600: An Anthology of Sources*. Oxford: Blackwell.

Erasmus, Desiderius. 1962. *Epistles of Erasmus*, Vol. 2. Translated by F. Morgan Nichols. New York: Russel & Russel.

Evangelisti, Silvia. 2007. *Nuns: A History of Convent Life: 1450–1700*. Oxford: Oxford University Press.

Evans, Edward Payson. 2006. *The Criminal Prosecution and Capital Punishment of Animals*. Clark, NJ: The Lawbook Exchange.

Evans, Michael. 2007. *Death of Kings: Royal Deaths in Medieval England*. London: Hambledon Continuum.

Evelyn, John. 1955. *The Diary of John Evelyn*, Vol. II. Edited by E.S. de Beer. Oxford: Clarendon Press.

Fancy Drills for Evening and Other Entertainments. 1897. London: Butterick Publishing Company.

Farmer, Craig Steven. 1997. *The Gospel of John in the Sixteenth Century: The Johannine Exegesis of Wolfgang Musculus*. Oxford: Oxford University Press.

Febvre, Lucien, 1982. *The Problem of Unbelief in the Sixteenth Century: The Religion of Rabelais*. Translated by B. Gottlieb. Cambridge, MA: Harvard University Press.

Ficino, Marsilio. 2006. "On Obtaining Life from the Heavens." In *Marsilio Ficino*, Angela Voss, ed. Berkeley, CA: North Atlantic Books.

Fiennes, Celia. 1949. *The Journeys of Celia Fiennes*. London: Cresset Press.

Finucane, Ronald C. 1995. *Miracles and Pilgrims: Popular Beliefs in Medieval England*. New York: St. Martin's Press.

Fissell, Mary Elizabeth. 2004. *Vernacular Bodies: The Politics of Reproduction in Early Modern England*. Oxford: Oxford University Press.

Flanagan, Sabina. 1998. *Hildegard of Bingen, 1098–1179: A Visionary Life.* London: Routledge.

Flanders, Judith. 2003. *The Victorian House: Domestic Life from Childbirth to Deathbed.* London: Harper Collins.

———. 2006. *Consuming Passions: Leisure and Pleasure in Victorian Britain.* London: HarperPress.

Flandrin, Jean-Louis. 1989. "Distinctions through Taste." In *A History of Private Life.* Vol. III: *Passions of the Renaissance.*

Foucault, Michel. 1979. *Discipline and Punish: The Birth of the Prison.* Translated by A. Sheridan. New York: Vintage Books

Freedman, Paul. 1999. *Images of the Medieval Peasant.* Stanford, CA: Stanford University Press.

Fudge, Erica. 2002. *Perceiving Animals: Humans and Beasts in Early Modern English Culture.* Urbana: University of Illinois Press.

———. 2004. "Saying Nothing Concerning the Same: On Dominion, Purity, and Meat in Early Modern England." In *Renaissance Beasts: Of Animals, Humans, and Other Wonderful Creatures.* Edited by Erica Fudge. Urbana: University of Illinois Press.

F. W. Woolworth & Co. 1954. *Woolworth's First 75 Years: The Story of Everybody's Store (1879–1954).* New York: Rudge and Sons.

Gage, John. 1993. *Colour and Culture: Practice and Meaning from Antiquity to Abstraction.* London: Thames and Hudson.

Gascoigne, George. 1870. *The Complete Poems of George Gascoigne,* Vol. II. Edited by William Carew Hazlitt. London: Whittingram and Wilks.

Gay, John. 1730. *Trivia, Or, The Art of Walking the Streets of London.* London: Bernard Lintot.

Gay, Peter. 1984. *The Bourgeois Experience, Victoria to Freud.* Vol. I, *The Education of the Senses.* Oxford: Oxford University Press.

Geary, Patrick. 1983. "Humiliation of Saints." In *Saints and Their Cults: Studies in Religious Sociology, Folklore and History.* Edited by Stephen Wilson. Cambridge: Cambridge University Press.

———. 1990. *Furta Sacra: Thefts of Relics in the Middle Ages.* Princeton, NJ: Princeton University Press.

George, Wilma. 1985. "Alive or Dead: Zoological Collections in the Seventeenth Century." In *The Origins of Museums: The Cabinet of Curiosities in Sixteenth and Seventeenth-Century Europe.* Edited by Oliver Impey and Arthur MacGregor. Oxford: Clarendon.

Giblin, James Cross. 1987. *From Hand to Mouth, Or, How We Invented Knives, Forks, Spoons, and Chopsticks, & the Table Manners to Go with Them.* New York: Thomas Y. Crowell.

Giedion, Siegfried. 1955. *Mechanization Takes Command: A Contribution to Anonymous History.* Oxford: Oxford University Press.

Gies, Frances, and Joseph Gies. 1990. *Life in a Medieval Village.* New York: Harper & Row.

Gies, Joseph, and Frances Gies. 1969. *Life in a Medieval City.* New York: Cromwell.

Gilman, Sander. 1993. "Touch, Sexuality and Disease." In Bynum and Porter, *Medicine and the Five Senses.*

Gloag, John. 1934. *English Furniture, A History and Guide.* London: A. & C. Black.

Glynn, Ian, and Jenifer Glynn. 2004. *The Life and Death of Smallpox.* New York: Cambridge University Press.

Goethe, Johann Wolfgang von. 1974. *Roman Elegies and Venetian Epigrams.* Translated by L. R. Lind. Lawrence: University Press of Kansas.

Goodall, Jane. 2002. *Performance and Evolution in the Age of Darwin: Out of the Natural Order.* London: Routledge.

The Goodman of Paris. 2006. Translated by Eileen Power. Woodbridge, UK: Boydell Press.

Gowing, Laura. 2003. *Common Bodies: Women, Touch and Power in Seventeenth-Century England.* New Haven, CT: Yale University Press.

Grant, Edward. 1996. *Planets, Stars and Orbs: The Medieval Cosmos, 1200–1687.* Cambridge: Cambridge University Press.

Grant, Teresa. 2007. "Entertaining Animals." In Boehrer, *A Cultural History of Animals in the Renaissance.*

Griffin, Emma. 2007. *Blood Sport: Hunting in Britain since 1066.* New Haven, CT: Yale University Press.

Grossmith, George, and Weedon Grossmith. 1962. *The Diary of a Nobody.* London: J.M. Dent & Sons.

Guerrini, Anita. 2003. *Experimenting with Humans and Animals: From Galen to Animal Rights.* Baltimore: Johns Hopkins University Press.

Guibert of Nogent. 1984. *Self and Society in Medieval France: The Memoirs of Abbot Guibert of Nogent.* Edited and translated by John F. Benton. Toronto: University of Toronto Press.

Guy-Bray, Stephen, 2002. *Homoerotic Space: The Poetics of Loss in Renaissance Literature.* Toronto: University of Toronto Press.

Hale, Rosemary Drage. 1995. "'Taste and See, for God is Sweet': Sensory Perception and Memory in Medieval Christian Mystic Experience." In *Vox Mystica: Essays on Medieval Mysticism in Honor of Professor Valerie M. Lagoria.* Anne Clark Bartlett Thomas Bestul, Janet Goebel, and William F. Pollard, ed. Cambridge: D.S. Brewer.

Hall, James. 1999. *The World as Sculpture: The Changing Status of Sculpture from the Renaissance to the Present Day.* London: Chatto & Windus.

Hallisey, Margaret. 1987. *Venomous Woman: Fear of the Female in Literature.* New York: Greenwood Press.

Hamilton, Bernard. 2000. *The Leper King and His Heirs: Baldwin IV and the Crusader Kingdom of Jerusalem.* Cambridge: Cambridge University Press.

Hare, Augustus J. C. 1896. *The Story of My Life.* London: George Allen

Harrison, William. 1994. *The Description of England: The Classic Contemporary Account of Tudor Social Life.* Edited by Georges Edelen. Toronto: Folger Shakespeare Library.

Harvey, Elizabeth D., ed. 2002. *Sensible Flesh: On Touch in Early Modern Culture.* Philadelphia: University of Pennsylvania Press.

Haskell, Francis, and Nicholas Penny. 1981. *Taste and the Antique: The Lure of Classical Sculpture, 1500–1900.* New Haven, CT: Yale University Press.

Hassall, W.O., ed. 1957. *They Saw It Happen: An Anthology of Eye-witnesses' Accounts of Events in British History, 55 B.C.–A.D. 1485.* Oxford: Basil Blackwell.

Hayden, Ruth. 1980. *Mrs. Delany: Her Life and Her Flowers* New York: New Amsterdam Books.

Hays, J. N. 2003. *The Burdens of Disease: Epidemics and Human Response in Western History.* Piscataway, NJ: Rutgers University Press.

Head, Thomas. 2000. "Saints, Heretics, and Fire: Finding Meaning through the Ordeal." In *Monks & Nuns, Saints & Outcasts: Religion in Medieval Society.* Edited by Sharon Farmer and Barbara H. Rosenwein. Ithaca, NY: Cornell University Press.

Hecker, Justus Friedrich Carl. 1970. *The Dancing Mania of the Middle Ages.* New York: Burt Franklin.

Heller-Roazen, Daniel. 2007. *The Inner Touch: Archaeology of a Sensation.* New York: Zone Books.

Henderson, Katherine Usher, and Barbara E. McManus, ed. 1985. *Half Humankind: Contexts and Texts of the Controversy about Women in England, 1540–1640*. Urbana: University of Illinois Press.

Henderson, W. O. 2006. *The Industrial Revolution on the Continent: Germany, France, Russia 1800–1914*. Oxford: Routledge.

Herder, Johann Gottfried. 2002. *Sculpture: Some Observations on Shape and Form from Pygmalion's Creative Dream*. Edited and translated by Jason Gaiger. Chicago: University of Chicago Press.

Hergemöller, Bernd-Ulrich. 2004. "Black Sabbath Masses: Fictitious Rituals and Real Inquisitions." In *The Fall of the Angels*. Edited by Christoph Auffarth and Loren T. Stuckenbruck. Leiden: Brill.

Herlihy, David. 1995. *Women, Family and Society in Medieval Europe: Historical Essays, 1978–1991*. Oxford: Berghan Books.

Herrin, Judith. 1999. *A Medieval Miscellany*. London: Weidenfeld and Nicholson.

Herrmann, Frank, ed. 1972. *The English as Collectors*. London: Chatto and Windus.

Heywood, Colin. 2001. *A History of Childhood: Children and Childhood in the West from Medieval to Modern Times*. Cambridge: Polity Press.

Heywood, John. 1905. "A Merry Play between the Pardoner and the Friar, the Curate and Neighbour Pratt." In *The Dramatic Writings of John Heywood*. Edited by John S. Farmer. London: Early English Drama Society.

Hibbert, Christopher. 1975. *Daily Life in Victorian England*. New York: American Heritage Publishing.

A History of Private Life. Vol. II: *Revelations of the Medieval World*. 1988. Edited by Georges Duby and Philippe Ariès. Translated by Arthur Goldhammer. Cambridge, MA: Belknap Press of Harvard University.

———. Vol. III: *Passions of the Renaissance*. 1989. Edited by Roger Chartier. Translated by Arthur Goldhammer. Cambridge, MA: Belknap Press of Harvard University.

Hivet, Christine. 2005. "Needlework and the Rights of Women in England at the End of the Eighteenth Century." In *The Invisible Woman: Aspects of Women's Work in Eighteenth-century Britain*. Edited by Isabelle Baudino, Jacques Carré, and Marie-Cécile Révauger. Aldershot, England: Ashgate Publishing.

Hobgood-Oster, Laura. 2008. *Holy Dogs and Asses: Animals in Christian Tradition*. Urbana: University of Illinois Press.

Hoffer, Peter Charles. 2005. *Sensory Worlds in Early America*. Baltimore: Johns Hopkins University Press.

Holman, Susan R. 2001. *The Hungry are Dying: Beggars and Bishops in Roman Cappadocia*. Oxford: Oxford University Press.

"The Holy Oil." 1831. *The Royal Lady's Magazine and Archives of the Court of St. James*, Vol. I. London: W. Sams and Sherwood and Co.

"Home Intelligence." 1888. *The Animal's Defender and Zoophilist* 8: 28–29.

Horrox, Rosemary, ed. and trans. 1994. *The Black Death*. Manchester: Manchester University Press.

Howes, David. 2003. *Sensual Relations: Engaging the Senses in Culture and Social Theory*. Ann Arbor: University of Michigan Press.

Howes, David, ed. 1991. *The Varieties of Sensory Experience: A Sourcebook in the Anthropology of the Senses*. Toronto: University of Toronto Press.

————. 2005. *Empire of the Senses: The Sensual Culture Reader.* Oxford: Berg.

Hudson, Kenneth. 1975. *A Social History of Museums: What the Visitors Thought.* London: Macmillan.

Hughes, Muriel Joy. 1968. *Women Healers in Medieval Life and Literature.* Freeport, NY: Books for Libraries Press.

Hugo, Victor. 1887. *Les Miserables.* Translated by Isabel F. Hapgood. New York: Thomas Y. Crowell Company.

Huizinga, Johan. 1948. *The Waning of the Middle Ages.* Translated by Fritz Hopman. London: Edward Arnold.

Hull, Suzanne W. 1982. *Chaste, Silent & Obedient: English Books for Women, 1475–1640.* San Francisco: Huntingdon Library.

Humphrey, Chris. 2001. *The Politics of Carnival: Festive Misrule in Medieval England.* Manchester: Manchester University Press.

Huneycutt, Lois L. 2003. *Matilda of Scotland: A Study in Medieval Queenship.* Woodbridge, UK: Boydell Press.

Hussey, Christopher. 1938. "A-la-Ronde, Exmouth Devon," *Country Life,* April 30.

Hutchinson, F. E. 1965. *Cranmer and the English Reformation.* London: English Universities Press.

Hutton, William. 1818. *A Journey to London.* London: n.p.

Hylson-Smith, Kenneth. 1988. *Evangelicals in the Church of England, 1734–1984.* Edinburgh: T. & T. Clark.

Ickert, Scott. 1998. "Luther and Animals: Subject to Adam's Fall?" In Linzey and Yamamoto, *Animals on the Agenda: Questions about Animals for Theology and Ethics.*

Imbert de Saint-Amand. 2006. *The Duchess of Berry and Charles X.* Teddington, England: The Echo Library.

Isidore of Seville. 2006. "Etymologia." In *Gender and Sexuality in the Middle Ages: A Medieval Source Documents Reader.* Edited by Martha A. Brozyna. Jefferson, NC: McFarland.

Ives, George. 1914. *History of Penal Methods: Criminals, Witches, Lunatics.* London: Stanley Paul & Co.

Jackson-Stops, Gervase. 1991. "A la Ronde, near Exmouth, Devon." *The Magazine Antiques,* June.

Jacquart, Danielle, and Claude Thomasset. 1988. *Sexuality and Medicine in the Middle Ages.* Princeton, NJ: Princeton University Press.

Jameson, Anna. 1844. *Companion to the Most Celebrated Private Galleries of Art in London.* London: Saunders and Otley.

Jephson, Henry. 1978. *The Sanitary Evolution of London.* New York: Arno Press.

Johansen, T. K. 1998. *Aristotle on the Sense Organs.* Cambridge: Cambridge University Press.

John of the Cross. 2007. *The Living Flame of Love.* Translated by David Lewis. New York: Cosimo.

Johnson, Geraldine A. 2002. "Touch, Tactility, and the Reception of Sculpture in Early Modern Italy." In *A Companion to Art Theory.* Edited by Paul Smith and Carolyn Wilde. Oxford: Blackwell.

Jolley, Nicholas. 2000. "Malebranche on the Soul." In *The Cambridge Companion to Malebranche.* Edited by Steven M. Nadler. Cambridge: Cambridge University Press.

Jones, Karen. 2006. *Gender and Petty Crime in Medieval England: The Local Courts in Kent, 1460–1560.* Woodbridge, England: Boydell Press.

Jones, William. 1880. *Credulities Past and Present.* London: Chatto and Windus.

Jordan, Constance. 1990. *Renaissance Feminism: Literary Texts and Political Models.* Ithaca, NY: Cornell University Press.

Jordan, Sarah. 2003. *The Anxieties of Idleness: Idleness in Eighteenth-Century British Literature and Culture.* Cranbury, NJ: Rosemont Publishing.

Jordan, William Chester. 1996. *The Great Famine: Northern Europe in the Early Fourteenth Century.* Princeton, NJ: Princeton University Press.

Jütte, Robert. 2005. *A History of the Senses: From Antiquity to Cyberspace.* Cambridge: Polity Press.

Kadri, Sadakat. 2005. *The Trial: A History from Socrates to O. J. Simpson.* New York: Random House.

Kaeuper, Richard W. 1999. *Chivalry and Violence in Medieval Europe.* Oxford: Oxford University Press.

Karras, Ruth Mazo. 2005. *Sexuality in Medieval Europe: Doing Unto Others.* New York: Routledge.

Keller, Eve. 2003. "The Subject of Touch: Medical Authority in Early Modern Midwivery." In Harvey, *Sensible Flesh: On Touch in Early Modern Culture.*

Kelso, Ruth. 1956. *Doctrine for the Lady of the Renaissance.* Urbana: University of Illinois Press.

Kempe, Margery. 1936. *The Book of Margery Kempe.* Edited by William Butler-Bowden. London: J. Cape.

————. 2004. *The Book of Margery Kempe.* Edited by Barry Windeatt. Cambridge: Brewer.

Kermode, Frank. 1971. *Shakespeare, Spenser, Donne: Renaissance Essays.* New York: Viking Press.

Kete, Katherine. 2007. "Animals and Human Empires." In *A Cultural History of Animals in the Age of Empire.* Edited by Katherine Kete. Oxford: Berg.

Kettle, Ann J. 1995. "Prostitutes and Servant Girls in Later Medieval England." In *Matrons and Marginal Women in Medieval Society.* Edited by Robert R. Edwards and Vickie Ziegler. Woodbridge, UK: Boydell Press.

Kieckhefer, Richard. 1987. "Major Currents in Late Medieval Devotion." In *Christian Spirituality: High Middle Ages and Reformation.* Edited by Jill Raitt. London: Routledge and Kegan Paul.

————. 2000. *Magic in the Middle Ages.* Cambridge: Cambridge University Press.

Kimmelman, Burt. 1999. "The Language of the Text: Authorship and Textuality in *Pearl, The Divine Comedy,* and *Piers Plowman.*" In *The Book and the Magic of Reading in the Middle Ages.* Edited by Albrecht Classen. New York: Garland Publishing.

Klapisch-Zuber, Christine. 1985. *Women, Family and Ritual in Renaissance Italy.* Translated by Lydia G. Cochrane. Chicago: University of Chicago Press.

Kleinschmidt, Harald. 1995. "The Military and Dancing: Changing Norms and Behaviour, 15th to 18th Century." *Ethnologia Europaea* 25: 157–76.

————. 2005. *Perception and Action in Medieval Europe.* Woodbridge, UK: Boydell Press.

Knight, Alan E. 1983. *Aspects of Genre in Late Medieval French Drama.* Manchester: Manchester University Press.

Kolofsky, Craig. 2005. "The Kiss of Peace in the German Reformation." In *The Kiss in History.* Edited by Karen Harvey. Manchester: Manchester University Press.

Kramer, Heinrich, and James Sprenger. 1971. *The Malleus Maleficarum of Heinrich Kramer and James Sprenger.* Edited and translated by Montague Summers. New York: Dover

Krug, Rebecca. 1999. "The Fifteen Oes." In *Cultures of Piety: Medieval English Devotional Literature in Translation.* Edited by Anne Clark Bartlett and Thomas Howard Besttul. Ithaca, NY: Cornell University Press.

Kwint, Marius, Christopher Breward, and Jeremy Aynsley, ed. 1999. *Material Memories.* Oxford: Berg.

Lamb, Charles. 1841. *The Letters of Charles Lamb: With a Sketch of His Life.* Edited by Thomas Noon Talfourd. London: Bradbury and Evans.

Lancaster, William. 1995. *The Department Store: A Social History.* Leicester: Leicester University Press.

Langbein, John H. 2004. "The Legal History of Torture." In *Torture: A Collection.* Edited by Sanford Levinson. Oxford: Oxford University Press.

Langland, William. 1935. *The Vision of Piers Plowman.* Translated by Henry W. Wells. New York: Sheed & Ward.

Lansbury, Coral. 1985. *The Old Brown Dog: Women, Workers and Vivisection in Edwardian England.* Madison: University of Wisconsin Press.

Lansing, Carol. 1998. *Power & Purity: Cathar Heresy in Medieval Italy.* Oxford: Oxford University Press.

Laqueur, Thomas. 1990. *Making Sex: Body and Gender from the Greeks to Freud.* Cambridge, MA: Harvard University Press.

Largier, Niklaus. 2007. *In Praise of the Whip: A Cultural History of Arousal.* New York: Zone Books.

La Roche, Sophie. 1933. *Sophie in London, 1786: Being the Diary of Sophie Von La Roche.* Translated by C. Williams. London: Jonathan Cape.

Lawrence, David R. 2009. *The Complete Soldier: Military Books and Military Culture in Early Stuart England, 1603–1645.* Leiden: Brill.

Lazarillo de Tormes. 1971. In *Two Spanish Picaresque Novels.* Translated by Michael Apert. Harmonsworth, England: Penguin.

Lea, Henry Charles. 1957. *Materials Toward a History of Witchcraft.* New York: Yoseloff.

LeBrun, François. 1989. "The Two Reformations: Communal Devotion and Personal Piety." In *A History of Private Life*, Vol. III: *Passions of the Renaissance.*

Le Goff, Jacques. 1984. *The Birth of Purgatory.* Translated by Arthur Goldhammer. Chicago: University of Chicago Press.

———. 1988. *Medieval Civilization, 400–1500.* Translated by Julia Barrow. Oxford: Blackwell.

———. 1998. "Reims, City of Coronation." In *Realms of Memory: The Construction of the French Past.* Edited by Pierre Nora and Lawrence D. Kritzman. Translated by Arthur Goldhammer. New York: Columbia University Press.

———. 2004. *Saint Francis of Assisi.* Translated by Christine Rhone. London: Routledge.

———. 2009. *Saint Louis.* Translated by Gareth Evan Gollrad. Notre Dame, IN: University of Notre Dame Press.

Lentes, Thomas. 2002. "Counting Piety in the Late Middle Ages." In *Ordering Medieval Society: Perspectives on Intellectual and Practical Modes.* Edited by Bernhard Jussen. Philadelphia: University of Pennsylvania Press.

Leshem, Ayval. 2003. *Newton on Mathematics and Spiritual Purity.* Dordrecht, The Netherlands: Kluwer Academic Publishers.

Levy, Michael. 1970. *A Brief History of the National Gallery with a Representative Selection of Pictures.* London: Pitkin Pictorials.

Levy, William Hanks. 1872. *Blindness and the Blind.* London: Chapman and Hall.

Lewalski. Barbara K. 2003. *The Life of John Milton.* Oxford: Blackwell.

Lewis, C. S. 1946. *The Problem of Pain.* London: The Centenary Press.

———. 1964. *The Discarded Image: An Introduction to Medieval and Renaissance Literature.* Cambridge: Cambridge University Press.

Linzey, Andrew. 1995. *Animal Theology.* Urbana: University of Illinois Press.

Linzey, Andrew, and Dorothy Yamamoto, ed. 1998. *Animals on the Agenda: Questions about Animals for Theology and Ethics.* London: SCM Press.

The Little Flowers of St. Francis. 1907. Translated by T. W. Arnold. London: Dent.

Lloyd, Genevieve. 1984. *The Man of Reason: "Male" and "Female" in Western Philosophy.* London: Methuen and Co.

Llull, Ramon. 1926. *The Book of the Order of Chyvalry.* Translated by William Caxton. Oxford: Oxford University Press.

Locke, John. 1779. *Some Thoughts Concerning Education.* London: J. and R. Tonson.

Logan, Thad. 2001. *The Victorian Parlour.* Cambridge: Cambridge University Press.

Luther, Martin. 1967. "Table Talk." In *Luther's Works.* Vol. 54. Translated and edited by Theodore G. Tappert. Philadelphia: Fortress Press.

Lutz, Tom. 1999. *Crying: The Natural and Cultural History of Tears.* New York: W. W. Norton & Company.

Lynch, Kathryn L. 1988. *The High Medieval Dream Vision: Poetry, Philosophy, and Literary Form.* Stanford, CA: Stanford University Press.

MacGregor, A. 1983. *Tradescant's Rarities.* Oxford: Clarendon.

Mackay, Charles. 1980. *Extraordinary Popular Delusions and the Madness of Crowds.* New York: Three Rivers.

MacKinney, Loren Carey. 1979. *Early Medieval Medicine: With Special Reference to France and Chartres.* Baltimore, Johns Hopkins Press.

Maclean, Ian. 1980. *The Renaissance Notion of Woman: A Study in the Fortunes of Scholasticism and Medical Science in European Intellectual Life.* Cambridge: Cambridge University Press.

Malory, Thomas. 1998. *Le Morte D'Arthur: The Winchester Manuscript.* Edited by Helen Cooper. Oxford: Oxford University Press.

Mandrou, Robert. 1976. *Introduction to Modern France, 1500–1640: An Essay in Historical Psychology.* Translated by R. E. Hallmark. New York: Holmes & Meier.

Manzoni, Alessandro. 1834. *The Betrothed.* London: Richard Bentley.

Markham, Gervase. 1986. *The English Housewife.* Edited by Michael R. Best. Montreal: McGill-Queens University Press.

Marks, Laura U. 2002. *Touch: Sensuous Theory and Multisensory Media.* Minneapolis: University of Minnesota Press.

Marshall, Peter. 2006. *Religious Identities in Henry VIII's England.* Aldershot, England: Ashgate.

Martin, John Jeffries. 2006. *Myths of Renaissance Individualism.* New York: Palgrave Macmillan.

Marx, Karl. 1988. *The Civil War in France.* New York: International Publishers.

Marx, Karl, and Friedrich Engels. 1996. "The Manifesto of the Communist Party. " In *Marx: Later Political Writings.* Edited by Terrell Carver. Cambridge: Cambridge University Press.

Masson, David. 1877. *The Life of John Milton: Narrated in Connexion with the Political, Ecclesiastical, and Literary History of his Time.* Vol. 5. London: Macmillan and Co.

Matthews, William Henry. 1922. *Mazes and Labyrinths: A General Account of Their History and Development.* London: Longmans, Green and Co.

Maxwell-Stuart, P. G. 2003. *Witch Hunters: Professional Prickers, Unwitchers & Witch Finders of the Renaissance.* Stroud, UK: Tempus.

Mayhew, Henry, and John Binny. 1862. *The Criminal Prisons of London and Scenes of Prison Life.* London: Griffin, Bohm and Company.

Mays, Simon A. 2005. "Paleopathological Study of Halux Valgus." *American Journal of Physical Anthropology* 126, no. 3: 139–49.

McCabe, James Dabney. 1869. *Paris by Sunlight and Gaslight*. Philadelphia: National Publishing Company.

McClellan, Andrew. 1994. *Inventing the Louvre: Art, Politics, and the Origins of the Modern Museum in Eighteenth-Century Paris*. Berkeley: University of California Press.

McDonnell, Myles Anthony. 2006. *Roman Manliness: Virtus and the Roman Republic*. Cambridge: Cambridge University Press.

McNamer, Sarah. 2010. *Affective Meditation and the Invention of Medieval Compassion*. Philadelphia: University of Pennsylvania Press.

Mearns, Rodney, ed. 1985. *The Vision of Tundale*. Heidelberg: Carl Winter.

Mercier, Louis-Sébastien. 1929. *The Picture of Paris Before & After the Revolution*. Translated by Wilfrid Jackson and Emilie Jackson. London: George Routledge & Sons.

Michie, Helena. 2006. *Victorian Honeymoons: Journeys to the Conjugal*. Cambridge: Cambridge University Press.

Midelfort, H. C. Erik, 1999. *A History of Madness in Sixteenth-Century Germany*. Stanford, CA: Stanford University Press.

Milhaven, John Giles. 1993. *Hadewijch and Her Sisters: Other Ways of Loving and Knowing*. Albany: State University of New York.

Miller, Edward. 1974. *That Noble Cabinet: A History of the British Museum*. Athens, OH: Ohio University Press.

Miller, James. 1963. "The Humours of Oxford." In *Three Centuries of English and American Plays: England, 1500–1800*. Vol. 3. Edited by Henry Willis Wells. New York: Redex Microprint Corporation.

Miller, John D. 2002. *Beads and Prayers: The Rosary in History and Devotion*. London: Burnes & Oates.

Miller, Michael B. 1981. *The Bon Marché: Bourgeois Culture and the Department Store, 1869–1920*. Princeton, NJ: Princeton University Press.

Minowski, W. L. 1994. "Physician Motives in Banning Medieval Traditional Healers." *Women and Health* 21: 1.

Mocarelli, Luca. 2009. "The Attitude of Milanese Society to Work and Commercial Activities." In *The Idea of Work in Europe from Antiquity to Modern Times*. Edited by Josef Ehmer and Catharina Lis. Farnham, England: Ashgate Publishing.

Modiano, Raimonda. 1978. "Coleridge's Views on Touch and Other Senses." *Bulletin of Research in the Humanities* 81: 28–41.

Molloy, J. Fitzgerald. 1885. *Royalty Restored, or London under Charles II*. London: Ward and Downey.

Mommsen, Theodor E. 2002. "Petrarch's Conception of the 'Dark Ages.'" In *Italian Renaissance: The Essential Readings*. Edited by Paula Findlen. Oxford: Blackwell.

Montaigne, Michel de. 1943. *Selected Essays*. Translated by Donald M. Frame. New York: W. J. Black.

———. 2003. *Apology for Raymond Sebond*. Translated by Roger Ariew and Marjorie Grene. Indianapolis, IN: Hacklett Publishing Company.

Moore, James R., ed. 1988. *Religion in Victorian Britain*. Vol. III, *Sources*. Manchester: Manchester University Press.

More, Thomas. 2000. *The Last Letters of Thomas More.* Edited by Alvaro de Silva. Grand Rapids, MI: William B. Eerdmans.

————. 2002. *The Four Last Things: The Supplication of Souls; A Dialogue on Conscience.* New York: Scepter Publishers.

————. 2008. *Utopia.* Rockville, MD: Arc Manor.

Moreira, Isabel. 2000. *Dreams, Visions, and Spiritual Authority in Merovingian Gaul.* Ithaca, NY: Cornell University Press.

Morgan, Kenneth. 1993. *Bristol and the Atlantic Trade in the Eighteenth Century.* Cambridge: Cambridge University Press.

Morison, James Cotter. 1884. *The Life and Times of Saint Bernard, Abbot of Clairvaux, A.D. 1091–1153.* London: Macmillian and Co.

Mormando, Franco. 1999. *The Preacher's Demons: Bernardino of Siena and the Social Underworld of Early Renaissance Italy.* Chicago: University of Chicago Press.

Morris, David B. 2005. "Sex, Pain and the Marquis de Sade." In Classen, *The Book of Touch.*

Most, Glenn W. 2005. *Doubting Thomas.* Cambridge, MA: Harvard University Press.

Muir, Edward. 2005. *Ritual in Early Modern Europe.* Cambridge: Cambridge University Press.

Mumford, Lewis. 1938. *The Culture of Cities.* New York: Harcourt, Brace and Company.

Murray, David. 1904. *Museums: Their History and Use,* Vol. 1. Glasgow: James MacLehose and Sons.

Musson, Albert Edward, and Eric Robinson. 1969. *Science and Technology in the Industrial Revolution.* Manchester, University of Manchester Press.

Nagy, Doreen Evenden. 1988. *Popular Medicine in Seventeenth-Century England.* Bowling Green, OH: Bowling Green State University Popular Press.

Naqvi, Nassim H., and M. Donald Blaufox. 1998. *Blood Pressure Measurement: An Illustrated History.* Pearl River, NY: Parthenon Publishing Group.

Nichols, Marden Fitzpatrick. 2006. "Plaster Cast Sculpture: A History of Touch." *Archaeological Review from Cambridge* 21: 114–30.

Nichols, Stephen G., Andreas Kablitz, and Alison Calhoun, ed. 2008. *Rethinking the Medieval Senses: Heritage, Fascinations, Frames.* Baltimore: Johns Hopkins University Press.

Nihell, Elizabeth. 1760. *A Treatise on the Art of Midwifery.* London: A. Morley.

Nordenfalk, Carl. 1990. "The Sense of Touch in Art." In *The Verbal and the Visual: Essays in Honor of William Sebastian Heckscher.* Edited by Karl-Ludwug Selig and Elizabeth Sears. New York: Italica Press.

Norman, A. V. B. 1971. *The Medieval Soldier.* New York: Thomas Y. Cromwell.

Norton, Robert E. 1990. *Herder's Aesthetics and the European Enlightenment.* Ithaca, N.Y.: Cornell University Press.

Nutton, Vivian. 1993. "Galen at the Bedside: The Methods of a Medical Detective." In Bynum and Porter, *Medicine and the Five Senses.*

Nye, David E. 1992. *Electrifying America: Social Meanings of a New Technology.* Cambridge, MA: MIT Press.

Nyrop, Christopher. 1901. *The Kiss and Its History.* Translated by W. F. Harvey. London: Sands & Co.

Olin, Margaret. 2000. "Alois Riegl." In *Medieval Scholarship: Biographical Studies on the Formation of a Discipline.* Vol. 3: *Philosophy and the Arts.* Edited by Helen Damico. New York: Garland Publishing.

Oliphant, Margaret O. W. 1896. "The Anti-Marriage League." In *Blackwood's Edinburgh Magazine.*

Orme, Nicholas. 2001. *Medieval Children*. New Haven, CT: Yale University Press.

————. 2006. *Medieval Schools: From Roman Britain to Renaissance England*. New Haven, CT: Yale University Press.

Orwell, George. 1937. *The Road to Wigan Pier*. London: Victor Gollancz.

Osborne, Catherine. 2007. *Dumb Beasts and Dead Philosophers: Humanity and the Humane in Ancient Philosophy and Literature*. Oxford: Oxford University Press.

Osterberg, Eva, and Dag Lindström. 1988. *Crime and Social Control in Medieval and Early Modern Swedish Towns*. Uppsala: Academia Upsaliensis.

Ovenell, R. F. 1986. *The Ashmolean Museum, 1683–1894*. Oxford: Clarendon Press.

"Pangur Ban," 1987. Translated by Robin Flower. In *Irish Literature: A Reader*. Edited by Maureen O'Rourke Murphy and James MacKillop. Syracuse, NY: Syracuse University Press.

Park, Katherine. 1998. "Medicine and Society in Medieval Europe." In *Medicine in Society: Historical Essays*. Edited by Andrew Wear. Cambridge: Cambridge University Press.

Parker, William Riley. 1996. *Milton: The Life*. Edited by Gordon Campbell. Oxford: Clarendon.

Parker, Rozsika. 1984. *The Subversive Stitch: Embroidery and the Making of the Feminine*. New York: Routledge.

Paterson, Mark. 2007. *The Senses of Touch: Haptics, Affects, and Technologies*. Oxford: Berg.

Pearsall, Derek, ed. 1999. *Chaucer to Spenser: An Anthology of Writings in English, 1375–1575*. Oxford: Blackwell.

Peña, Carolyn Thomas de la. 2005. "The Golden Age of Electrotherapy." In Classen, *The Book of Touch*.

Penn, Alan, 1999. *Targeting Schools: Drill, Militarism, and Imperialism*. London: Woburn Press.

Pepper, Simon. 2002. "Body, Diagram, and Geometry in the Renaissance Fortress." In *Body and Building: Essays on the Changing Relation of Body and Architecture*. Edited by George Dodds and Robert Tavenor. Cambridge, MA: MIT Press.

Pepys, Samuel. 1976. *The Diary of Samuel Pepys*. Edited by R. Latham and W. Matthews. Berkeley: University of California Press.

Petkov, Kiril. 2003. *The Kiss of Peace: Ritual, Self, and Society in the High and Late Medieval West*. Leiden: Brill.

Petrarch, Francesco. 1898. *Petrarch: The First Modern Scholar and Man of Letters*. Edited and translated by James H. Robinson. New York: Haskell House Publishers.

Philo, 1961. *Questions and Answers on Genesis*. Translated by Ralph Marcus. Cambridge, MA: Harvard University Press.

Pleij, Herman. 2001. *Dreaming of Cockaigne: Medieval Fantasies of the Perfect Life*. Translated by Diane Webb. New York: Columbia University Press.

————. 2004. *Colors Demonic and Divine*. Translated by Dianne Webb. New York: Colombia University Press.

The Plough, the Loom and the Anvil. Vol. 4. 1852. New York: Myron Finch.

Plumptre, James. 1816. *The Experienced Butcher*. London: Darton, Harvey, and Co.

Pointon, Marcia. 1999. "Materializing Mourning: Hair, Jewelry and the Body." In Kwint, Breward, and Aynsley, *Material Memories*.

Porter, Roy. 1999. *The Greatest Benefit to Mankind: A Medical History of Humanity*. New York: Harper Collins.

————. 2005. *Flesh in the Age of Reason: The Modern Foundations of Body and Soul*. New York: W. W. Norton.

Porter, Dorothy, and Roy Porter. 1989. *Patient's Progress: Doctors and Doctoring in Eighteenth-Century England.* Stanford, CA: Stanford University Press.

Power, Eileen. 1995. *Medieval Women.* Cambridge: Cambridge University Press.

———. 2006. "Introduction." In *The Goodman of Paris.* Translated and edited by Eileen Power. Woodbridge, UK: Boydel Press.

Preece, Rod. 2002. *Awe for the Tiger, Love for the Lamb: A Chronicle of Sensibility to Animals.* Vancouver: University of British Columbia Press.

———. 2008. *Sins of the Flesh: A History of Ethical Vegetarian Thought.* Vancouver: University of British Columbia Press.

Priestley, Philip. 1985. *Victorian Prison Lives: English Prison Biography, 1830–1914.* London: Methuen & Co. .

Quillen, Carol E. 1998. *Rereading the Renaissance: Petrarch, Augustine, and the Language of Humanism.* Ann Arbor: University of Michigan Press.

Quiviger, François. 2010. *The Sensory World of Italian Renaissance Art.* London: Reaktion Books.

Ranum, Orest. 1989. "The Refuges of Intimacy." In *A History of Private Life.* Vol. III: *Passions of the Renaissance.*

Rappaport, Erika. 2004. "A New Era of Shopping." In *The Nineteenth-Century Visual Culture Reader.* Edited by Vanessa R. Schwartz and Jeannene M. Przyblyski. London: Routledge.

Rawcliffe, Carole. 2006. *Leprosy in Medieval England.* Woodbridge, UK: Boydell Press.

Rémy, Nicholas. 1930. *Demonolatry.* Translated by E. A. Ashwin. London: John Rodker.

Rey, Roselyne. 1998. *The History of Pain.* Translated by Louise Elliot Wallace, J. A. Cadden, and S. W. Cadden. Cambridge, MA: Harvard University Press.

Reynolds, Barbara. 2006. *Dante: The Poet, the Political Thinker, the Man.* London: L.B. Tauris & Co.

Reynolds, Myra. 1964. *The Learned Lady in England.* Gloucester, MA: Peter Smith.

Reynolds, Philip Lyndon. 1999. *Food and the Body: Some Peculiar Questions in High Medieval Theology.* Leiden: Brill.

Rice, Shelley. 2000. *Parisian Views.* Cambridge, MA: MIT Press.

Rickaby, Joseph. 1888. *Moral Philosophy: or Ethics and Natural Law.* London: Longmans, Green & Co.

Rigaux, Dominique. 2005. *Le Christ du dimanche, histoire d'une image médiévale.* Paris: L'Harmattan.

Riskin, Jessica. 2002. *Science in the Age of Sensibility.* Chicago: University of Chicago Press.

Ritvo, Harriet. 1987. *The Animal Estate: The English and Other Creatures in the Victorian Age.* Cambridge, MA: Harvard University Press.

Rolle, Richard. 2000. "The Fire of Love." In *English Spirituality in the Age of Wyclif.* Edited by David Lyle Jeffrey. Vancouver, BC: Regent College.

Rossiaud, Jacques. 1995. *Medieval Prostitution.* Translated by Lydia G. Cochrane. Oxford: Blackwell.

Rowling, Marjorie. 1973. *Life in Medieval Times.* New York: Berkley Publishing Group.

Rubin, Miri. 1991. *Corpus Christi: The Eucharist in Late Medieval Culture.* Cambridge: Cambridge University Press.

Rudy, Gordon. 2002. *The Mystical Language of Sensation in the Later Middle Ages.* New York: Routledge.

Russell, Jeffrey Burton. 1997. *A History of Heaven: The Singing Silence.* Princeton, NJ: Princeton University Press.

Ryder, Richard D. 2000. *Animal Revolution: Changing Attitudes toward Speciesism.* Oxford: Berg.

Salisbury, Deb, ed. 2009. *Elephant's Breath & London Smoke: Historic Colour Names, Definitions & Uses.* Neustadt, ON: Five Rivers Chapmanry.

Salisbury, Joyce E. 1994. *The Beast Within: Animals in the Middle Ages.* London: Routledge.

Sankovitch, Tilde A. 1988. *French Women Writers and the Book: Myths of Access and Desire.* Syracuse, NY: Syracuse University Press.

Savage, Anne, and Nicholas Watson. 1991. *Anchoritic Spirituality: Ancrene Wisse and Associated Works.* Mahwah, NJ: Paulist Press.

Schaffer, Simon. 1998. "Regeneration: The Body of Natural Philosophy in Restoration England." In *Science Incarnate: Historical Embodiments of Natural Knowledge.* Edited by Christopher Lawrence and Steven Shapin. Chicago: University of Chicago Press.

Schiller, Friedrich. 1982. *On the Aesthetics and Education of Man.* Edited and translated by E. M. Wilkinson and L. A. Willoughby. Oxford: Clarendon.

Schivelbusch, Wolfgang. 1995. *Disenchanted Night: The Industrialization of Light in the Nineteenth Century.* Translated by Angela Davies. Berkeley: University of California Press.

Schleif, Corine, and Richard G. Newhauser, ed. 2010. "Pleasure and Danger in Perception: The Five Senses in the Middle Ages and the Renaissance." Special issue of *The Senses & Society* 5, no. 1.

"The Schoolboy's Lament." 1999. In Pearsall, *Chaucer to Spenser.*

Schott, G. D. 2004. "The Sick Dürer—a Renaissance Prototype Pain Map." *British Medical Journal* 7474–7480: 1492.

Scot, Reginald. 1964. *The Discoverie of Witchcraft.* London: Centaur Press.

Scully, Terence. 2005. *The Art of Cookery in the Middle Ages.* Woodbridge, UK: Boydell Press.

"Segunda Pastorum." 1897. In *The Timothy Plays.* Edited by G. England. London: Oxford University Press for the Early English Text Society.

Sells, Michael Anthony. 1994. *Mystical Languages of Unsaying.* Chicago: University of Chicago Press.

Sennett, Richard. 1994. *Flesh and Stone: The Body and the City in Western Civilization.* New York: W. W. Norton.

Sewell, Anna. 1922. *Black Beauty: The Autobiography of a Horse.* Garden City, NY: Doubleday.

Shackford, Martha Hale. 1913. *Legends and Satires from Medieval Literature.* Boston: Ginn and Company.

Shadwell, Thomas. 1927. *The Complete Works.* Edited by Montague Summers. London: The Fortune Press.

Siebers, Alisha. 2006. "Marie Corelli's Magnetic Revitalizing Force." In *Victorian Literary Mesmerism.* Edited by Martin Willis and Catherine Wynne. Amsterdam: Rodopi.

"Sight-seeing in the Time of Queen Anne." 1881. In *All the Year Round*, February 19.

Simmons, James R. Jr., ed. 2007. *Factory Lives: Four Nineteenth-Century Working-Class Autobiographies.* Peterborough, ON: Broadview Press.

Sir Gawain and the Green Knight. 1992. Edited and translated by James Winny. Peterborough, ON: Broadview Press.

Smith, Ann D. 1962. *Women in Prison: A Study in Penal Methods.* London: Stevens.

Smith, Bruce R. 1999. *The Acoustic World of Early Modern England: Attending to the O-Factor.* Chicago: University of Chicago Press.

Smith, Mark. M. 2006. *How Race is Made: Slavery, Segregation and the Senses.* Chapel Hill: University of North Carolina Press.

————. 2007. *Sensing the Past: Seeing, Hearing, Smelling, Tasting, and Touching in History.* Berkeley: University of California Press.

Smith, Virginia Sarah. 2007. *Clean: A History of Personal Hygiene and Purity.* Oxford: Oxford University Press.

Smollet, Tobias George. 2008. *Humphry Clinker.* Edited by Angus Ross. London: Penguin.

Snoek, Godefridus, J. 1995. *Medieval Piety from Relics to the Eucharist: A Process of Mutual Interaction.* Leiden: Brill.

The Song of Roland. 2002. Translated by Robert Harrison. New York: New American Library.

Sorrell, Roger Daniel 1988. *St. Francis of Assisi and Nature: Tradition and Innovation in Western Christian Attitudes Toward the Environment.* Oxford: Oxford University Press.

Sousa, Geraldo U. de. 1996. "The Peasants' Revolt and the Writing of History in 2 Henry VI." In *Reading and Writing in Shakespeare.* Edited by David M. Bergeron. Cranbury, NJ: Associated University Presses,

Southey, Robert. 1808. *Letters from England.* Vol. I. New York: David Longworth.

Spearing, A. C. 1987. *Readings in Medieval Poetry.* Cambridge: Cambridge University Press.

Spierenburg, Pieter. 2008. *A History of Murder: Personal Violence in Europe from the Middle Ages to the Present.* Cambridge: Polity Press.

Stallybrass, Peter, and Allon White. 1986. *The Politics and Poetics of Transgression.* London: Methuen and Co.

Steel, Carlos G., Guy Goldentops, and Pieter Beuliens, ed. 1999. *Aristotle's Animals in the Middle Ages and Renaissance.* Leuven, Belgium: Leuven University Press.

Steiner, Gary. 2005. *Anthropocentrism and its Discontents: The Moral Status of Animals in the History of Western Philosophy.* Pittsburgh, PA: University of Pittsburgh Press.

Stendhal. 1927. *On Love.* Translated by H. B. V. New York: Boni & Liveright.

Stewart, Susan. 1999. "Prologue: From the Museum of Touch." In Kwint, Breward, and Aynsley, *Material Memories.*

The Story of Grettir the Strong. 1869. Translated by Eiríkr Magnússon and William Morris. London: F.S. Ellis.

Strutt, Joseph. 1801. *The Sports and Pastimes of the People of England.* London: Methuen & Co.

Stuart, Tristram. 2006. *The Bloodless Revolution: A Cultural History of Vegetarianism from 1600 to Modern Times.* London: Harper Press.

Sturges, Robert S. 2000. *Chaucer's Pardoner and Gender Theory: Bodies of Discourse.* New York: St. Martin's Press.

Summers, David. 1987. *The Judgement of Sense: Renaissance Naturalism and the Rise of Aesthetics.* Cambridge: Cambridge University Press.

Synnott, Anthony. 2005. "Handling Children: To Touch or Not to Touch?" In Classen, *The Book of Touch.*

Tattlewell, Mary, and Joan Hit-Him-Home. 1985. "The Women's Sharp Revenge." In Henderson and McManus, *Half Humankind.*

Tatton-Brown, Tim. 2002. "Canterbury and the Architecture of Pilgrimage Shrines in England." In *Pilgrimage: The English Experience from Becket to Bunyan.* Edited by Colin Morris and Peter Roberts. Cambridge: Cambridge University Press.

Taylor, John. 1985. "A Juniper Lecture." In Henderson and McManus, *Half Humankind.*

Teather, Lynne. 1984. "Museology and Its Traditions: The British Empire, 1845–1945," Ph.D. dissertation. Leicester: University of Leicester.

Teresa of Avila. 2002. "Relation V." In *Complete Works of Teresa of Avila*. Vol. 1. Translated by E. Allison Peers. London: Burns & Oates.

―――――. 2007. *The Book of My Life*. Translated by Mirabai Starr. Boston: Shambala Publications.

Thewelaite, Karl. 2005. "Sexuality and the Drill." In Classen, *The Book of Touch*.

Thomas, Keith. 1983. *Man and the Natural World: Changing Attitudes in England, 1500–1800*. Oxford: Oxford University Press.

―――――. 1986. "Literacy in Early Modern England." In *The Written Word: Literacy in Transition*. Edited by Gerd Baumann. Oxford: Clarendon Press.

―――――. 1997. *Religion and the Decline of Magic: Studies in Popular Beliefs in Sixteenth- and Seventeenth-Century England*. Oxford: Oxford University Press.

―――――. 2005. "Magical Healing." In Classen, *The Book of Touch*.

Thomas, Nicholas. 1991. *Entangled Objects: Exchange, Material Culture, and Colonialism in the Pacific*. Cambridge, MA: Harvard University Press.

Thomas à Kempis. 1912. *St. Lydwine of Schiedam*. Translated by Vincent Scully. London: Burns & Oates.

Thomas Aquinas. 1970. *Summa Theologiae*. Translated by Timothy Suttor. New York: Blackfriars.

Thomson, James. 1876. *The Seasons and the Castle of Indolence*. London: Chatto and Windus.

Thorndike, Lynn. 1958. *History of Magic and Experimental Science*. Vol. 4. New York: Columbia University Press.

Thurston, Herbert. 1898. *The Life of Saint Hugh of Lincoln*. London: Burns and Oates.

Torrell, Jean-Pierre. 2005. *Saint Thomas Aquinas: The Person and His Work*. Translated by Robert Royal. Washington, DC: Catholic University of America Press.

Trevor-Roper, H. R. 1967. *The European Witch-Craze of the Sixteenth and Seventeenth Centuries and Other Essays*. New York: Harper & Row.

Trollope, Anthony. 1859. *The Bertrams*. Vol. I. New York: Harper & Brothers.

Tryon, Thomas. 1691. *The Way to Health. Long Life and Happiness*. London: R. Baldwin.

Tuchman, Barbara W. 1978. *A Distant Mirror: The Calamitous 14th Century*. New York: Ballantine Books.

Tudor, M. L. R. . 1970. *A la Ronde (The Round House) Exmouth and the Parminter Collection*. Exeter: W. V. Coles & Sons.

Turner, Alice K. 1993. *The History of Hell*. San Diego: Harcourt Brace & Co.

Uffenbach, Zacharias Conrad von. 1928. *Oxford in 1710: From the Travels of Zacharius Conrad von Uffenbach*. Translated and edited by William Henry Quarrell and William James Chance Quarrell. Oxford: Basil Blackwell.

―――――. 1934. *London in 1710: From the Travels of Zacharius Conrad von Uffenbach*. Translated by William Henry Quarrell and Margaret Mare. London: Faber & Faber.

Ure, Andrew. 1967. *The Philosophy of Manufactures: or, An Exposition of the Scientific, Moral, and Commercial Economy of the Factory System of Great Britain*. London: Frank Cass and Company.

Van Horn Melton, James. 1988. *Absolutism and the Eighteenth-Century Origins of Compulsory Schooling in Prussia and Austria*. Cambridge: Cambridge University Press.

Van Sant, Ann Jessie. 1993. *Eighteenth-Century Sensibility and the Novel: The Senses in Social Context*. Cambridge: Cambridge University Press.

Vauchez, André. 1997. *Sainthood in the Later Middle Ages*. Translated by Jean Birrell. Cambridge: Cambridge University Press.

Vaughan, Richard. 2002. *Philip the Good: The Apogee of Burgundy*. Woodridge, UK: Boydell Press.

Vila, Anne C. 1998. *Enlightenment and Pathology: Sensibility in the Literature and Medicine of Eighteenth-Century France.* Baltimore: Johns Hopkins University Press.

Viladesau, Richard. 2006. *The Beauty of the Cross: The Passion of Christ in Theology and the Arts, from the Catacombs to the Eve of the Renaissance.* Oxford: Oxford University Press.

Villon, François. 1994. *Complete Poems.* Edited and translated by Barbara N. Sargent-Baur. Toronto: University of Toronto Press.

Vinge, Louise. 1975. *The Five Senses: Studies in a Literary Tradition.* Lund, Sweden: The Royal Society of Letters at Lund.

Walsh, James, ed. 1981. *The Cloud of Unknowing.* Mahwah, NJ: Paulist Press.

Waterman, Catharine Harbeson. 1853. *The Book of Parlour Games.* Philadelphia: H.C. Peck & Theo. Bliss.

Weinstein, Donald, and Rudolph M. Bell. 1982. *Saints & Society: The Two Worlds of Western Christendom, 1000–1700.* Chicago: University of Chicago Press.

Weygand, Zina. 2009. *The Blind in French Society from the Middle Ages to the Century of Louis Braille.* Translated by Emily-Jane Cohen. Stanford, CA: Stanford University Press.

Wheeler, Michael. 1990. *Heaven, Hell, and the Victorians.* Cambridge: Cambridge University Press.

Wilkins, Sally E. D. 2002. *Sports and Games of Medieval Cultures.* Westport, CT: Greenwood Press.

Williams, Deanne. 2004. *The French Fetish from Chaucer to Shakespeare.* Cambridge: Cambridge University Press.

Wilson, Katharina M., ed. 1987. *Women Writers of the Renaissance and Reformation.* Athens, University of Georgia Press.

Windham, William. 1841. *Select Speeches of the Right Honourable William Windham and the Right Honourable William Huskisson.* Edited by Robert Walsh. Philadelphia: Edward C. Biddle.

Winny, James. 1992. "Introduction." In *Sir Gawain and the Green Knight.*

Woolf, Daniel R. 2003. *The Social Circulation of the Past: English Historical Culture, 1500–1730.* Oxford: Oxford University Press.

Woolgar, C. M. 2006. *The Senses in Late Medieval England.* New Haven, CT: Yale University Press.

Woolley, Hannah. 1684. *The Queen-like Closet or Rich Cabinet.* 5th ed. London: R. Chiswel.

Yamamoto, Dorothy. 2000. *The Boundaries of the Human in Medieval English Literature.* Oxford: Oxford University Press.

Zaleski, Carol. 1987. *Otherworld Journeys: Accounts of Near-death Experience in Medieval and Modern Times.* Oxford: Oxford University Press.

Zola, Emile. 1886. *The Ladies' Paradise.* London: Vizetelly.

Zwijnenberg, Robert. 2003. "Presence and Absence: On Leonardo da Vinci's *Saint John the Baptist.*" In *Compelling Visuality: The Work of Art in and out of History.* Edited by C. Farago and R. Zwijnenberg. Minneapolis: University of Minnesota Press.

INDEX

Adair, James, 80–81

Adam and Eve, 17, 73, 75, 91, 101, 118, 148

Adams, Thomas, 118

Aelfric, 18, 19

agriculture, 16–17

A la Ronde, 134–36

Albertus Magnus, 87

Alice of Schaerbeek, 62

anaesthetics, 164

Ancrene Wisse, 33, 62, 87

Angela of Foligno, 41, 87, 88

angels, 111–12, 114–15

animals, xv, xvii, 16–17, 58, 93, 172; as companions, 95–103; and experimentation, 117–22, as food, 94–97, 101, 105–6; and rationality, 109–17; trials of, 113–15

Annales School, xv

Anthropology of the Senses, xvi

Ariès, Philippe, xv

Aristotle, 74, 108

art, 123–66

asceticism, 31–35

Au bonheur des dames, 191, 194

Aucassin & Nicolette, 68

Augustine of Hippo, 43–44, 118, 148

Ayrault, Pierre, 129

baiting, 107–8

Baldwin IV of Jerusalem, 56

bathing, 3, 20–21, 32, 86

Beard, George, 184–85

Becket, Thomas, 5, 33, 44, 56

beds, 3–4, 9–10, 11–12

Benedict of Aniane, 32

Bentham, Jeremy, 120

Beowulf, 124

Berenson, Bernard, 126–27

Bernardino of Siena, 69, 117

Bernard of Clairvaux, 29–30, 35, 48, 62, 128, 129

bestiary, 75, 93, 113, 117

Bible, 30, 36, 44–45, 65, 75, 111–12, 115, 152

Bingley, William, 96, 109

birds, 104, 116

Birgitta of Sweden, 29

Black Beauty, 121

blindness, 51–56, 123, 160–61

Bloch, Marc, xv, 1

Boccaccio, Giovanni, 15, 58

Bonardo, Giovanni, 94

Born, Bertran de, 25

Bougeant, Guillaume-Hyacinthe, 120

Boyle, Robert, 159

Braille, 160–61

Braunstein, Philippe, 123

Bruegel the Elder, Pieter, 22, 59

Bueil, Jean de, 25

Burney, Frances, 162
butchers, 97

Cade, Jack, 6
Canterbury Tales, The, 98, 151
capital punishment, 63–64, 69, 114–15, 158–59, 173–74
Carew, Thomas, 95
Carnival, 15
carving, 29
Castelein, Martin, 52
Castiglione, Baldassare, 129
castles, xvi–xvii, 1–2, 23–24
Catherine of Ricci, 86, 88, 89
Catherine of Siena, 44, 70, 85, 86, 88
cats, 100
Cavendish, Margaret, 82–83, 88, 120, 154
celestial spheres, 27–9
Chadwick, Edwin, 180–81
Charlemagne, 70
Charles I, 54, 158
Charles II, 158–59
Charles X, 165–66
Chaucer, 123, 151
Chauliac, Guy de, 55
Cheyne, George, 120–21
childbirth, 38, 48, 71, 73, 77, 190
children, 17, 77–78, 86–87, 104, 114; disciplining of, 19, 61, 170, 172, 190–91
chimneys, 11–12
cities, 2, 12–15, 178–83, 194
Civilizing Process, The, 154–55
Claire Montefalco, 34
clothing, 4, 8–9, 57, 94, 155, 162–64
Cloud of Unknowing, The, 8, 30
Cockaigne, 16, 22, 95
cold, 7–8, 20, 27–28, 71–74, 77
Coleridge, Samuel, 180
collage, 134
colors, 127–29
Columban, Saint, 46
compassion, 68–70
Condillac, Etienne Bonnot de, 160
Condition of the Working Class in England, The, 170

Confessions of an Opium Eater, 164
Confessions of Augustine, 19, 148
Connor, Steven, xvi
consumer culture, 187, 191–97
Cooke, John, 158
Corbin, Alain, xv
Corelli, Marie, 185
Corpus Christi, 41–43, 149
cosmology, 27–9, 157–58
Cowper, William, 103
craft, 18, 28, 52, 123, 133–36
Cranmer, Thomas, 63
crusades, 45
crying, 70

dancing manias, 59–60, 128
Danse Macabre, 60
Dante, 5, 28, 66
Dark Ages, xii–xiv, 147
darkness, xii–xiii, 11
Darwin, Charles, 109, 120, 187
David I of Scotland, 57
deafness, 120
death, 15, 35, 36–37, 40, 60, 63–64, 118, 129–30
Decameron, The, 151
Defeux, Louis, 1
Defoe, Daniel, xi, 156, 163
Delany, Mary, 133, 134
deodand, 113
department stores, 191–97
De Quincey, Thomas, 164
Descartes, René, 118–19
Des Roches, Catherine, 82
Des Roches, Madeleine, 64
Diderot, Denis, 152
Digby Play, 31
disabilities, 50, 56. *See also* blindness
Discarded Image, The, 123
discipline, 19, 31–32, 61, 88–89, 165–73
Discipline and Punish, 173
disease, 15, 48–60, 62, 89
Divine Comedy, 5, 67
dogs, 24, 95, 98–99, 113, 116, 117
Dowsing, William, 131

drill, military, 167–71, 173–74, 189–90
Du Moulin, Pierre, 54–55
Dürer, Albrecht, 126

eating, 3, 22, 155. *See also* food; taste
Ebner, Margaret, 87, 130
Edmund the Martyr, 37–38, 39
Ekirch, A. Roger, 10
electricity, 183–85
elements, 26–27
Elias, Norbert, 2, 154–55
Elizabeth I, 25
Engels, Friedrich, 121, 170
Erasmus, 4, 152
etiquette, 2–4, 98, 143, 154–56
Eucharist, 41–43, 44, 106, 149
Evelyn, John, 139, 141
evolutionary theory, 109, 182
Expedition of Humphrey Clinker, The, 178
eyeglasses, 123, 153–54

Fable of the Bees, 171
factories, 169–70, 171–72
fairs, 14, 196
famine, 47, 106
Febvre, Lucien, xv
festivals, 14–15
feudalism, 1–2
Fiennes, Celia, 136–37
fire, 7–8, 11–12, 188–89; in cosmology, 26,
    27–28; ordeals by, 43–51; punitive use of,
    63, 65, 69, 92
flagellants, 34–5
fleas, 47–8
Florentius, Saint, 116
food, 2–3, 7, 22, 71, 90, 95–97; animals as,
    101, 105–6, 122; and health, 48–99; in
    museums, 140
Formosus, Pope, 130
Foucault, Michel, 173
Francis de Sales. 62
Francis of Assisi, 36, 58, 70, 100–101, 116
Franciscans, 116–17
Frederick the Great, 169–70
free will, 28

French Revolution, 165, 173, 177
Freud, Sigmund, 182
furniture, 9–10, 11–12, 163–64, 187–89
Futurism, 185–86

Galen, 48–49
games, 22–24, 188
gardens, 10, 157
Gascoigne, George, 97, 121
Gassendi, Pierre, 119–20
Gay, John, 178
Gay, Peter, 189
gestures, 8–9, 31–35, 172
Ghiberti, Lorenzo, 132
Giles, Saint, 100
Gilman, Sander, xv
Giorgio Martini, Francesco di, 12
gloves, 4, 57, 155
God, 27–46, 111–12, 118, 152, 161, 185
Godiva, 32
Goethe, Johann Wolfgang von, 132
Goodman of Paris, The, 20, 21, 47, 110
Gowing, Laura, xvi
Greatrakes, Valentine, 159
Gregory the Great, 41, 100
"Grettir's Saga," 23
Guibert of Nogent, xiv, 150

Hadewijch of Brabant, 30
hair, 92, 104, 187
hair shirts, 9, 32, 33
handholding, 4–5
hands, 104
hares, 103
Harold of Wessex, 36, 39
Harrison, William, 11–12
Harvey, Elizabeth, xvi
Haussmann, Baron, 181–82
Hayes, Mary, 162
healing, 48–9, 55, 124, with electricity,
    184–85; mystical, 38, 50–51, 56, 150–60;
    165–66; and women, 79–81
hearing, xv–xvi, xvii, 14, 19, 26, 64, 69, 75, 85
heat, 3, 7–8, 11–12, 99; symbolism of 28,
    71–74, 77, 89. *See also* fire

Heaven, 26, 27–28, 46, 64, 67, 68, 114
Hell, 5, 27–28, 45–6, 64–68, 89, 97, 157–58, 185
Henry II, 5, 33
Henry IV, 33
Henry VI, Part 2, 6, 111
Henry VIII, 63
Herder, Johann Gottfried, 132
heretics, 8
Heywood, John, 151
Hildegard of Bingen, 72, 128
history of the senses, xi–xvii
Hobbes, Thomas, 119
Holy Ampulla. See *sainte ampoule*
Holy Nail, 37
homosexuality, 4, 21, 69
Hooke, Robert, 140–41
horses, 96, 104, 198, 115
housing, 7–8, 162–64, 181–82, 186–89
Howes, David, xvi
Hugh of Lincoln, 38, 57–58
Huizinga, Johan, 20
humoral theory, 27–28, 49, 71–73
hunger, 20, 22, 47, 106
hunting, 24–25, 98–99, 122
Hutten, Ulrich von, 3

iconoclasm, 130–31
Ida of Louvain, 86
idleness, 171–72
Ignatius of Loyola, 70
illiteracy, xiii, 5, 6
individualism, 153, 187
Industrial Revolution, 169–70
Isaac II Angelus, 55
itchiness, 47–48

Jacoba de Almania, 80
James II, 54
Jameson, Anna, 144–45
Jerome, Saint, 100
Jesus, 29–31, 34, 42, 49, 54, 86–88, 98, 116, 185
Jews, 23, 35, 41, 54, 105
Joan of Arc, 44 45
John I of Bohemia, 55

John of the Cross, 30
Jonson, Ben, 75, 99
Journal of a Plague Year, 156
Jütte, Robert, xv

Kelso, Ruth, 78
Kempe, Margery, 47–48, 87
King Lear, 54
kin group, 1–2
kissing, 4–5, 31, 58–59, 152, 190
knights, 2–3, 16, 17, 24, 39, 98–99

labor-saving devices, 163–64
labyrinths, 124–25
ladies' work, 133–36
Langland, William, 6, 11
language, xvi, 5, 75–76, 110, 111–12, 120
La Roche, Sophie von, 142–43
Launay, Vicomte de, 182
Le Goff, Jacques, xv
Leonardo da Vinci, 130
leprosy, 56–58, 62
Le Roy Ladurie. Emmanuel, xv
Lewis, C.S., 114, 123
Life of Lazarillo Tormes, The, 53
lighting, 10–11, 183–85
literacy, 6, 110
Little Flowers of Saint Francis, The, 101
Llull, Ramon, 19
Locke, John, 160
Louis IX, 37, 50, 53, 70, 124
Luddites, 170
Luther, Martin, 77, 117, 151–52
Lydwine of Schiedam, 62, 89

machinery, 18, 168–69, 180
Magnus IV, 52, 55
Malebranche, Nicolas, 118
Malleus maleficarum, 91
Mandeville, Bernard de, 171
Mandrou, Robert, xi, xv
Margaret of Oignt, 86, 87
Marinelli, Lucrezia, 73–74
Marinetti, F. T., 185–86
Marten, Henry, 158
Marx, Karl, 121, 182

Mary Magdalene, 30–31, 37, 39, 151, 185
Mary of Oignies, 31, 32
Master of Game, The, 113
Matilda of Scotland, 57
Maurice of Nassau, 167
men, 15, 30, 71–77, 88, 80; and aggression, 25–26, 30, 61; and home life, 20–21, 188–89; in public life, 194
Mercier, Louis-Sébastien, 177
Mesmer, Franz Anton, 160
Michelangelo, 126–27
midwives, 81
military, 167–71
Milton, John, 54–55, 77, 157, 158
Molyneux's Question, 160
Montaigne, Michel de, 8, 119
More, Thomas, 63–64, 154
Morte D'Arthur, 98, 99, 124
Muffet, Thomas, 95
museums, 136–46, 176–78
mysticism, 29–31, 85–90, 159

Native Americans, 108–9, 110
nerves, 161–62
Newton, Isaac, 161
New World, 96, 108–9, 154
night, 11
Nihell, Elizabeth, 81
nobility, 6, 163
Nordenfalk, Carl, 125
nuns, 85–90, 99
nursing, 79–81

Odo de Beaumont, 56
Oedipus, 52
"Of Englische Dogges," 99
ordeals, 43–46
Oken, Lorenz, xii
O'Rourke Boyle, Marjorie, xvi
Overton, Richard, 118, 119

pain, 17–18, 20, 47–70, 161–62, 164; of animals; 95, 117–21; religious use of 29–35, 88–90, 95
painting, 123, 125–31
Paracelsus, 59

Paradin, Claude, 135
paralysis, 51, 89
Parminter, Jane and Mary, 134–36
Paston, John, 79
Paterson, Mark, xvi
Patrick, Saint, 44
peasants, 6, 10, 16, 105–6, 108
Pencz, Georg, 125
Pepys, Samuel, 139, 142–43
Peter Bartholomew, 45
Peter Damian, 12, 42
Peter the Venerable, 33
Petrarch, 19, 147–48, 153
Philip II, 4
Philip Neri, 100
Philips, Katherine, 82
Philo, 73
physicians, 48–49, 55, 58, 79–81, 89, 161
pigs, 52–53, 58, 101, 107, 114
pilgrimage, 37, 47–48, 50–51
Pisan, Christine de, 79
plague, xi, 15, 34–35, 42, 50–51, 58–59, 150
pleasure, 20–26, 41, 96, 161–62, 163–64, 187–88, 193
Porete, Marguerite, 69–70
poverty, 10, 53, 78, 180–81, 188–89
prayers, 31–32
pregnancy, 81
priests, 16, 31, 34
Primatt, Humphrey, 120
prisons, 173–76
prostitution, 3, 20–21, 195
Protestantism, 63, 85, 92, 117, 131, 151–52, 154
pulse-reading, 48–49
Purgatory, 28, 46

railway, 178
reading 19, 152
reason, 73, 110, 120
relics, 35–45, 49–51, 149–51
Remi, Saint, 165
Remy, Nicholas, 91
Rickaby, Joseph, 122
Richard of Chichester, 100, 110
Richard the Lionhearted, 4

Riegl, Alois, 127

riots, 6, 15, 170, 181

Ripamonte, Giuseppe, 156–57

Robinson Crusoe, 163

Roche, Saint, 100

Rolle, Richard, 26

Roman Catholicism, 5, 21, 27–46, 63, 85, 122, 131, and the Counter Reformation, 150, 152

Romuald, Saint, 36

Roper, Margaret More, 83

rosaries, 32

royal touch, 50, 158–59, 165–66

Rühl, Philippe, 165

Rupert of Deutz, 88

Sade, Marquis de, 161–62

sainte ampoule, 165–67

Salimbene di Adam, 102

Salomon, Ernst von, 190–91

Salvation Army, 170–71

sanitary reform, 180–81, 183

Satan, 5, 28, 31, 157–58

Saunderson, Nicholas, 152

Schiller, Friedrich, 132

Schreber, Daniel, 190–91

schools, 6, 19, 171–73

science, xv

sculpture, 131–32

Scot, Reginald, 91

servants, 3, 61, 154

sewing, 81–85, 133–34

sexuality, xv, 3, 4, 20–21, 71–73, 75; transgressive, 32, 52, 56, 91, 106–7, and Victorians, 189, 195

Shadwell, Thomas, xiv

Shakespeare, William, 6, 54, 56, 96, 111

sheep, 18, 94, 111, 113, 119

shopping, 14, 191–97

sight, xiv, xv–xvi, xvii, 10–11, 13, 52, 54–55, 75–76, 123; in modernity, 148, 153–54, 157, 164; in religion, 26, 32, 69, 149–50; as superficial, 30, 141, 160; as tactile, 58, 91, 146. *See also* lighting, surveillance

sin, 20, 45–46, 48, 88–89

Sinclair, George, 91

Sir Gawain and the Green Knight, 17, 123–24

skins, 94, 105, 110–11

slavery, 108–9

sleeping, 3–4, 10, 11–12, 32

Sloane, Hans, 139, 142

smell, xvi, xvii, 26, 53, 69, 74, 75, 89, 159; in afterworld, 40, 64; of cities, 13, 14; of sanctity, 40, 165, 181

Smith, Mark, xv

Smollet, Tobias, 178–79

Song of Roland, The, 70

sorrow, 68–70

Southey, Robert, 144

speed, 178–79

spinning, 75, 82, 180

spiritual senses, 30

sports, 22–24

St. Anthony's Fire, 60

Stendahl, 162.

Stensen, Niels, 119

Stephen VI, Pope, 130

stigmata, 88

Sundays, 16

surgery, 49, 79

surveillance, 175, 183

Symonds, John, 189

tactile values, 126–27

tarantism, 60

taste, xvi, 22, 64, 75, 96, 125, 139–40

Taylor, John, 84

telegraph, 185

Teresa of Avila, 85–86, 89

textiles, 9, 18, 128–29, 191

Thackeray, William, 179

Thomas, Keith, xiii, 6, 94, 96

Thomas the Apostle, 30–31

Thomas Aquinas, xi, 36–37, 43, 108, 111–12, 117

Thomson, James, 163

toothache, 50–51

Toplady, Augustus, 117

torture, 26, 29, 63–64, 69–70, 92, 173–74

tournaments, 24

trades, 14, 18

traffic, 13, 178–79

Travies, Charles-Joseph, 125

Tristan and Isolde, 99

Tyler, Watt, 6

Uffenbach, Zacharias Conrad von, 137–40, 176

Ure, Andrew, 171

Varchi, Benedetto, 132

variety stores, 196

Villon, Francois, 21–22

violence, 61

Virgin Mary, 42, 86

virtus, 40, 89

Vision of Piers Plowman, The, 6, 7, 11

Vision of Tundale, The, 66

Vitellesco, Hippolito, 132

vivisection, 118–22

walking, 8, 11, 13–14, 67–68, 104–5, 178

war, 15, 17, 25–26, 167–68

waste, 13, 180–81

Watson, John B., 190

weather, 14, 192

weaving, 18, 75, 82

Wesley, John, 117

whipping, 19, 32, 33, 34–35, 62

Wilberforce, William, 109

wild men, 106–8

William Longbeard, 35

William the Conqueror, 36, 39

Windham, William, 121

windows, 7, 11, 128, 186

winter, 7, 22

witchcraft, 31, 90–92

wolves, xvii, 97, 100

Woolley, Hannah, 79, 81

women, 10, 20–21, 71–77; and art, 133–36; as consumers, 194–96; as homemakers, 77–81, 188–91; in religion, 85–92; as writers, 81–85

work, 16–20, 77–81

working classes, 121–22, 163, 170–71, 176–77, 189–90

wrestling, 23

writing, 18–19, 81–84, 85, 88, 110–11, 153

Zola, Emile, 191, 192, 194

CONSTANCE CLASSEN is an award-winning writer and researcher based in Montreal, Canada. Her other books include *Worlds of Sense: Exploring Senses in History Across Cultures, The Color of Angels,* and the anthology *The Book of Touch.*

The University of Illinois Press
is a founding member of the
Association of American University Presses.

———————————————

Designed by Kelly Gray
Composed in 11/13 Perpetua
by Jim Proefrock
at the University of Illinois Press
Manufactured by Thomson-Shore, Inc.

University of Illinois Press
1325 South Oak Street
Champaign, IL 61820-6903
www.press.uillinois.edu